What is Academic Freedom?

This book explores the history of the debate, from 1915 to the present, about the meaning of academic freedom, particularly as concerns political activism on the college campus. The book introduces readers to the origins of the modern research university in the United States, the professionalization of the role of the university teacher, and the rise of alternative conceptions of academic freedom challenging the professional model and radicalizing the image of the university. Leading thinkers on the subject of academic freedom—Arthur Lovejoy, Angela Davis, Alexander Meiklejohn, Edward W. Said, among others—spring to life. What is the relationship between freedom of speech and academic freedom? Should communists be allowed to teach? What constitutes unacceptable political "indoctrination" in the classroom? What are the implications for academic freedom of creating Black Studies and Women's Studies departments? Do academic boycotts, such as those directed against Israel, violate the spirit of academic freedom? The book provides the context for these debates. Instead of opining as a judge, the author discloses the legal, philosophical, political, and semantic disagreements in each controversy. The book will appeal to readers across the social sciences and humanities with interests in scholarly freedom and academic life.

Daniel Gordon is a Professor of History at the University of Massachusetts Amherst, USA and Co-Editor in Chief of the journal *Society*. He received a Ph.D. in history from the University of Chicago and a Master of the Study of Law degree from the Yale Law School. He is the author of *Citizens Without Sovereignty: Equality and Sociability in French Thought*, 1670–1789 (Princeton University Press, 1994), the editor of *The Anthem Companion to Alexis de Tocqueville* (Anthem Press, 2019), and the author of many articles on free speech and religious freedom in France and the United States.

"A welcome addition to the rather large library of essays and books on academic freedom, Daniel Gordon's book departs from the assumption that history is a purifying mechanism in the course of which succeeding generations refine and distill a concept or a program. Gordon offers a much more complex account of academic freedom, telling a multi-faceted story from which 'academic freedom' emerges not as a term with a single meaning, but as something of a floating signifier that has meant different things at different times and different things at the same time, depending on social and political circumstances inside and outside of the academy."

—*Stanley Fish, Florida International University, USA*

"This is a nuanced account of academic freedom controversies—from World War I-era disputes over wartime limits on academic expression, to the mid-century debate about whether Communists should be allowed to teach, to the current fracas over BDS and academic boycotts. This book's combination of strong legal and philosophical analysis with vivid personal profiles (of leading figures such as Arthur Lovejoy, Alexander Meiklejohn, and Angela Davis) makes it an original and thought-provoking contribution to academic freedom studies."

—*Nadine Strossen, John Marshall Harlan II Professor of Law,*
New York Law School, Emerita Former President,
American Civil Liberties Union, 1991–2008

"A very smart tour through the people and ideas behind a century of debate over academic freedom."

—*Kenneth S. Stern, director of the Bard Center and author of The Conflict*
over The Conflict: The Israel/Palestine Campus Debate

"I thought I was familiar with the history of academic freedom in the United States, but Daniel Gordon's fascinating and lively history taught me that there are complexities within the complexities. I recommend this book for anyone who isn't sure what 'academic freedom' means and has meant—that is to say, almost everybody."

—*Michael Bérubé, Edwin Erle Sparks Professor of Literature, Pennsylvania*
State University and co-author (with Jennifer Ruth) of It's Not Free Speech:
Race, Democracy, and the Future of Academic Freedom

"Daniel Gordon's superb '*What is Academic Freedom?*' brings a new level of sophistication to an intensifying debate. At a moment when politicians, activists and even some academics question the ideal of academic freedom, this shrewd and compelling history gives readers a richer understanding of the concept, its past, and its potential future."

John McGreevy, Francis A. McAnaney Professor of History at the
University of Notre Dame and author of Catholicism and
American Freedom: A History

What is Academic Freedom?

A Century of Debate, 1915–Present

Daniel Gordon

Routledge
Taylor & Francis Group
LONDON AND NEW YORK

Cover image: © Getty Images

First published 2023
by Routledge
2 Park Square, Milton Park, Abingdon, Oxon OX14 4RN

and by Routledge
605 Third Avenue, New York, NY 10158

Routledge is an imprint of the Taylor & Francis Group, an informa business

British Library Cataloguing-in-Publication Data
A catalogue record for this book is available from the British Library

Library of Congress Cataloging-in-Publication Data
Names: Gordon, Daniel, 1961- author.
Title: What is academic freedom? : a century of debate, 1915-present / Daniel Gordon.
Description: Abingdon, Oxon ; New York, NY : Routledge, 2023. | Includes bibliographical references and index.
Identifiers: LCCN 2022016374 | ISBN 9780367511708 (hardback) | ISBN 9780367511715 (paperback) | ISBN 9781003052685 (ebook)
Subjects: LCSH: Academic freedom—United States. | College teaching—Political aspects—United States. | Universities and colleges—United States—History. | Education, Higher—Aims and objectives—United States.
Classification: LCC LC72.2 .G67 2023 | DDC 378.1/2130973—dc23/eng/20220601
LC record available at https://lccn.loc.gov/2022016374

ISBN: 9780367511708 (hbk)
ISBN: 9780367511715 (pbk)
ISBN: 9781003052685 (ebk)

DOI: 10.4324/9781003052685

Typeset in Bembo
by codeMantra

An electronic version of this book is freely available, thanks to the support of libraries working with Knowledge Unlatched (KU). KU is a collaborative initiative designed to make high quality books Open Access for the public good. The Open Access ISBN for this book is 9781003052685. More information about the initiative and links to the Open Access version can be found at *www.knowledgeunlatched.org*.

Contents

Acknowledgements

I wish to thank the journal *Society* and its publisher, Springer Nature, for permission to publish a revised version of my article, "The Firing of Angela Davis at UCLA, 1969–1970: Communism, Academic Freedom, and Freedom of Speech," vol. 57, no. 6 (November/ December 2020); as well as the journal *Philosophy and Literature* and its publisher, the Johns Hopkins University Press, for permission to publish a revised version of "'The Politics of the Classroom Are Not the Politics of the World': An Unpublished Speech by Edward W. Said," vol. 44, no. 2 (October 2020).

My deepest gratitude is to my wife Catherine Epstein and our children Nathan, Dora, and Stella, for providing, in their own scholarly and other endeavors, sources of inspiration and joy.

Figures

Introduction

Abstract
This is a historical work, but the Introduction is philosophical in spirit. Instead of providing a timetable of the major debates covered in the book, I discuss the principle of "debate" itself as a feature of historical inquiry. I suggest that the primary role of the historian is to explain the conditions which have made rival conceptions of academic freedom plausible. I also discuss some of the leading scholars who have written about academic freedom. Some act as sitting judges on past controversies and do not inform us properly about any arguments with which they disagree. But when one takes pains to portray debates over academic freedom with precision, one is likely to change one's ideas in the process of writing. The book offers no prescriptions other than the imperative to be well informed about past controversies before taking any position on what academic freedom ought to mean.

What makes a fire burn
is space between the logs,
a breathing space. (Judy Sorum Brown, "Fire,"[1])

God alone knows history in its totality; only fragments are shown to man. (Elie Wiesel, *Sages and Dreamers*[2])

For over a century, the meaning of academic freedom has been contested in the United States. There has been no agreement on who the beneficiaries of academic freedom are. Professors of course, but what about students and university administrators: are they also legatees of academic freedom? Who is *homo academicus?* Putting aside the question of *Who*, we may ask *What?* What constitutes academic activity as distinct from other endeavors? How to draw the line separating academic inquiry from political activism? What is the difference between academic freedom and freedom of speech?

The queries can be multiplied. Competing doctrines arise as a matter of course, for ideas are conflictual in nature. With a compound term like "academic freedom," rival constructions are inevitable. Different conceptions of *academic* freedom reflect different understandings of closely related terms such as professor, knowledge, university, teaching, and research. Different conceptions of academic *freedom* reflect different understandings of rights and democracy. In 2006, the authors of a textbook on law and higher education wrote:

> Academic freedom traditionally has been considered to be an essential aspect of American higher education . . . It has been a major determinant of the missions of higher educational institutions, both public and private, and a major factor in shaping

DOI: 10.4324/9781003052685-1

the roles of faculty members as well as students. Yet the concept of academic freedom eludes precise definition.[3]

And in 1987, Mark G. Yudof, then Dean of the University of Texas School of Law, observed:

> In my judgment the attempt to create only one face for academic freedom is a form of plastic surgery that ill serves the ends of justice and public policy. If, in our enthusiasm to protect the academy, we wish to etch the concept into a stone image oblivious to the changes wrought by time, perhaps we should aspire to the multiple faces of Mt. Rushmore. Even so stalwart a defender of academic freedom as Robert O'Neil is quick to admit that we use the term "with a degree of confidence that may surpass our common understanding."[4]

With these cautions in mind—against positing a transcendent idea of academic freedom—I have written the present book. It discloses debates in which mutually exclusive ideas about academic freedom are in play. These debates have not achieved closure; the history of academic freedom is an accumulation of uncertainties. This approach differs from that of most commentators on academic freedom, for they purport to have discovered its singular essence. When a historian discusses a case in which a professor was fired, the reader is likely to hear that the termination was plainly right or wrong, as if there is an obvious trans-historical standard of truth; as if there is no ground on which one can explore how each side in the controversy was *plausible*. I have tried to avoid right-versus-wrong judgments and have focused instead on explaining the intricacy of disagreements. The book is a series of complex case studies, not a collection of prophetic op-eds. I use history to resurrect knotty controversies and to disclose competing discourses.

Some readers may find the chapters that follow too inconclusive. But we are exploring variations of a highly contested term. The meaning of academic freedom is not to be found in one abstract definition; there is "no simple and handy appendage" that is the meaning of this concept.[5] Particularly when a term is a matter of dispute over a long period, the meaning can only be plural. It is a totality of designations and contexts: the wide array of controversies in which contestants wield the term as the answer to specific problems that concern them. I have aspired to map out a significant portion of these controversies. There is no "conclusion" to the inquiry, except an enriched understanding of an idea that is sometimes wielded with nonchalant over-confidence.

Historical scholarship, it is true, is no guarantee of detachment. In fact, erudition makes it easier to pass off one's opinions as authoritative: to embed prescriptions in the interstices of scholarly description. If one aims to study academic freedom *sine ira et studio*, it helps to have a skeptical disposition. It is sometimes said that we always write from a particular point of view and that neutrality is impossible; better to wear one's political colors on one's sleeve than mask one's biases. But why can't one's "particular" point of view be pluralistic and inquisitive? Are there not people who derive satisfaction from contemplating ideas in their multiplicity? Impartiality is not to be confused with claims to objective knowledge. Impartiality seeks only to portray rival solutions to a problem, while objectivity decrees which solution is true. As the Swiss historian Jacob Burckhardt said, history "coordinates," philosophy "subordinates."[6] History, or at least the kind I cultivate here, brings out the meaning of ideas by contrasting them to other ideas, as when the outlines of two or more shapes in a collage appear more vivid by being juxtaposed. The deeper meaning of academic freedom, in fact, is to be discerned in the spaces between discrete conceptions of it.

Hannah Arendt observed:

> Impartiality, and with it all true historiography came into the world when Homer decided to sing the deeds of the Trojans no less than those of the Achaeans, and to praise the glory of Hector no less than the greatness of Achilles.[7]

What Arendt describes as a miraculous cognitive breakthrough by Homer is explicable linguistically. The classicist Gregory Nagy states that "the Homeric poems are prodigiously versatile in integrating a plethora of various different traditions in epic narrative." Focusing on the etymology of words through the *Iliad*, Nagy detects an "intercultural synthesis," the inclusion of words drawn from different pre-existing accounts of the war.[8] What tends to make a work inclusive and impartial is, more than anything else, *the interlacing of the language of others into one's story.* That Arendt understood impartiality in this way is evident when she praises "the speeches in which Thucydides makes articulate the standpoints and interests of the warring parties."[9]

To be impartial does not mean that one begins an inquiry without preferring some ideas over others. It means that one accepts the scholarly task of delineating with care even the ideas one finds irritating. After a while, one begins to notice a change: some of the ideas one disliked start to make sense. A calming of the nerves occurs, and one may even change one's mind on fundamental issues. Michel Foucault famously said:

> I don't feel that it is necessary to know exactly what I am. The main interest in life and work is to become someone else that you were not in the beginning. If you knew when you began a book what you would say at the end, do you think that you would have the courage to write it? . . . The game is worthwhile insofar as we don't know what will be the end.[10]

When I began to write this book—indeed, it was one of my reasons for writing it—I had an Achillean rage against professors at my university who used the classroom to broadcast their political opinions against Israel. I continue to see "activism" in the classroom, as its defenders call it (critics call it "indoctrination"), as something to avoid. Yet, in writing this book, I realized that the issue cannot be settled easily. With the creation of politically oriented departments, such as Black Studies and Women's Studies, departments whose founders rejected traditional models of academic freedom, a platform for combining academics and politics was installed in the heart of the university. One may disapprove of this fact, but it remains a fact. Also, sophisticated social theorists, from the founders of the departments just mentioned to postmodernist thinkers, have questioned the distinction between politics and academics.

Rather than attempt to *resolve* this debate, I have provided illustrations of how the debate has *evolved* over a century—to the point where even the American Association of University Professors (AAUP) reversed its position. At the time of its founding in 1915, the AAUP articulated the ideal of a professional separation of academics and politics. In our century, the AAUP has encouraged academics to be politically engaged in the classroom and elsewhere. The transformation is discussed in Chapter 4. As for Israel, Chapter 5, which is about the Boycott, Divestment, and Sanctions movement, reflects again how my ideas changed in the process of writing. It is not that my relationship to Israel has altered; rather, I now perceive some of the American defenders of Israel as violating academic freedom as much as the advocates of anti-Israel boycotts do.

★

Let us take the discussion of impartiality further, into a consideration of some scholarly studies of academic freedom. In *Versions of Academic Freedom* (2014), Stanley Fish declared that he was forging an original line of scholarship: "I am announcing the inauguration of a new field—Academic Freedom Studies."[11] How could Fish claim to invent the subject, given the seminal tome by Hofstadter and Metzger, *The Development of Academic Freedom in the United States* (1956), and subsequent historical studies of academic freedom?

There is a relatively simple answer, one which suggests that Fish's approach is indeed unusual. Those who write about the history of academic freedom often presuppose that it is a glorious idea with one meaning, which becomes the telos of their story. Competing meanings are ignored or treated as obstructions in the rise of academic freedom. Fish, to whom I will return, avoids this style of narrative, which is the norm in much that has been written about the past of academic freedom. Beginning their story in the Middle Ages, Hofstadter and Metzger adhere to a conventional periodization of Western Civilization; they inscribe academic freedom in their account of how the Enlightenment and modern science "displaced religion." The book revolves around dichotomies such as medieval versus modern, doctrine versus debate, and faith versus reason. Progress culminates in the formation of the American research university around 1890. The end of the book proclaims that the acceptance of academic freedom is "one of the remarkable achievements of man."[12] There is little sense that conflict over academic freedom might emanate from the concept's intrinsic ambiguity. Conflict is between academic freedom and obscurantism. The meaning of academic freedom is never in doubt. Western society just needed to become secularized and rational enough to make room for it.

If we fast forward to a more recent book by an accomplished historian, Henry Reichman, we feel, at times, that we are in the same groove. Entitled *The Future of Academic Freedom*, the book is largely an account of past controversies, interlaced with warnings about current threats to academic freedom. This study by a long-term officer of the AAUP is highly nuanced in one regard. The many brief chapters draw attention to a kaleidoscopic array of controversies around academic freedom ranging from "Can I Tweet That?" to "Are Invited Speakers Entitled to a Platform?"

However, Reichman is able to move with assurance among so many topics because he has few doubts about what academic freedom means—and it usually means what the AAUP says it is. Repeatedly praising the AAUP for its role in defending academic freedom over the years, he is not distracted by inconsistencies in AAUP doctrines over time, such as the fact that the 1915 "General Declaration of Principles on Academic Freedom and Academic Tenure" (the AAUP's founding document) differs markedly from the AAUP's next major statement on academic freedom, the 1940 "Statement of Principles on Academic Freedom." Reichman amalgamates the two texts as if they are in fundamental accord; he suggests that they comprise the solid foundation of academic freedom.[13] However, the 1915 text is considerably more liberal on the extra-mural speech rights of faculty (the right to be politically engaged off campus), while the 1940 text is more permissive in its teaching guidelines. The two documents certainly do not comprise a consistent whole (discussed further in Chapter 1).

Reichman's treatment of historic controversies is at times melodramatic, featuring victims and oppressors. The termination of Angela Davis's position as a philosophy instructor at UCLA in 1970 was one of the most important academic freedom disputes of the twentieth century. When discussing this case, Reichman treats it as an obvious lesson in the abuse of administrative power. He quotes one member of the California Board of Regents who dissented in the decision to dismiss Davis, or more precisely, the decision not to renew her expired one-year contract.[14] He does not discuss the carefully crafted report of the majority of Regents. Thus, the reader does not encounter the actual reasons for the dismissal, which I explore fully in Chapter 1.

Reichman's discussion of the Steven Salaita controversy also leaves out the contending viewpoints. Salaita's appointment at the University of Illinois Urbana-Champaign was withdrawn in 2014, as a result of his tweets concerning Israel and Palestine. Reichman is willing to stipulate that the tweets were offensive, and perhaps even antisemitic; but he considers it "obvious" that prohibiting "emotionally provocative speech" poses "dangers to democracy."[15] Yet, those who supported the un-hiring of Salaita argued that his tweets were directly related to the academic subject, indigenous studies, which he was being hired to teach. The tweets, they argued, had an impact on whether students would perceive this professor, and hence the university, as fair. Reichman does not include the voices of Salaita's opponents. One of these voices was Cary Nelson, a former president of the AAUP.

My point is not to condemn Salaita but to observe that the historian's job is not to play the role of a judge but to explain the context in which a past decision was made. Reichman does not even present any of the tweets to the reader. I have given my own version of the Salaita affair, including the tweets and Nelson in Chapter 4. Readers will find many sketches of high-profile cases embedded in the chapters which follow.

No review of the historical scholarship on academic freedom, however selective, would be complete without considering *For the Common Good: Principles of American Academic Freedom* by Matthew W. Finkin and Robert C. Post. The book provides a concise overview of basic ideas concerning the freedom to teach, do research, and engage in political expression inside and outside the university. Yet, here again, I discern a tendency to overstate the unity of academic freedom. The authors bemoan the proliferation of debate about the meaning of academic freedom in the twenty-first century. They suggest that current disagreements stem from a lack of knowledge about the core principles of academic freedom as codified in the past. The past is thus a way to end debate, to discover "a common understanding of the history and structure of American academic freedom" and "a consensus vision of the purposes of American higher education."[16] I agree with Finkin and Post on this point: "For too many members of the American scholarly community, academic freedom has become a hortatory ideal without conceptual clarity or precision."[17] But I do not share their view that there has been a perennial canon of concepts—what they call the "essential ideas of American academic freedom."[18] I believe there are endless controversies and leading minds within these controversies whose ideas are at odds with each other. The past century is saturated with complex and often unresolved disagreements about the meaning of academic freedom. We must not take flight from indeterminacy.

Finkin and Postman share with Reichman a tendency to portray the AAUP as the source of authoritative interpretations of academic freedom. But there is a fundamental problem with this approach, apart from the fact that the AAUP has changed its doctrines over time. Unlike the American Bar Association, the AAUP's pronouncements on professional matters are not binding on anyone. The organization plays a purely advisory role to universities. Hence, the founding of the AAUP in 1915 and the various positions this organization has taken in important controversies must be part of the story of academic freedom in the United States; but the AAUP is only one role in the cast of characters.

Over the past century, there has been a profusion of ideas concerning academic freedom *outside* the AAUP. The AAUP has no power to contain them. Nor do leaders of the AAUP have any technical expertise that gives them higher intellectual authority. The history of academic freedom cannot be centered on the AAUP because this history is essentially (if we are going to use that word at all) a story about the de-centering of a concept which the AAUP helped to make popular but has not been able to stabilize. The ideas of the philosopher Arthur Lovejoy when he co-founded the AAUP in 1915 must be recorded, but no less worthy of being traced is his later divorce with the AAUP over the question of whether communists should be allowed to be faculty members. The influence of Lovejoy, who opposed hiring communists, greatly overshadowed the AAUP in the discussion of this issue around 1950. The ideas of Cedric Clark (later Syed Malik Khatib) on academic freedom were unorthodox, to say the least, in relation to the doctrines of the AAUP; but his ideas undergirded the creation of Black Studies departments (see Chapter 3 on both Lovejoy and Clark).

What the proliferation of competing visions of academic freedom means for getting university policy today "right" is not a subject I address in detail. I will only suggest that university policies already vary a great deal. At my own university, the academic freedom policy is construed every three years in the faculty union contract with the state of Massachusetts. The language is brief and open-ended; and it says nothing about academic duties, only academic rights, as one might expect in a text based on a union bargaining process. It is up to us, the faculty, to flesh out through discussion what academic freedom means as both right and obligation. It is helpful to refer to AAUP policies, but they are evolving, not constant, and are sometimes ambiguous (see Chapter 5 on academic boycotts against Israel for an instance of acute ambiguity in the AAUP). I agree, then, with Edward W. Said, who wrote that "each community of academics, intellectuals, and students must wrestle with the problem of what academic freedom in that society at that time actually is and should be."[19]

It ought to be helpful, then, to have a historical record of some major disputes over the past century which illustrate competing understandings of academic freedom. My own preferences are traditional: for example, no academic boycotts and no political preaching in the classroom. But one cannot pretend that a given conception of academic freedom can be restored simply by asserting that it is a historically dominant one or the only "correct" one; there are now multiple traditions. Professors on each campus need to know the intellectual history of academic freedom, as Finkin and Post suggest. But not because the past is a repository of unambiguous wisdom. One needs to know this history so that one can see the spectrum of possibilities and choose among them with a sense of what one is not choosing and with a knowledge of the benefits and costs of one's choice.

★

Returning to Fish, his *Versions of Academic Freedom* is indeed exemplary. As an inventory of competing understandings of academic freedom, the book offers ample materials for critically assessing even the author's own take. Fish discerns five schools of thought about academic freedom ranging from "professionalism" to "revolution." He does not refer to J. L. Austin in *Versions,* but a fascination with Austin and the study of incongruent understandings of a given term is a hallmark of Fish's scholarship. Austin wrote:

> This is by way of a general warning in philosophy. It seems to be too readily assumed that if we can only discover the true meanings of each of a cluster of key terms, usually historic terms, that we use in some particular field (as, for example, "right," "good," and the rest in morals), then it must without question transpire that each will fit into place in some single, interlocking, consistent, conceptual scheme. Not only is there no

reason to assume this, but all historical probability is against it, especially in the case of a language derived from such various civilisations as ours is. We may cheerfully use, and with weight, terms which are not so much head-on incompatible as simply disparate, which just don't fit in or even on. Just as we cheerfully subscribe to, or have the grace to be torn between, simply disparate ideals—why *must* there be a conceivable amalgam, the Good Life for Man?[20]

Nearly all commentators on academic freedom presuppose not only that there is one correct way to define it but also that this proper definition will mesh easily with other key concepts, such as free speech, knowledge, research, teaching, and university. Fish does not presuppose such coherence; the world of ideas that he portrays is contradictory and open-ended.

If I were to quibble with Fish, I would make two points. First, his inventory of the versions of academic freedom does not reach back into the past; his classification is centered on ideas in the present. Can such a "synchronic" approach to the language of academic freedom be sufficient? Don't we also need a "diachronic" approach in order to understand not only where current usages come from but also how some older usages have been forgotten? Secondly, while Fish provides a suggestive classification of competing versions of academic freedom, he overlays it with a heavy-handed judgment as to which of the five is the best. What he calls the "professional" version is better than the others. The professional model of academic freedom places an accent on the first word: *academic* and not on freedom. Academic freedom is not the right of academics to do what they wish. It is certainly not to be confused with free speech, according to Fish, who is a vociferous critic of professors who give political sermons in the classroom. Academic freedom is the right to teach and conduct research within the limits of one's discipline.

The problem here is not so much the coexistence of an "is" (the five versions) with an "ought" (the "professional" version). The problem is that the "ought" conditions the "is": the classification is structured so as to make it relatively easy to uphold one version over all the others. Given that the hallmark of the professional version is the distinction between what is academic and what is political, all of the other models are simply variations of the argument that academics and politics are intertwined, so they can be refuted simultaneously. What appears at first to be a fivefold classification is only twofold: Fish versus the rest.

Nevertheless, Fish does bring a unique spirit of skepticism and intellectual diversity to his analysis. He fully represents the viewpoints of his opponents through copious quotation, which I have suggested is the key to impartial representation. A high point is when he debates one of the superstars of literary and social theory, Judith Butler, who argues that academic freedom must be more than conformity to the existing canons of a discipline, otherwise one would have no room to transform a discipline. Though Fish sets out to refute Butler, her intelligent voice comes through, as we will see in Chapter 6. Finally, it should be noted that the central issue which is generative of Fish's classification of the five versions—whether academic inquiry is separable from politics—is one of the recurrent issues in the history of academic freedom. It is a plausible basis for his book and informs much of my book.

Did Fish really inaugurate a new field of Academic Freedom Studies, or was he engaging in a conceit? Splitting the difference, I would say that he brought a different style of inquiry to the field. Instead of portraying an arc of progress, he reveals disputes that remain open. The present book is likewise designed to enable the reader to be a witness to high-level debates over the meaning of one of the most important ideas of modern times.

Notes

1   https://www.judysorumbrown.com/blog/breathing-space.

2   Elie Wiesel, *Sages and Dreamers* (New York: Simon & Schuster, 1991), 173.

3   William A. Kaplin and Barbara A. Lee, *The Law of Higher Education* (4th ed., San Francisco: Jossey-Bass, 2006), 613. Curiously, a later edition does not describe academic freedom as elusive but treats academic freedom simply as interchangeable with freedom of expression under the First Amendment: (5th ed., San Francisco: Jossey-Bass, 2014), 248f. The shift is consistent with a trend over the past two decades to submerge academic freedom in freedom of speech. For criticism of this trend, see Robert C. Post, "Discipline and Freedom in the Academy," *Arkansas Law Review*, vol. 65, no. 2 (2012), 203–216; the argument is amplified in Post, *Democracy, Expertise, and Academic Freedom: A First Amendment Jurisprudence for the Modern State* (New Haven: Yale University Press, 2013). Stanley Fish goes even further than Post in separating academic freedom from constitutional rights. See Daniel Gordon, "Is Free Speech an Academic Value? Is Academic Freedom a Constitutional Value?" review of Stanley Fish's book, *The First: How to Think About Hate Speech, Campus Speech, Religious Speech, Fake News, Post-Truth, and Donald Trump*, in *FIU Law Review*, vol. 14, no. 4 (2021), 717–720.

4   Mark G. Yudof, "Three Faces of Academic Freedom," *Loyola Law Review*, vol. 32, no. 4 (Winter, 1987), 831–832, quoting O'Neil, "Academic Freedom and the Constitution," *Journal of College and University Law*, vol. 61 (1984), 280. Yudof criticizes the growing tendency to presume that academic freedom is interchangeable with free speech and the ideal of personal autonomy. He thus questions the trend I mention in the previous note.

5   J. L. Austin, "The Meaning of a Word," in *Logic and Philosophy for Linguists,* ed. J.M.E. Moravcsik (The Hague: Mouton & Co., 1974), 192 (commenting on words in general, not academic freedom).

6   Jacob Burckhardt, *Reflections on History* (London: George Allen & Unwin, 1950), 15.

7   Hannah Arendt, "The Concept of History Ancient and Modern," in *The Portable Hannah Arendt*, ed. Peter Baehr (Harmondsworth: Penguin Books, 2000), 286. See also Peter Euben, "Hannah Arendt on Politicizing the University and other Clichés," in *Hannah Arendt and Education*, ed. Mordechai Gordon (Boulder: Westview Press, 2001), 193: whereas "impartiality rests on our ability to see the world from different points of view that are themselves partial in the double sense of being incomplete and self-serving, objectivity presumes we could stand outside the world as if we were not part of it."; and Peter Baehr, "Education: Arendt against the Politicization of the University," in *The Bloomsbury Companion to Arendt*, ed. Peter Gratton and Yasemin Sari (London: Bloomsbury Academic, 2020), 565–575, esp. 572 and note 34 on 574–575.

8   Gregory Nagy, *The Best of the Achaeans: Concepts of the Hero in Ancient Greek Poetry* (Baltimore: Johns Hopkins University Press, 1980), 6–7.

9   Arendt, "The Concept of History Ancient and Modern," 286.

10   Michel Foucault, "Truth, Power, Self: An Interview with Michel Foucault," in *Technologies of the Self: A Seminar with Michel Foucault*, ed. Luther H. Martin, Huck Gutman, Patrick H. Hutton (London: Tavistock, 1988), 9.

11   Stanley Fish, *Versions of Academic Freedom: From Professionalism to Revolution* (Chicago: University of Chicago Press, 2014), 6–7.

12   Richard Hofstadter and Walter P. Metzger, *The Development of Academic Freedom in the United States* (New York: Columbia University Press, 1955), viii, 16–17, 506.

13   Henry Reichman, *The Future of Academic Freedom* (Baltimore: Johns Hopkins University Press, 2019), xiv, 3.

14   Ibid, 22; see also 57–58.

15   Ibid, 21; see also 20, 22, 59 on the Salaita case.

16   Matthew W. Finkin and Robert C. Post, *For the Common Good: Principles of American Academic Freedom* (New Haven: Yale University Press, 2011), 5, 7.

17   Ibid, 6.

18   Ibid.

19   Edward W. Said, "Identity, Authority, and Freedom: The Potentate and the Traveler," in *The Future of Academic Freedom*, ed. Louis Menand (Chicago: University of Chicago Press, 1996), 216.

20   J. L. Austin, "A Plea for Excuses," *Proceedings of the Aristotelian Society*, vol. 57 (1956-1957), 29, note 16 (italics in original). Fish's career-long fascination with linguistic instability appears to owe more to Jacques Derrida than to Austin. See Stanley Fish, "With the Compliments of the Author: Reflections on Austin and Derrida," *Critical Inquiry*, vol. 8, no. 4 (Summer, 1982), 693–721. I happen to find Austin's "A Plea for Excuses" (a relatively neglected text, compared to *How to Do Things With Words*)

to be an especially clear exposition of the value of focusing on the "overlapping, conflicting, or more generally simply disparate" meanings of popular words and phrases. The primary difference with Derrida is that the French thinker encouraged one to discern contradictions within specific texts, while Austin encourages one to look for discordant nuances in the language as a whole: how a given term is used throughout a society. This is largely what Fish does in *Versions,* and what I attempt to do, but with a longer time horizon.

1 The Firing of Angela Davis

Abstract

In 1969, the Board of Regents of the University of California fired Angela Davis for her membership in the Communist Party. After the courts ruled that a university could not fire a professor merely for *being* a communist, the Regents managed to fire her again, this time for *speaking* in public like a communist. In her speeches, Davis defined academic freedom as the right to engage in political struggles on campus. She also held that those who do not engage in progressive struggles do not have academic freedom. The legal system protected her First Amendment right to associate with the Party but did not protect her against the Regents' judgment that her statements about academic freedom made her unfit to be a professor. The Davis case is saturated with competing conceptions of academic freedom and can serve as a textbook for understanding the structure of debate about this topic.

Introduction

On September 19, 1969, the Board of Regents of the University of California fired Angela Yvonne Davis. She had just begun a one-year, renewable appointment as an Acting Assistant Professor of Philosophy at the University of California Los Angeles. The reason for dismissing Davis had nothing to do with her academic performance. She was fired for being a member of the Communist Party. In a press release on September 23, Davis stated,

> The Regents seem intent on meting out punishments which concur with the fascist tendencies of the times. The sole reason they give for their intention to fire me is my membership in the Communist Party. They have not questioned my qualifications, my academic training, or my ability to teach.[1]

In 2016, Ibram X. Kendi described Davis as one of the most prominent and provocative racial theorists of our time.[2] She is a pioneer in the development of integrative race, gender, and class studies, and a leader in the prison abolition movement.[3] When she was hired at UCLA in the summer of 1969, as part of an initiative to increase the number of Black faculty members,[4] Davis was only 25. She was unknown to the world but already committed to activism; she was not afraid of contending with the powerful Regents.

Growing up in Alabama, Davis had experienced racial segregation and violence.[5] She had joined the Black Panthers as well as the Communist Party shortly before starting at UCLA. She was working on a doctorate in Philosophy at the University of California San Diego, under the supervision of the German-American Marxist, Herbert Marcuse, known as "the Father of the New Left." Marcuse considered Davis to be "the best student I ever had."[6] She

DOI: 10.4324/9781003052685-2

in turn was inspired by his conviction that being a philosopher and an activist are not mutually exclusive.[7] The title of her thesis, "A Kantian Theory of Violence," hinted at the idea of turning abstract notions of justice into revolutionary action. Davis was in the process of combining Marcuse's generic analysis of modernity—of alienation and repression in all capitalist nations—with a critique of racist practices specific to the United States.[8] She was aggrieved, brilliant, and courageous. The Regents had no idea of the battle that would ensue.

The Los Angeles Times described the Davis controversy as "the most explosive academic freedom case" of the past 20 years.[9] I would go further by suggesting that no other contest has raised so many acute issues about academic freedom. Two factors explain why the case was so protracted and raised so many deep questions. The first has to do with Davis' strategy in the conflict. Her priority was never to keep her job. Instead, her goal was to highlight contradictions in the academy and to agitate for radical change. She pushed the battle with the Regents to its limits. Even though she was successful in her legal appeal of the 1969 firing, which was based on the premise that communists could be excluded from the professoriate, she created a second wave of conflict by challenging conventional understandings of knowledge and academic freedom. Hence, more was at stake than her own academic freedom: the dispute morphed into a battle over the very meaning of academic freedom.

The second factor has to do with law. The Davis case reached the Supreme Court, in the form of a petition for certiorari by the Regents, who persisted in their contention that membership in the Communist Party was ipso facto incompatible with academic freedom. The petition was denied, so no Supreme Court decision resulted; but the lower court cases, plus the petition itself, provide an extensive body of material through which we can better understand how academic freedom interacted with constitutional law (particularly the First Amendment) at that time. Though the law was on Davis' side in 1969, the status of communists under the law and within the university had shifted only a few years before. Had she been fired in 1964, her legal action would have been unsuccessful. We thus have an opportunity to reconstruct a major change in the 1960s in the American understanding of the relationship between communism, freedom of speech, and freedom of expression.

As regards law, there is more. Though Davis won decisively in the courts, the Regents were still able to dismiss her in 1970 for being a communist. When her one-year contract came up for renewal, the Regents declined to reappoint her for reasons related to her actual speech rather than her Party membership. The Regents exploited the fact that university administrators have considerable discretion in academic affairs; indeed, this is a kind of academic freedom—known as institutional academic freedom, as opposed to individual academic freedom—over which the courts generally exercise no jurisdiction. How to define academic competency and worthiness for hiring, rehiring, and promotion are matters that courts generally leave to university administrators, out of respect for their autonomy, i.e., their academic freedom. The Davis case is a reminder that judicial review coexists with a wide margin of administrative discretion to which courts defer. The Davis case occurred at a time when the law was plainly on her side as concerns her Communist Party *membership,* but the norms of academic life that administrators oversaw were stacked against her as concerns her communist *speech.* She was dismissed with finality in 1970 because certain speeches she gave about the nature of academic freedom were understood at the time—not only by the Regents but by some UCLA faculty members—as a threat to academic freedom.

The complexity of the Davis case, which was really two cases (the firing in 1969, the non-renewal in 1970), makes it challenging to explicate. In fact, there is no scholarly treatment of it to date. But since the case is saturated from beginning to end with competing conceptions of academic freedom, it can serve as a textbook for understanding the structure of debate about this elusive concept.

Overview of the Two Tiers of the Davis Case

At the beginning of the battle with the Regents, Davis had one advantage: the law was in her favor. In *Elfbrandt v. Russell* (1966), the Supreme Court turned its back on numerous prior decisions that consecrated the exclusion of communists from public educational institutions and other governmental agencies. The case concerned Barbara Elfbrandt, an Arizona junior high school teacher and a Quaker. She refused to sign an oath stating that she was not a communist or a member of any other organization designed to overthrow the American government. The Court held that it is unconstitutional to assume that every person who belongs to the Communist Party endorses the Party's commitment to violent revolution. Speaking for a 5–4 majority, Justice William O. Douglas stated that one can support the "legitimate aims" of an organization without supporting its criminal precepts. He stated that "the doctrine of 'guilt by association' . . . has no place here."[10] Previously, the Court held that employers were entitled to presume that Party members subscribed to all the principles that the Party espoused. Thus, what fundamentally shifted was not the attitude toward communism but the attitude toward *membership* in a political party: membership no longer implied a total commitment to the party's precepts.

In 1967, in *Keyishian v. Regents of the State University of New York,* the Court reaffirmed the principle that communists cannot automatically be excluded from public employment. Henry Keyishian was an English instructor at SUNY Buffalo who refused to sign a certificate attesting that he had never been a communist. He was on a renewable year-to-year contract, making his academic position similar to what Davis' would be at UCLA. Speaking for another 5–4 majority, Justice William J. Brennan found the certificate requirement illegal not only because it barred Communist Party membership but also because it prohibited any "seditious" political affiliation. The term seditious was not defined in the New York statute underpinning the certificate requirement. As Brennan explained, the vagueness of the word meant that the authorities could arbitrarily stifle speech they simply did not like.[11]

As a result of these two Supreme Court cases, the California Supreme Court invalidated, in December 1967, an oath required of all public employees in the state. The oath dated to 1950 and proscribed membership in any party advocating the overthrow of the government through violence or other unlawful means.[12]

This flurry of court decisions, in 1966–1967, transformed the legal landscape. When Judge Jerry Pacht of the Los Angeles Superior Court received a motion for summary judgment from Davis' attorneys, it was a clear-cut case for him. On October 24, 1969, he granted the motion. Pacht declared that the Regents cannot

> automatically exclude from faculty employment by the University of California, solely by virtue of such membership, any person who is a member of the Communist Party . . . there is no defense to the action and no triable issue of fact is presented.[13]

In their appeals, the Regents failed. First, they lost in the California Supreme Court; then, their petition to be heard in the US Supreme Court was denied. Davis was the victor, so it seemed.

Yet, on June 19, 1970, the Regents dismissed Davis from the UCLA faculty again. They now offered a multi-faceted rationale for the dismissal, or more precisely, for their decision not to renew her contract. One of their reasons was that they did not need to have a reason. They were not releasing Davis in the middle of her service but merely refraining from appointing her for an additional year. They also purported that budget cuts were necessary on the UCLA campus. The Regents cited a letter of April 22, 1970, from Franklin Rolfe, UCLA's Dean of the College of Letters and Sciences, to David Saxon, Vice-Chancellor (effectively the Provost). The letter was a response to Saxon's request for Rolfe's opinion on the re-appointment of Davis. Rolfe wrote that given impending reductions of the faculty, it was not advisable to renew.

> But if I were to request such a provision, I would be elevating this appointment to the Number 1 priority of the College and giving it sudden precedence over fifty-two already needed positions in nearly every Department of the College. In my opinion, to do so would be unfair and not in the best interests of the College. I therefore do not recommend the appointment.[14]

Saxon, however, was partial to Davis. As a young Physics professor at UCLA, he had been one of 31 tenured professors in the UC system who refused to take the oath forswearing communism.[15] He was dismissed in 1950 but reinstated in 1952. Saxon asked Rolfe to report again and to limit his advice to whether he favored the reappointment of Davis apart from budgetary considerations. Rolfe said that he supported the renewal. Saxon assured Rolfe that he would take care of the funding from a pool designated for minority faculty.[16]

The Regents nevertheless used the budget to justify their decision not to reappoint Davis. Throughout the Davis controversy, the Regents elected to exercise their reserve of authority over personnel and other matters in the university. This authority was grounded in a powerful source, Article 9, Section 9, of the California Constitution, which gave the Regents "full powers of organization and government" in university administration. The US Supreme Court recognized the Regents' constitutional authority in *Hamilton v. Board of Regents of the University of California* (1934).[17] The case upheld the authority of the Regents to require students to do military service and to deny religious students the right to claim conscientious exemption.

However, in their report of June 1970, on Davis' dismissal, the Regents went beyond citing the budgetary factor. They evaluated Davis' performance. The non-renewal thus acquired the tone of a firing because it faulted the employee's behavior. The Regents noted that Davis had made no progress on her doctoral dissertation during the 1969–1970 academic year. This was true; she never finished her thesis. Above all, the Regents referred to several public speeches that Davis gave while employed at UCLA, speeches "so extreme" and "so antithetical to the protection of academic freedom" that her continued employment would impinge upon "the individual and collective rights of all the Faculty."[18] To make it appear that their judgment was not unilateral but rather based on an ethos shared by the faculty, the Regents cited a report written in April 1970 by a faculty committee appointed by UCLA Chancellor Charles E. Young. The committee's function was to assess Davis' teaching and political speeches. The committee wrote, "We also find . . . that Miss Davis' choice of language in some of her public statements is inconsistent with academic freedom."[19]

The non-renewal of Davis' contract is unusually rich in its documentation of competing conceptions of academic freedom. We have Davis' speeches, the faculty committee's report of April 1970, and the Regents report of June 1970. The American Association of

University Professors (AAUP) also weighed in with a report in September 1971. All of these texts addressed the broad question of the meaning of academic freedom, and the specific question of whether radical criticism of the dominant discourse of academic freedom can be a violation of academic freedom. Davis' views on academic freedom, we will see, were influenced by Marcuse and specifically by his theory of "repressive tolerance." Marcuse argued that academic freedom is never impartial. It is always the pillar of a particular system of power. According to Marcuse, the logic of repressive tolerance applies to the socialist future as well as to the capitalist present. Just as the right-wing bourgeois estab- lishment represses critical ideas, so a revolutionary government will need to stifle ideas that "counteract the possibilities of liberation."[20]

We will examine more fully Davis' variations on Marcuse's theme of repressive tolerance, but here is a sample of the discourse that disturbed the Regents, from a lecture Davis gave at UC Berkeley on October 24, 1969. Davis said:

> A lot of professors think that they have a monopoly over academic freedom. Now I think that *students* ought to have a monopoly over academic freedom because it ought to be an inherent element in the process of learning itself.
>
> . . . we can't allow it [academic freedom] to be a mere reflection of the atrocities and injustices which are being perpetuated in the society today, such as the fact that the University of California has I don't know how many research grants for developing more efficient ways of murdering in Vietnam. Sociologists attempt to explain away the existence of social problems within the university . . . This is *not* a reflection of academic freedom. These people are *exploiting* the notion of academic freedom.
>
> The *real* academic freedom, the real free intellectual atmosphere of the university ought to consist in the ability to link up with *concrete struggles*, to link up with the black libera- tion struggle, the Chicano liberation struggle, the struggle in Vietnam, and to not only criticize what's going on in the society but to pose solutions, *revolutionary* solutions . . . If we *aren't* able to link up with these struggles, then that's when academic freedom becomes a *farce*.[21]

It had been illegal when the Regents fired Davis for *being* a communist. Now, they dismissed her legally—for *talking* like one.

The rest of this chapter explores more fully issues involved in the Regents' two-tiered effort to get rid of Davis. I focus on ambiguities in the meaning of academic freedom at that time, including ambiguities in the relationship between academic freedom and freedom of speech. In no way do I mean to suggest that dismissing Davis was a *good* decision. But I also refrain from condemning the Regents, who are the natural villains in any Manichean account. The register of discussion here is historical and analytical rather than editorial. The goal is to highlight what made the Regents' decision *plausible* in the context of unresolved ambiguities about the meaning of academic freedom around 1970.

These uncertainties persist. It remains unclear today, for example, whether academic freedom necessarily protects professors from being disciplined for provocative statements they make outside of the classroom or whether academic freedom means that professors bear responsibility for public remarks that undermine the university's reputation and values. Conflicting visions of the status of a professor's "extramural utterances" were central in the Davis case; these visions still hang in the balance. I am aware that emphasizing what is am- biguous and unresolved will not yield any clear-cut policy recommendations. But policy- making should be preceded by a full exploration of the *complexity* of a topic. The deepest way to comprehend academic freedom is not to establish what it "is" through an authoritative definition or to trace its "origin" and "triumph" in a linear historical narrative. Instead, we need to understand, through intensive case studies, the accumulation of questions that have never been settled. This kind of non-linear intellectual history will not tell us what to think, but it will enable us to be lucid about fundamental issues, such as:

- When do a professor's words comprise harm to the academy or suggest that the professor is not fit to be a member of the academy?
- Does one professor's academic freedom include the right to deny that other professors have academic freedom?
- Since academic freedom presumably does not mean exactly the same thing as freedom of speech, what are the competing ways of articulating the difference?
- Do university educators, irrespective of their political orientation and field of specialization, have any duties in common? In other words, what does it mean to be a *professional* as opposed to being a conservative or progressive academic?
- What does academic freedom suggest about the balance of power between administrators and academics in the university? Is academic freedom primarily a protection of professors against university administrators (individual academic freedom), or a protection of the administrators against legislators and judges (institutional academic freedom)?

In regards to the last item, before rushing to judgment that institutional academic freedom (the freedom of administrators) is the "conservative" take on academic freedom, one should consider that this concept is mentioned in *Bakke*, the landmark affirmative action case of 1978.[22] By invoking the idea of institutional academic freedom, the court authorized administrators (not professors) to define "diversity" as an essential component of college education and to frame admissions policies accordingly.

The Supreme Court has never defined academic freedom with precision. As Stanley Fish observes, "Academic freedom is rhetorically strong but legally weak."[23] An excellent example of Fish's point is the *Keyishian* case, cited above; it is one of the first Supreme Court cases to use the term academic freedom. Brennan wrote:

> Our Nation is deeply committed to safeguarding academic freedom, which is of transcendent value to all of us and not merely to the teachers concerned. That freedom is therefore a special concern of the First Amendment, which does not tolerate laws that cast a pall of orthodoxy over the classroom . . . The classroom is peculiarly the 'marketplace of ideas.' The Nation's future depends upon leaders trained through wide exposure to that robust exchange of ideas which discovers truth 'out of a multitude of tongues, (rather) than through any kind of authoritative selection.'[24]

Here, it is individual academic freedom that is in question. However, this passage is an example of "dicta"—words of wisdom in a judicial opinion that are not part of its central legal holding. In *Keyishian*, the main question was whether the New York anti-communist test was so vague that it chilled freedom of speech; academic freedom was not mentioned in the resolution of this central issue. In several other cases, the Court has referred to academic freedom but only to embellish more important constitutional points. The Court is reluctant to pin down the meaning of academic freedom because to do so would impinge on academic freedom itself, that is, on the right of the university to define its governing principles. Hence, it is perennially unclear what academic freedom, which is not mentioned in the First Amendment, adds to the free-speech rights of professors. Is academic free-dom redundant, restrictive, or expansive in relationship to freedom of speech? The Davis case illustrates a spectrum of possibilities, a spectrum that continues to haunt us with its uncertainty.

The Gap

Angela Davis is iconic and much written about. Yet, there is no scholarly study of her removal from the faculty at UCLA.[25] Davis herself did not discuss the conflict with the Regents in detail in her 1974 *Autobiography*. Other portraits of Davis' life and work typically devote only a paragraph or two to the UCLA controversy. The reason for such a proverbial "gap in the literature," starting with the *Autobiography*, is not hard to explain. Davis' conflict with the Regents over her $9,684-per-year position was soon overshadowed by a life-or-death struggle with the criminal law system: her trial for murder. She became a suspect in the kid-napping and murder of a California Judge, Harold Haley. The crime occurred on August 7, 1970. On August 18, J. Edgar Hoover placed Davis on the FBI's Ten Most Wanted list. On October 13, 1970, Davis was apprehended in a Howard Johnson Motor Lodge in New York City. She spent almost two years in jail awaiting trial as an alleged principal—not merely an accessory—in the murder, even though she had not been present at the scene of the crime.[26]

Davis was charged as a principal because the weapons used in the crime were registered under her name. She also had a close relationship with 17-year-old Jonathan Jackson, who stormed the courthouse on August 7. The death of Haley occurred when Jackson, heavily armed, attempted to seize the judge in order to negotiate the freedom of the "Soledad Brothers"—three Black inmates of Soledad State Prison who were accused of murder. In the resulting shootout with police outside the courtroom, five people died, including Jackson and Haley. One of the Soledad Brothers whom Jackson intended to liberate was his older brother, George Jackson. According to Bettina Aptheker, one of Davis' legal advisors at the time, Davis was "in love" with George.[27]

Transmitting arms to Jonathan Jackson was not enough to hold Davis responsible for the murder, so the prosecution relied on her letters to both George and Jonathan, letters which discussed the possibility of using violence to achieve racial justice. The letters, however, did not urge the brothers to commit specific acts. In light of the dearth of evidence against her, Davis was acquitted by an all-white jury on June 4, 1972. The dismissal of Davis at UCLA may look inconsequential compared to her imprisonment and murder trial. Since Davis went on to become one of America's premier critics of the "Prison Industrial Complex,"[28] it is natural to magnify Davis' early engagement with the penitentiary system and to reduce her dismissal at UCLA to background detail. Yet, Davis' clash with the Regents has a his-torical importance of its own. It illustrates an important moment of transition in American law and culture when dismissal from public employment could no longer occur merely for belonging to a certain political party but could still occur for engaging in certain types of speech deemed professionally irresponsible.

The Relationship between Academic Freedom and Freedom of Speech

Before the 1960s, the dominant academic ethos discouraged political partisanship. As the AAUP's 1915 "General Declaration of Principles on Academic Freedom and Academic Tenure," drafted by Arthur Lovejoy and Edward R. A. Seligman,[29] stated:

Since there are no rights without corresponding duties, the considerations heretofore set down with respect to the freedom of the academic teacher entail certain correlative obligations. The claim to freedom of teaching is made in the interest of the integrity and of the progress of scientific inquiry; it is, therefore, only those who carry on their work in the temper of the scientific inquirer who may justly assert this claim.[30]

In his 1937 entry on "Academic Freedom" in the *Encyclopaedia of Social Sciences,* Lovejoy wrote that the opinions of a professor should have not only a "competent" but also a "disinterested" character. It is not the role of an academic to take a partisan position on a moral or political question that remains unresolved. Rather, the academic's job is to inform students and the public of the "diversity of opinion among specialists" and to take "special care to avoid the exclusive or one-sided presentation of his personal views."[31]

In 1915, when the AAUP began to champion academic freedom, this professional version of academic freedom was more authoritative than the libertarian version that is popular today: that is, the equation of academic freedom with freedom of speech. Indeed, there was no libertarian version, for there was scarcely any constitutional guarantee of freedom of speech in the United States until later.[32] The idea that the Constitution broadly protects incursions on free speech is not what the First Amendment originally meant. The Constitution's primary purpose was to limit the federal power so that state and local governments could have a wide range of action, which included the regulation of speech and religion. The First Amendment said, "*Congress* shall make no law" abridging the freedom of speech or religion. In contrast, the Fourteenth Amendment, ratified in 1868, declared, "*No State* shall make or enforce any law which shall abridge the privileges or immunities of citizens of the United States." Prior to the Fourteenth Amendment, it would have been incongruous to evoke the First Amendment against a university, private or public, that fired an academic for speaking provocatively. This changed when the Supreme Court began to consider the possibility of "incorporation"—of reading the First Amendment through the lens of the Fourteenth. Freedom of speech then became, in principle, applicable against state institutions.[33]

It took a long time for the Supreme Court to take the Fourteenth Amendment and incorporation seriously. In matters of religion, the first case in which the Court acknowledged that the "Free Exercise" clause was justiciable against the states was the previously mentioned *Hamilton* case. While granting that the claims of religious students who opposed military service at the University of California deserved scrutiny under the First Amendment, the Court held that their religious freedom had *not* actually been violated, because the service did not require them to bear arms. Likewise, the first case in which the Court recognized the possibility of incorporating freedom of speech against the states was *Gitlow v. New York* (1925) concerning the conviction of a socialist journalist for publishing a "Left Wing Manifesto." But the Court upheld the conviction. These are landmark cases because they acknowledge the formal possibility of finding state laws unconstitutional under the First Amendment. But it would take an additional factor, the liberalization of the substance of First Amendment jurisprudence, to make incorporation a pillar of individual liberty.

The liberalization of First Amendment doctrine occurred slowly prior to the 1960s. It consisted primarily of the adoption of Oliver Wendell Holmes' "clear and present danger" test for assessing whether utterances could be regulated. This standard supplanted the "bad tendency" test that states used, throughout the nineteenth and early twentieth centuries, to justify the repression of speech. The "bad tendency" standard was applicable to any kind of speech whose effects could be construed as harmful in any way and at any time.[34] "Clear and present danger" did not give states such wide power to limit speech, but it still enabled the criminalization of political discourse that could be construed as having dangerous effects.

It was only in the 1960s and 1970s that the idea of free speech as a constitutive principle of the American public sphere, comparable to the principle of private property in the economic sphere, gained wide currency. The Supreme Court then began to invalidate many state and municipal restrictions on speech. The remaining legal limits, such as obscenity regulations, came to be classified as exceptions to a general right of free speech. The Davis controversy thus took place at a time when, in contrast to the era of the founding of the AAUP, it was possible to envision the professoriate as a kind of special guild of free speakers: the primary bearer of a constitutional value, freedom of speech, that the entire society officially cherished. The timing of the Davis case was such that her dismissal cut in different directions. It inevitably struck some as a violation of her academic freedom, in the sense of her right to speak freely. Yet, the Regents were still able to justify the dismissal of Davis, in June 1970, on the basis of the same concept: academic freedom, in the traditional sense of the university's corporate right to set its own standards and to discipline its members.

From Davis' perspective, her dismissal was part of a right-wing conspiracy intertwined with structural racism. In one of her first press releases, she said:

> Joseph McCarthy's irrational attacks on the basic rights of man are explained away by many Americans as an unfortunate scar in the past history of this country. They do not realize that we may now be embarking upon an era marked by far greater destruction of human rights. The first target will continue to be Black and Brown people active in the movement for their liberation in the community and on the campus . . . These overt acts of repression must be met with an opposition which makes clear this reactionary intention. This is why I did not attempt to hide my political affiliation—I am a member of the Che-Lumumba Club, an all Black collective of the Communist Party of Southern California . . . As a Black woman, my politics and political affiliation are bound up with and flow from participation in my people's struggle for liberation, and with the plight of oppressed people all over the world against American Imperialism.[35]

Davis' accusations are plausible. As Governor of California since 1966, Ronald Reagan filled vacancies on the Board of Regents. The Regents were a conservative group, with exceptions such as leftist attorney William K. Coblentz, an appointee of Reagan's predecessor, Governor Pat Brown; Coblentz dissented from the Regents' decision in 1970. As the historian Lisa McGirr has shown, Orange County formed the base of Reaganite conservatism. In the wake of massive Black migration to southern California, racial bias in housing and other areas of public policy was widespread. Urban insurrections, such as the Watts uprising of 1966 against police brutality, led to the intensification of racist law-and-order discourse.[36] The firing of Davis, a Black radical, is consistent with Reagan's efforts to consolidate electoral support among white conservatives in the Los Angeles area.

The limitation of this formulation is that it focuses on Reagan rather than the Regents, and it underscores motives that are hard to link to the documentary evidence, notably the Regents' report on the termination of Davis. What we need is an account of the competing languages of academic freedom—the semantic space in which the conflict actually played out and in which Davis managed to be partially victorious. The principles articulated by the Regents were traditional but not racist. Even when they fired Davis for being a communist, they deployed arguments that had been used frequently, by both conservatives and progressives, until the mid–1960s.

An Unorthodox Philosopher

The events leading to Davis' firing traced to July 9, 1969, when a student named William Tulio Divale published an article in the *UCLA Daily Bruin*. "The Philosophy Department has recently made a two-year appointment of an acting assistant professor . . . this person is C.P. member."[37] Divale did not mention Davis' name, but on July 9, 1969, Ed Montgomery, of the *San Francisco Examiner*, did.

> . . . Miss Angela Davis [is] a known Maoist, according to U.S. intelligence reports, and active in the SDS and the Black Panthers. On April 7 Miss Davis purchased a Plainfield .30 caliber carbine and a Lama.45 caliber automatic pistol from the Western Surplus store at 8505 South West Ave. in Los Angeles.[38]

On July 16, Vice-Chancellor Saxon wrote to Davis. After referring to the two articles, he said, "I am constrained by Regental policy to request that you inform me whether or not you are a member of the Communist Party."[39]

Davis was traveling in the summer and did not receive the letter until late August. Instead of evading the question by invoking the First or Fifth amendment, Davis replied directly on September 5.

> My answer is that I am now a member of the Communist Party. While I think this membership requires no justification here, I want you to know that as a black woman I feel an urgent need to find radical solutions to the problems of racial and national minorities in white capitalist United States. I feel that my membership in the Communist Party has widened my horizons and expanded my opportunities for perceiving such solutions and working for their effectuation. The problems to which I refer have lasted too long and wreaked devastation too appalling to permit complacency or half-measures in their resolution.[40]

Davis stated that she was a member of the Che-Lumumba Club, a branch of the Communist Party for young black people in Los Angeles.[41]

Saxon was "under constraint" to write to Davis because, while the state-wide loyalty oath had been abolished in 1967, several older resolutions by the Board of Regents against communism were still on the books. One of these, from October 11, 1940, said that

> membership in the Communist Party is incompatible with membership in the faculty of a State University. Tolerance must not mean indifference to practices which contradict the spirit and the purposes of the way of life to which the University of California as an instrument of democracy is committed.

Another resolution, of June 24, 1949, announced that "the Regents reaffirm their declaration of policy adopted in 1940 that membership in the Communist Party is incompatible with objective teaching and with [the] search for truth." A third resolution of March 22, 1950, reaffirmed the earlier ones, this time noting that the Regents were "gratified that the Academic Senate . . . has concurred in this policy by an overwhelming vote, reported on March 22, 1950."[42]

When Judge Pacht granted the motion for summary judgment in October 1969, he referred to the three resolutions as unconstitutional in light of *Elfbrandt* and *Keyishian*. The Regents might have responded quickly by trying to fire Davis again on the basis of her job performance, but there were two problems here. The first is that they had more in mind than ousting Davis: they wished to convince the courts that all communists could be excluded from the faculty. To this end, they tried to revive a tradition of judicial anti-communism that predated *Elfbrandt*. The second reason for not sacking Davis right away on the basis of her performance was that there was nothing in her record to hold against her.

Davis had been fired on the assumption that any member of the Communist Party would try to spread the orthodoxy of Marxism-Leninism, but her classroom demeanor refuted that supposition. Davis was originally given the fall term off from teaching. She was supposed to concentrate on finishing her doctoral thesis. However, after the firing in September, she asked the Philosophy department to let her lecture on a non-credit, unpaid basis while she awaited a judge's decision on her complaint against the Regents. She was also waiting for the results of an appeal to the Faculty Senate's Committee on Tenure and Academic Freedom. As the Chair of Philosophy, Donald Kalish, reported to Saxon, Davis wanted to teach in order "to refute by her conduct the charge that she would use the classroom to indoctrinate [students]."[43]

On October 7, the *Los Angeles Times* covered the first lecture Davis gave in her course entitled "Recurrent Philosophical Themes in Black Literature." Two thousand students were present in Royce Hall when Davis entered.

> She is tall. She wore a dress with mixed green, yellow, and pink coloring and empire waist, and the dress was well above the knee as is the fashion . . . Her face is the color of well-creamed coffee, the hair two shades darker and evenly shaped in the natural style.[44]

Many factors have contributed to Davis' fame over her career, including her "natural" (Afro) hairstyle. In 1994, Davis commented, "I am remembered as a hair-do. It . . . reduces a politics of liberation to a politics of fashion."[45] But the apparently superficial description of Davis in the *Times* gave way to a nuanced summary of Davis' class. The Black journalist, William J. Drummond, captured the complexity of Davis' lecture, in which she developed a major criticism of Marx.

As Drummond described, Davis began by stating that Western civilization had devised lofty theories of freedom but also created institutions of slavery. Black literature, she stated, has philosophical importance because it is situated at the heart of this paradox. Drummond observed that the students chuckled knowingly when Davis used certain terms in the Marxist vocabulary. But he also tracked the independent quality of her thinking, particularly when she began "disputing Marx," as he put it, on the subject of religion. In fact, as a transcript of Davis' lectures shows, much of the first two lectures was about the inadequacy of Marx's conception of religion as the "opium of the people."[46] Davis demonstrated how Christianity was a liberating resource for Frederick Douglass and Nat Turner. Slaveowners used the idea of the equality of souls in heaven to distract slaves from oppression on the plantation. But some slaves were able to educate themselves. Acting on their own reading of the gospels, they moved the spiritual onto the social plane, turning, as Davis put it, "eternity into history."[47] All this Drumond captured in his fine summary, and it is evident that Davis did not strike her listeners as ideologically overbearing. A professor who attended one of Davis' lectures reported, "There was absolutely nothing that could be remotely regarded as indoctrination. Indeed, the heavy and apparent emphasis was on getting students to think for themselves." Evaluations by students confirmed this judgment.[48]

The Regents had access to the favorable assessments of Davis' teaching. But they also had access to recordings of her speeches outside of class. In line with some statements by the AAUP in the early twentieth century, notably the AAUP's 1940 Statement of Principles on Academic Freedom and Tenure, which spoke of a special obligation to exercise restraint in one's public utterances,[49] the Regents believed that a professor could be disciplined for statements made outside of class. Today, the issue is still pressing and unresolved. Professors who make comments deemed to be offensive on social media platforms are sometimes punished.[50] The fact that Davis was an excellent teacher did not change the Regents' position that communists are generally more committed to party ideology than academic inquiry.

Militant Democracy

The Regents were keen to create a test case. On May 23, 1969, President Nixon nominated Warren Burger to the Supreme Court to replace Earl Warren. In the same month, Abe Fortas resigned. He would be replaced by Harry Blackmun. Davis was hired when the moment of opportunity had arrived for a reversal of *Elfbrandt* and *Keyishian*. That the legal community understood what the Regents were up to is evident from a report on the Davis case in *The College Law Digest in* January 1970. "This case is probably on its way to the Supreme Court."[51]

The Regents began by appealing to the California Court of Appeal. The Court affirmed Judge Pacht's decision in a brief opinion that referenced *Elfbrandt* and *Keyishian*. One judge on the panel dissented.

> A plenary examination of the communist dogma, its objectives and the conduct of the Communist Party member in connection therewith while on the teaching faculty of the University pose potentially valid constitution grounds for the exclusion of such a person from such a position . . . I am unable to subscribe to the view that the resolutions herein were, as a matter of law, violative of the California or United States Constitutions. The position which the majority feels compelled to take herein suggests the need for an immediate reevaluation of the subject.[52]

The Regents appealed to the Supreme Court of California, which denied a hearing without issuing a reason. In their petition to the US Supreme Court, the Regents' attorneys framed the central question in this way: "Whether the University of California can exclude from its faculty members of the Party by reason of their want of academic integrity and opposition to the principles of academic freedom." The Regents argued that *Elfbrandt* and *Keyishian* were not conclusive. These cases invalidated state policies that presumed Communist Party members to be committed to violent revolution. The Regents argued that no prior case held that a state university may not reasonably determine that persons who join and remain members of the Communist Party are disqualified from service on its faculty *by reason of lack of academic integrity or want of professional ethics . . .*[53]

In other words, the law established that one could not assume a communist to be committed to overthrowing the government, but one could still presume that a communist wished to undermine impartial academic inquiry.

Thus far the argument appears weak. For in *Elfbrandt* and *Keyishian*, the Court opposed the principle of guilt by association. To say that one cannot assume every communist to be in favor of violent revolution implies that one cannot make any particular assumptions about what a Party member believes. But the Regents thought they had a strong card in their hand, which they described as "the single most analogous authority" to the question of whether a university could exclude communists for university-related reasons.[54] This authority was the 1950 case of *American Communications Association v. Douds*, which takes us into the heart of judicial anti-communism in the mid-twentieth century America.

In *Douds*, the Court upheld the constitutionality of section 9(h) of the 1947 Labor Management Relations Act, also known as the Taft-Hartley Act. This section required officers of unions certified by the National Labor Relations Board to swear that they were not members of the Communist Party. Congress claimed that 9(h) was based on the public interest in preventing political strikes. Justice Fred M. Vinson wrote the majority opinion.

> Congress could rationally find that the Communist Party is not like other political parties in its utilization of positions of union leadership as a means by which to bring about strikes and other obstructions of commerce for purposes of political advantage.[55]

The Regents pointed out that in the 1969 case of *Bryson v. United States*, the Supreme Court acknowledged that *Douds* had never been overruled. On the basis of *Douds*, the Regents argued that universities, like unions, are special zones that need to be immune from the influence of communism.

In their petition, the Regents made extensive use of Justice Robert H. Jackson's "illuminating analysis of the Communist Party" in his concurring opinion in *Douds*. Jackson is a key figure in understanding judicial anti-communism prior to its demise in the *Elfbrandt* case. A distinguished New Dealer and civil libertarian, Jackson, represents a highly principled type of anti-communism that is distinguishable from the demagoguery of Senator Joseph McCarthy. As Solicitor General under FDR, Jackson defended the legality of economic controls against challenges in the Supreme Court. He served as the Chief Prosecutor at the Nuremberg Trials in 1945–1946, taking a break from the Supreme Court which he joined in 1941. He died in 1954, shortly after joining the majority in *Brown v. Board of Education*.

Today, Jackson is honored for his progressive judicial opinions, including his dissent in *Korematsu v. U.S.* (1944) against the majority which upheld the internment of Japanese American citizens. Also famous is the majority opinion he wrote in *West Virginia v. Barnette* (1943). The case concerned Jehovah's Witnesses who refused to salute the American flag in school during World War II. The following is one of the most frequently quoted sentences in the Supreme Court's First Amendment jurisprudence.

> If there is any fixed star in our constitutional constellation, it is that no official, high or petty, can prescribe what shall be orthodox in politics, nationalism, religion, or other matters of opinion, or force citizens to confess by word or act their faith therein.[56]

Cass Sunstein has described Jackson's opinion as the greatest moment in Supreme Court history.[57] Jackson appears to express the libertarian free-speech ethos of the 1960s before its time. Yet, he was never in favor of tolerating radical political discourse. In a dissenting opinion in *Terminiello v. Chicago* (1949), he argued that a priest who delivered an anti-Black and anti-Jewish diatribe was not protected by the First Amendment. Jackson described the discourse as "fascist." He argued that members of "totalitarian groups" seeking to undermine democracy and individual rights should not enjoy freedom of speech.

> The choice is not between order and liberty. It is between liberty with order and anarchy without either. There is danger that, if the Court does not temper its doctrinaire logic with a little practical wisdom, it will convert the constitutional Bill of Rights into a *suicide pact*.[58]

The reference to suicide is evocative of the transformation of Germany's Weimar Republic into Hitler's Nazi state.

Although we generally think of Cold War ideology as accentuating the difference between democracy and totalitarianism, judicial anti-communism in the early twentieth century was concerned about the affinity between the two. In his influential theory of "militant democracy," the German emigré scholar, Karl Loewenstein, provided an explanation for why the democracies of inter-war Europe became "breeding grounds" of political extremism.[59] He claimed that anti-democratic parties knew how to "perfectly adjust" to democratic conditions. "Democracy and democratic tolerance have been used for their own destruction. They [extremist parties] exploit the tolerant confidence of democratic ideology that in the long run truth is stronger than falsehood . . ." Democracy must awake from its "*suicidal lethargy*" and become "militant."[60] Loewenstein was explicit that democratic vigilance should include the curtailing of freedom of speech and association.[61]

The concept of militant democracy has influenced German constitutional law and the decisions of the European Court of Human Rights.[62] The German Constitutional Court banned the German Communist Party (KPD) in 1957; it remains banned to this day. In the United States, the theory of militant democracy has largely been forgotten. Its place has been taken by confidence that open debate will discredit bad political parties. Yet, before the 1960s, opponents of communism often deployed the argument that democracy is not a suicide pact. In "Communism versus Academic Freedom," an article of 1949, Arthur Lovejoy wrote that it seems "self-contradictory to argue for the restriction of freedom in the name of freedom." But the believer in freedom "is not thereby committed to the conclusion that it is his duty to facilitate its destruction by placing its enemies in strategic positions of power, prestige or influence." A proper conception of freedom

> is not one which implies the legitimacy and inevitability of its own *suicide*. It is, on the contrary, a conception which, so to say, defines the limits of its own applicability; what it implies is that there is *one* kind of freedom which is inadmissible—the freedom to destroy freedom.[63]

Lovejoy supported the exclusion of Communist Party members from faculty positions. In the Douds case, Jackson maintained that constitutional democracy need not be tolerant of totalitarian parties. He had made the point in *Terminiello* with regard to fascism; now, he made the argument with respect to communism. Citing numerous academic authorities, he stated that the inevitable result of communism is the destruction of a nation's constitution.

> In each country where the Communists have seized control they have so denationalized its foreign policy as to make it a satellite and vassal of the Soviet Union and enforced a domestic policy in complete conformity with the Soviet pattern, tolerating no deviation in deference to any people's separate history, tradition or national interests.[64]

In their petition to the Supreme Court, the Regents cited this passage and many others from Jackson's opinion. Yet, their reliance on the *Douds* case was a losing strategy. For one thing, *Douds* did not prevent communists from being union members; the case affirmed only that Congress could exclude communists from being union *leaders*. Davis was at the bottom of the academic ladder. At best, *Douds* could be used to suggest that she should not be an administrator.

More importantly from a legal perspective, by 1970, the Supreme Court had adopted a higher standard than that used in *Douds* for the examination of governmental policies that impinged on freedom of speech and association. Jackson operated with the assumption that government only needed a "rational basis" for its policy of excluding communists from the leadership of unions. The rational basis standard was associated with New Deal legal thinking. In the early twentieth century, progressives saw the capacity of federal courts to strike down state legislation as a problem. Conservative judges used judicial review to annul economic controls and pro-union legislation. The basic idea of the "rational basis" standard promoted by New Dealers was that courts should not strike down laws unless they appeared to be utterly capricious. If Congress or a state legislature had consulted experts on the causes of a social problem and the need for regulation, then the resulting policy was presumed to be reasonable, even if expertise could also be adduced against the law.

An important innovation of the Supreme Court in the 1960s was the adoption of a separate and higher standard for the review of state policies, when they impinged on basic liberties such as freedom of speech. By 1970, the Warren Court had determined that a "strict scrutiny" test rather than a "rational basis" test must apply when the First Amendment is jeopardized. Strict scrutiny served as the theoretical foundation of a new type of judicial activism, leading to the striking down of many state regulations on speech. The *Keyishian* case, for example, invoked the doctrine of strict scrutiny.[65] As Davis' attorneys pointed out when responding to the Regents' petition to the Supreme Court, the *Douds* case was a weak precedent in any situation in which free speech was at stake.[66] Even with the two new Nixon appointees, the Court would not turn back the clock on strict scrutiny.[67] The Regents failed to resuscitate the theory of militant democracy.

Extramural Speech

The Regents lost in court when it came to firing Davis for being a communist. But the non-renewal of her contract in June 1970 was more of an administrative matter than a constitutional one. Davis had never been guaranteed a second year. The Regents only needed to cite budgetary considerations to justify the non-renewal. Their criticism of Davis' speeches as "antithetical to the protection of academic freedom" raised the stakes by making the non-renewal a statement about the boundaries of the university.

We have seen already that Davis described academic freedom as a "farce" unless scholars "link up" with the political struggle against capitalism and other systems of oppression.

A key question is whether she simply intended to say that academic freedom means that radical scholars, such as herself, should be included in the academy, or that *all* scholars must be radically engaged in order to deserve academic freedom. Her intent may have been only to put radical faculty on an equal footing with others, but her speeches suggested at times that she wished to politicize the whole academy and purge non-radical professors from it.

Two of the four speeches which the UCLA faculty committee and the Regents examined are available today as audio recordings. A theme of both speeches is that American society is heading in the direction of dictatorship. The university is complicit in this trend. Academic freedom is widely abused to support injustice; it should be used to resist oppression. In a speech at UCLA's Pauley Pavilion, on October 8, 1969, Davis stated that "an era of fascism" is looming. Capitalism has utterly failed to provide decent jobs to racial minorities, so the system "is resorting to fascist techniques more and more" to silence people of color (she says "black and brown" people).[68] As a pillar of the status quo, the university is "inherently political."[69] Its "politics are defined by the controlling political apparatus in this country." Evidence of this "conspiracy" (a term she uses often) is the vast amount of funding for research that the university receives from the Defense Department.[70] The university also concentrates in itself the "institutional racism" of the educational system—the differential academic treatment of Black people that begins in elementary school and is preserved in the university's entrance requirements.[71]

The ideal for Davis is not a university detached from political partisanship, which she regards as impossible, but a university fully inscribed in the movement for progressive change. Knowledge, she stated, has no purpose except to facilitate the abolition of racism and misery. It is essential, then, to bring political opinions into the classroom: "education itself is inherently political, its goal ought to be political."[72] As for those who cultivate knowledge without regard to political considerations, they are abetting fascism. In a speech at Berkeley, on October 24, 1969, she derided those who believe that academic freedom is "the freedom to remain unaware, to be ignorant of pressing human problems." Those who think academic freedom is a right "to sever themselves off from society" do not realize "that they are either consciously or unconsciously accomplices in the exploitation and oppression of man." Academic freedom is "useless" unless one employs it "to unveil the predominant oppressive acts in this country."[73]

Davis singled out Berkeley psychologist Arthur Jensen for criticism. In February 1969, Jensen published "How Much Can We Boost IQ and Scholastic Achievement" in the *Harvard Education Review.* He called for "unfettered research" on intelligence differences between the races because "much of the current thinking behind civil rights . . . appeals to the fact that there is a disproportionate representation of different racial groups in the various levels of the educational, occupational, and socioeconomic hierarchy." "We are forced," he stated, "to examine all the possible reasons for this inequality among racial groups." Jensen tried to preempt criticism by evoking the ethos of scientific inquiry.

> I strongly disagree with those who believe in searching for the truth by scientific means only under certain circumstances and eschew this course in favor of ignorance under other circumstances, or who believe that the results of inquiry on some subjects cannot be entrusted to the public but should be kept the guarded possession of a scientific elite. Such attitudes, in my opinion, represent a danger to free inquiry and, consequently, in the long run, work to the disadvantage of society's general welfare. 'No holds barred' is the best formula for scientific inquiry. One does not decree beforehand which phenomena cannot be studied or which questions cannot be answered.[74]

The article led to intense controversy, not only about the validity of Jensen's claim that there may be intelligence differences between the races but about whether he even had a right to publish his views. The AAUP issued a statement, "On Issues of Academic Freedom in Studies Linking Intelligence and Race." Its position is evident in the first sentence, "Some of its own members are undermining the integrity of the academic community by attempting to suppress unpopular opinions . . ." The AAUP reprimanded those who urged that studies such as Jensen's "be condemned out of hand." Academic freedom means that there is an "open forum for the dissemination of ideas through publication, exposition, and debate." This forum also allows critics of published work to advocate "counter-positions" and to publish their refutations "without restraint."[75] Davis took the position that Jensen's work "is not a reflection of academic freedom." Rather, he was "exploiting the notion of academic freedom" to promote racism.[76]

Davis built on the ideas of Marcuse. At Berkeley, Davis spoke after Marcuse delivered a 16-minute introduction. He concluded his remarks by stating that Davis was "the ideal victim" of repression by the Regents because "she is black, she is militant, she is a communist, she is highly intelligent, and she is pretty."[77] Davis began her speech by saying that Marcuse had influenced her thinking on academic freedom, particularly with his insistence that knowledge is always political.[78] There is certainly an affinity between Davis' ideas on academic freedom and Marcuse's theory of "repressive tolerance." Marcuse wrote that "tolerance cannot be indiscriminate and equal with respect to the contents of expression."[79] The anti-liberal conception of academic freedom and freedom of speech held by Marcuse and Davis was congruent with the Regents' attempt to fire Davis for being a communist! In other words, Davis' political outlook was not so different from that of the Regents when they wished to reverse *Elfbrandt* and *Keyishian*. Both sides took the view that the academy should not harbor political enemies. The Regents wished to exclude communism; Davis opposed what she called fascist professors.

In a meeting of the Board of Regents in November 1969, one of the members, William French Smith, stated that he considered Davis' public statements to be grounds for dismissal, apart from the previous issue of membership in the Communist Party.[80] He was elected Chairman of the Regents in June 1970.[81] This future Attorney General of the United States was a moving force on the Board.

As it became evident that the Regents were looking closely at Davis' speeches, UCLA Chancellor Young appointed a faculty committee to assess both Davis' teaching and the speeches. Young was not aligned with the Regents; his intention presumably was to preempt the Regents from dismissing Davis for her speeches. Accordingly, the committee reported, in April 1970, that it found no grounds for firing Davis in the middle of her current contract. But the report did point to problems in Davis' speeches—enough to recommend that these problems "be taken into account . . . by the appropriate faculty and administrative authorities when consideration is given to the renewal of Miss Davis' present contract of employment."[82] That was a perfect setup for the Regents decision not to renew Davis's contract in June. It is also worth noting that by charging the committee to examine Davis' speeches and not just her teaching, Young confirmed that a faculty member's utterances outside the classroom could be the subject of an investigation.

With regard to the speeches, the faculty committee noted that Davis' view of academic freedom was not in accord with the AAUP's view.[83] The committee stated, "she does not hesitate to attack the motives, methods, and conclusions of those with whom she disagrees."[84] The committee expressed disapproval of her remarks about Jensen and even for a moment seemed to defend Jensen by describing him as a tenured professor who "after years of study published a lengthy article outlining an hypothesis that certain kinds of learning abilities vary in measurable degrees between races." At the same time, the committee observed that Jensen's views are debatable and that "scholarly debate is not always conducted in the genteel tradition."[85] It is important to note that in their June report, the Regents steered clear of anything having to do with race and Jensen; they never mentioned Davis' criticism of him. Some of the Regents may well have harbored more admiration for Jensen than for Davis. But the suppression of any reference to race, as well as any reference to Davis' graphic criticism of the Regents, gave the Regents' report a professional tone. The faculty committee, in contrast, stated, "she has frequently sacrificed accuracy and fairness for the sake of rhetorical effect. We deem particularly offensive such utterances as her statement that the Regents 'killed . . . brutalized [and] murdered' the 'People's Park' demonstrators . . . and her repeated characterization of the police as 'pigs'."[86]

In November 1969, the UCLA Faculty Senate asked the AAUP to intervene. The AAUP did not issue a report until September 1971. The report focuses not on the firing of Davis for being a communist but on the Regents' decision not to renew Davis' contract in June 1969. The committee consisted of University of Michigan Philosophy professor Richard Brandt and University of Oregon Law professor Hans A. Linde. Their report focused on Davis' speeches because "Davis' extracurricular utterances were the main basis of their [the Regents'] decision on the merits."[87] Their defense of Davis is based on the belief that extramural speech should rarely figure in the performance evaluation of a professor.

The AAUP's 1940 Statement of Principles on Academic Freedom was the most general declaration of its norms since the founding declaration of 1915. As noted above, the 1940 text urged professors to exercise discretion in their off-campus political statements; the document even suggested in a footnote that professors could be fired for intemperate speech outside of the classroom.[88] We should recall that in 1940, the incorporation of the First Amendment into the Fourteenth was barely under way. The First Amendment did not have the robust character it would acquire in the 1960s. Moreover, in the field of employment law, the legal tradition was that employers, including those in state institutions, had a right to regulate employee speech *no matter where it occurred*. A classic expression of this principle was by Oliver Wendell Holmes, when he was Chief Justice of the Massachusetts Supreme Court. Holmes upheld the firing of a policeman who had violated a rule against showing public support for a political candidate.

> The petitioner may have a constitutional right to talk politics, but he has no constitutional right to be a policeman. There are few employments for hire in which the servant does not agree to suspend his constitutional rights of free speech as well as of idleness by the implied terms of his contract. The servant cannot complain, as he takes the employment on the terms which are offered him.[89]

The 1960s, however, saw a reversal of the principle that one can contract away one's constitutional rights. *Pickering v. Board of Education*, 1968, was the seminal case. Marvin Pickering was a public school teacher who was fired for writing a letter to a newspaper complaining that the school board allocated too much money to athletics. In an 8–1 decision, Justice Thurgood Marshall ruled that Pickering's letter was constitutionally protected speech. The decision rested on a distinction between the individual as employee and the individual as citizen—with the First Amendment protecting speech uttered as a citizen; that is, speech outside of work that addresses political issues.

In its report on the Davis affair, the AAUP referred to the *Pickering* case. The AAUP also meticulously traced the evolution of its own policy on extra-curricular speech through various documents, such as its 1963 "Advisory Letter No. 11 on Extramural Utterances" and its 1966 "Statement on Professional Ethics." Based on these post-1940 sources, the AAUP's report on the Davis case upheld the position that "extramural utterances . . . rarely bear on an individual's fitness for his position."[90] The report also stated, "institutional sanctions imposed for extramural utterances can be a violation of academic freedom even when the utterances themselves fall short of the standards of the profession."[91] The AAUP concluded that the decision not to reappoint Davis for the reason that her speeches were antithetical to academic freedom was itself a violation of her academic freedom. "[C]riticism of the AAUP doctrine about academic freedom, or even utterances which on full inquiry were found to transgress the AAUP standard, would not ipso facto establish unfitness for an academic position."[92] In other words, the AAUP did not consider respect for academic freedom to be a precondition of belonging to the academy.

The AAUP's position is the appropriate one for an organization committed to maximizing the speech rights of academics. But the position contains several ambiguities. By itemizing these, I do not mean to discredit the AAUP's approach to extramural speech. I wish to explain, rather, why the AAUP's stance, though plausible in itself, was not conclusive—not sufficient to negate the Regents' arguments. The closeness of this debate helps to explain why the controversy over extramural speech is still unresolved.

The ambiguities in question all have to do with the uncertain meaning of "extramural." When Davis spoke at UC Berkeley after her dissertation supervisor introduced her, it was both an academic and a political event. In what sense was Davis' speech "extramural"? Her remarks were certainly "extracurricular"—outside the classroom. But the AAUP used the word "extramural." Do the two words mean the same thing? The answer is no. Speech at a meeting of a Faculty Senate or in a departmental meeting is extracurricular but not extramural; it is employment-related speech. "Extramural" literally means "outside the walls," which suggests that the *venue* is off campus. In *Pickering,* the Supreme Court held that a teacher could write editorials in newspapers. The newspaper is clearly outside the boundaries of the school. Yet, Davis gave two of the four contested speeches on UC campuses.

Suppose, instead, we assume that extramural refers to the *content* of speech—extramural then means something like "not academic." There is still a problem. In some of the speeches, Davis was introduced as a professor of philosophy, and she spoke as a philosopher about the meaning of education and academic freedom. Her discourse was that of an academic *and* of a citizen. Efforts to classify speech according to the binary distinction of extramural and work-related break down in many real situations.

The patent inadequacy of the binary (employee/citizen) articulated in *Pickering* has led the Supreme Court to modify the distinction in multiple ways. In a detailed survey of recent efforts by the Court to establish a clear doctrine concerning what types of speech can be regulated by a public employer, Mark Strasser finds a "dizzying set of rules" and a "muddled jurisprudence."[93] But one thing is clear: the Court has become more sympathetic to public employers wishing to limit employee speech. It should be noted too that the *Pickering* case concerned the *firing* of a teacher. The Regents did not fire Davis for her speeches; they only weighed her speeches as one factor, along with the budget and her unfinished thesis, in their decision not to renew her contract.

By a 15–6 vote on June 19, 1970, the Regents decided not to renew Davis' contract.[94] I have argued that what allowed them to get rid of Davis was their capacity to take

advantage of persistent ambiguities in the idea of academic freedom. AAUP pronouncements tilted toward free expression in the 1960s, but the organization still upheld professional values, and the Regents were able to draw on AAUP documents to make their case
against Davis. They quoted, for example, the AAUP's 1966 Statement on Professional
Ethics:

> As a colleague, the professor has obligations that derive from common membership in
> the community of scholars. He respects and defends the free inquiry of his associates.
> In the exchange of criticism and ideas he shows due respect for the opinions of others.[95]

For the evaluation of the content of the speeches, the Regents relied on the criticism for-
mulated in the UCLA faculty committee's "penetrating inquiry."[96] As for the unfinished
thesis, the Regents shrewdly linked it to Davis' own conception of academic freedom as
subordinate to political activism. In her UCLA speech, Davis told students and professors
that their research should not take priority over pursuing social justice.

> Miss Davis announced that, "I myself was supposed to have my Ph.D. dissertation fin-
> ished by the end of this quarter, but obviously that's not going to be the case," because,
> as she went on to explain, she would be devoting her time and energies to political
> purposes.[97]

Once the Regents added that the budget required them to reduce the faculty and quoted
dean Rolfe to the effect that Davis' position was not a high priority, they completed a
case that rested entirely on materials elicited from the UCLA academic community. The
Regents' report was not only plausible; it was a *tour de force*.

Conclusion

This is not to say that the Regents "won." The victor in the long run was Davis. In 1991,
she became a professor at the University of California Santa Cruz. Today, her writings are
regarded as essential reading for those who wish to comprehend the roots of racial protest.[98]
Davis has entered the mainstream of political discussion. But there is more. She was not just
victorious after her battle with the Regents; she won the battle itself.

While sentences such as "The Regents dismissed Davis," make it sound like she was a
victim or object, the reality is that she was the leading agent throughout the conflict. She
controlled the course of events. She could have refused to answer Saxon's inquiry about
her Communist Party membership. She answered bluntly because she wished to highlight the university's exclusionary policy. From a Marxist perspective, progress occurs
when social action brings out antagonism in society.[99] Polarization is more desirable than
compromise. Davis radicalized her disagreement with the Regents over communism,
and she won that battle in the courts. Likewise, when the Regents condemned Davis for
her speeches, the driving agent was Davis. She chose to give the speeches. She provoked
conflict by linking the Regents to the growth of "fascism" and by describing academic
freedom as a "farce." Keeping her job at UCLA was never Davis' priority. Her priority
was to illuminate contradictions in the self-image of the American university as a zone
of freedom.

Of the four speeches Davis gave which created consternation among the Regents, one of
the two for which there is no recording was her speech on October 12, 1969, at a banquet

in Santa Monica held by *The People's World*, the Communist Party newspaper. Fortunately, the excellent journalist, William J. Drummond, who covered her first classroom lecture at UCLA, was there.

> The proper use of the classroom, she said, is to "unveil those who perpetuate suffering" and to "unmask the predominant ideas for what they are." If no positive solutions are presented to students, "academic freedom is a real farce," she said . . . The way to test the validity of "bourgeois democratic concepts" such as freedom of speech, freedom of the press and freedom of thought is to test their application to suppressed peoples, Davis said . . . "We have to fight these proponents of selective democracy and expose the limits of bourgeois democracy," Miss Davis said.[100]

Davis drew applause when she declared, "Socialism alone can solve the problems created by capitalism."[101] This she never proved. But the conflict she instigated with the Regents amply demonstrated the existence of acute contradictions in our language of academic freedom and freedom of speech.

Notes

1 "Press Release Issued by Miss Angela Y. Davis," September 23, 1969, in "Angela Y. Davis Academic Freedom Case at UCLA (Leon Letwin file)," https://leonletwin.files.wordpress.com/2016/02/1969-1970-angela-davis-ucla-academic-freedom-battle-prof-leon-letwin-file.pdf. This is a collection of documents compiled by UCLA Law Professor Leon Letwin. Cited hereafter as Letwin Collection. The collection is not paginated continuously but the documents appear in chronological order.

2 Ibram X. Kendi, *Stamped from the Beginning: The Definitive History of Racist Ideas in America* (New York: Hachette Book Group, 2016), 8.

3 Bernice McNair Barnett, "Angela Davis and Women, Race, and Class: A Pioneer in Integrative RGC Studies," *Race, Gender, & Class*, vol. 10, no. 3 (2003), 9–22; Angela Y. Davis, *Women, Race, and Class* (New York: Vintage, 1983) and *Are Prisons Obsolete?* (New York: Seven Stories Press, 2011). For a bibliography of writings by and about Davis through 2003, see John L. Novak, "Angela Davis: A Bibliography," http://docplayer.net/184315036-Angela-davis-a-bibliography-compiled-by-john-l-novak.html.

4 "Academic Freedom and Tenure: The University of California at Los Angeles," *AAUP Bulletin*, vol. 57, no. 3 (September 1971), 385. Cited afterward as "AFT," this is the American Association of University Professors' report on the dismissal of Davis, which I will analyze in detail later in the article. It provides background on the hiring of Davis as well as her dismissal.

5 Angela Davis, *An Autobiography* (New York: International Publishers, 1974), discusses growing up under segregation and the death of her friends in the bombing of the 16th Street Baptist Church in 1963.

6 Stephen J. Whitfield, "A Radical in Academe: Herbert Marcuse at Brandeis University," *Journal for the Study of Radicalism*, vol. 9, no. 2 (Fall, 2015), 101.

7 Ibid, p. 102. See also Angela Davis, "Preface: Marcuse's Legacies," in *Herbert Marcuse: The New Left and the 1960s*, vol. 3., ed. Douglas Kellner (London: Routledge, 2005), xi.

8 This essay underscores common points between Marcuse and Davis on the subject of free speech and academic freedom. But Davis' focus on race was a major addition to the "critical theory" of Marcuse and Frankfurt School. For a provocative criticism of the "whiteness" of the Frankfurt School, see Charles W. Mills, *Black Rights/White Wrongs: The Critique of Racial Liberalism* (Oxford: Oxford University Press, 2017), 203–204.

9 Kenneth Reich and William Trombley, "Explosive Academic Freedom Case Confronts UC Regents," *Los Angeles Times* (September 10, 1969), 1.

10 *Elfbrandt v. Russell*, 384 U.S. 11 (1966), 15, 19. The phrase "guilt by association" was the subject of widespread debate in the 1950s and 1960s. See Sidney Hook (ed.), "What Is 'Guilt by Association'"? in *Heresy, Yes—Conspiracy, No* (New York: John Day Company, 1953), 84–93 for a discussion of

the competing viewpoints. Hook took the position that membership in the Communist Party was *prima facie* evidence that one is a hardened conspirator; according to Hook, the Party had "control" commissions that expelled non-compliant members. I discuss below how Robert H. Jackson and other Supreme Court justices in the 1950s agreed with this. The *Elfbrandt* case rejected this understanding of Party membership.

11 Keyishian v. Board of Regents of the State of New York, 385 U.S. 589 (1967), 597–598.

12 Vogel v. Los Angeles County, 68 Cal.2d (1967). The text of the oath is at 2–3. The oath originated with the Levering Act of 1950, which superseded the highly controversial oath of 1949 that applied only to faculty at the University of California. The Levering oath did not mention communism explicitly; the university oath did. In 1952, the California Supreme court ruled that the university oath was unconstitutional because it singled out academics for a loyalty test; but the Court also ruled that the Levering oath was constitutional because it applied equally to all public employees. See Tolman v. Underhill, 39 Cal.2d 708 (1952) and Pockman v. Leonard, 39 Cal.2d 267 (1952). The Vogel case thus set a new course by invalidating all oaths for public employees in California that banned membership in subversive organizations.

13 Superior Court of the State of California for the County of Los Angeles, No. 962388 (October 24, 1969), xxiv; accessed as Appendix B in *Regents of California v. Karst*, Petition for a Writ of Certiorari, United States Supreme Court No. 71-1609 (October term 1971); the Petition for Certiorari, containing Judge Pacht's decision as an appendix, is the principal document in the Making of Modern Law pamphlet entitled *Regents of the University of California v. Karst*, ed. Thomas J. Cunningham, John T. McTernan, and Charles H. Phillip (n.p.: Gale, 2011). There is no continuous pagination in the volume. Page numbers are internal to specific documents.

14 "Report of the Regents' Committee of the Whole" (June 19, 1970), in *University Bulletin: A Weekly Bulletin for Staff of the University of California,* vol. 18, no. 37 (June 29, 1970), 200; cited hereafter as "RRCW."

15 On Saxon, who became President of the UC system in 1975, see Blauner, *Resisting McCarthyism,* 88, 109, 157; and Ellen W. Schrecker, *No Ivory Tower: McCarthyism and the Universities* (New York: Oxford University Press, 1986), 118.

16 "AFT," 389.

17 29 U.S. 245 (1934), 256.

18 "RRCW," p. 200 (italics added).

19 Ibid, 199.

20 Herbert Marcuse, "Repressive Tolerance," in *A Critique of Pure Tolerance*, eds. Robert Paul Wolff, Barrington Moore, Jr., and Herbert Marcuse (Boston: Beacon Press, 1969; first pub. 1965), 80.

21 "Angela Davis and Herbert Marcuse at UC Berkeley, 1969," https://www.youtube.com/watch?v=HuyWj8BtjKc, starting at 20:07. I have italicized words to capture Davis' voice inflections.

22 Regents of the University of California v. Bakke, 438 U.S. 265 (1978), 312.

23 Stanley Fish, *Versions of Academic Freedom: From Professionalism to Revolution* (Chicago: University of Chicago Press, 2014), x. For a similar view, i.e., that academic freedom is a professional norm, not a legal concept, see Robert Post, "Discipline and Freedom in the Academy," *Arkansas Law Review,* vol. 65, no. 2 (2012), 203–216. For a contrary view, i.e., that academic freedom is a subset of the First Amendment, see William W. Van Alstyne, "Academic Freedom and the First Amendment in the Supreme Court of the United States: An Unhurried Historical View," *Law and Contemporary Problems,* vol. 55, no. 3 (Summer, 1990), 79–154.

24 Keyishian v. Board of Regents, 603. The "multitude of tongues" clause is a reference to Judge Learned Hand's decision in U.S. v. Associated Press, D.C., 52 F. Supp. 362 (1943), 372.

25 Stephen H. Aby discusses the Davis case in "Angela Davis and the Changing Paradigm of Academic Freedom in the 1960s," *American Educational History Quarterly,* vol. 34, no. 2 (Fall, 2007), 289–301. Unfortunately, the author confuses the Regents' June 1970 report on Davis' dismissal with a different document, the report of the UCLA faculty committee in April, 1970. Hence, his discussion of the reasons for Davis' termination contains basic errors. J. A. Parker, *Angela Davis the Making of a Revolutionary* (New Rochelle: Arlington House), 104–130, covers the UCLA dismissal; the analysis is biased by the author's frequent assertions to the effect that communists should never be allowed to teach.

26 Bettina Aptheker, *The Morning Breaks: The Trial of Angela Davis* (Ithaca: Cornell University Press, 1999), 21.

27 Ibid, 11. For Davis' account of the relationship as "very close," see her 1971 interview on the Thames TV program "This Week," https://www.youtube.com/watch?v=fnJPwdKsIjc at minute 9.

28 Angela Davis, *The Prison Industrial Complex* (CD, Chico: AK Press, 1971); "Masked Racism: Reflections on the Prison Industrial Complex," *Color Lines* (September 10, 1998), https://www. colorlines.com/articles/masked-racism-reflections-prison-industrial-complex.

29 Thomas Haskell, "Justifying the Rights of Academic Freedom in the Era of 'Power/Knowledge'," in *The Future of Academic Freedom*, ed. Louis Menand (Chicago: University of Chicago Press, 1996), 57 (on authorship of the 1915 text).

30 "General Declaration of Principles on Academic Freedom and Academic Tenure," *Indiana Law Journal*, vol. 91, no. 1 (Winter, 2015; first pub. 1915), 66.

31 Arthur Lovejoy, "Academic Freedom," *Encyclopaedia of the Social Sciences*, ed. R.A. Seligman (New York: Macmillan, 1937), vol. 1, 384.

32 David M. Rabban, "The First Amendment in Its Forgotten Years," *Yale Law Journal*, vol. 90, no. 3 (January 1981), 514–595.

33 Akhil Amar, *The Bill of Rights: Creation and Reconstruction* (New Haven: Yale University Press, 2000); William J. Brennan, Jr., "The Supreme Court and the Meiklejohn Interpretation of the First Amendment," *Harvard Law Review*, vol. 79, no. 1 (November 1965), 1–20.

34 Rabban's article, Ibid, is primarily about the "bad tendency" test. Holmes first referred to "clear and present danger" in *Schenk v. United States* (1919).

35 "Press Release Issued by Miss Angela Y. Davis," September 23, 1969.

36 Lisa McGirr, *Suburban Warriors: The Origins of the New American Right* (Princeton: Princeton University Press, 2001); Max Felker-Kantor, *Policing Los Angeles: Race, Resistance, and the Rise of the LAPD* (Chapel Hill: University of North Carolina Press, 2018).

37 William Tuilio Divale, "FBI Student Spy in CPUSA Answers Criticisms," *UCLA Daily Bruin*, July 1, 1959, 5.

38 Ed Montgomery, "Maoist Prof Poses Problems for Regents," *San Francisco Examiner*, July 9, 1969, 14.

39 Letter from Saxon to Davis, July 16, 1969, Letwin Collection (the first document in the collection).

40 "A Statement of Facts Concerning the Appointment and Threatened Dismissal of Angela Davis, Provided by the Department of Philosophy," September 29, 1969, 4–5. University of California Archives, Bancroft Library: http://content.cdlib.org/view?docId=hb1x0nb4kq&brand=oac4.

41 On Che-Lumumba and Davis' participation in it, see Beth Slutsky, *Gendering Radicalism: Women and Communism in Twentieth-Century California* (Lincoln: University of Nebraska Press, 2015), 155–164.

42 The three resolutions are in Cunningham et al., *Regents of the University of California v Karst* (there is no continuous pagination but see xxvii–xxxvi of the Regents' petition for certiorari; the resolutions are included as Appendices). The reference to a faculty vote against admitting CP members as professors is accurate; 90% of the UC faculty responded to a survey asking them to vote for or against a proposition stating that CP members "are not acceptable as members of the Faculty." About 90% of faculty at all campuses voted, and 79% were for the proposition. At UCLA, it was 83%. For the text of the ballot, which included a statement by Arthur Lovejoy for the proposition and a statement by the AAUP against, see "Letter, March 13, 1950: Memorandum on Proposition 1 and Proposition 2," Online Archive of California, https://oac.cdlib.org/view?docId=hb0199p04j&brand=oac4&doc. view=entire_text. For results of the ballot, see Blauner, R*esisting McCarthyism*, 108.

43 "AFT," 386.

44 William J. Drummond, "First Lecture: Paradoxes in Society Cited by Miss Davis," *Los Angeles Times*, October 7, 1969, 8. On the same day, the *Times* included a front-page story on Davis' lecture: Kenneth Reich, "2,000 Jam UCLA Hall to Hear First Lecture by Davis," 1, 29. Reich's article outlined the political controversy, while Drummond focused on the content of the lecture.

45 Brad Snyder, "Angela Davis Laments Her Legacy as a 'Hair-Do." *Baltimore Sun*, December 4, 1994. https://www.baltimoresun.com/news/bs-xpm-1994-12-04-1994338067-story.html

46 Angela Davis, "Lectures on Liberation," in *A Political Companion to Frederick Douglass*, ed. Neil Roberts (Lexington: University of Press of Kentucky, 2018), 110–134 (the first two lectures from Davis' 1969 course, apparently unaltered).

47 Drummond, "First Lecture," 8.

48 "AFT," 407–408.

49 "1940 Statement of Principles on Academic Freedom and Tenure," https://www.aaup.org/report/ 1940-statement-principles-academic-freedom-and-tenure; item number 3 on "Academic Freedom."

50 Some notable recent controversies are the Drexel University professor who tweeted, "All I want for Christmas is white genocide" (after being placed on leave, the professor resigned); the University

of Pennsylvania Law professor who wrote an op-ed stating that "All cultures are not equal" (the professor was barred from teaching mandatory first-year courses), and the University of Louisiana professor who posted a racial slur about President Barack Obama (the professor was put on leave and may be fired). Readers can easily find news reports on these cases. For a brief article that references several other cases and captures the unresolved nature of the principles at stake, see Emily Bohatch, "Professors Walk Tight Rope When Posting to Web," *USA Today*, June 26, 2017, www.usatoday. com/story/news/2017/06/26/professors-walk-tight-rope-when-posting-web/429486001/.

51 Thomas Blackwell, "Constitutionality of Dismissal Based on Membership in the Communist Party," *The College Law Digest* (January, 1970), 6.

52 Judge Alport (dissenting), Karst v. *Regents of the University of California*, 2 Civil No. 38,410 (January 26, 1972) in Cunningham et al. (eds), ix-x (Appendix A of the Regents petition for certiorari).

53 Petition for Writ of Certiorari, *Regents of University of California v. Karst*, in Cunningham et al. (eds.), 6-7 (italics in original).

54 Ibid, 8.

55 *American Communications Association v. Douds*, 399 U.S. 382 (1950), pp. 390–391; cited in the Regents' petition (see previous note), 8.

56 West Virginia State Board of Education v. Barnette, 310 U.S. 624 (1943), 642.

57 Robert H. Jackson Center website, "If There Is Any Fixed Star," https://www.roberthjackson.org/article/if-there-is-any-fixed-star-jackson-on-west-virginia-v-barnett/.

58 Terminiello v. Chicago, 337 U.S. 1 (1949), 37 (italics added).

59 Karl Loewenstein, "Militant Democracy and Fundamental Rights, I," *American Political Science Review*, vol. 31, no. 3 (June, 1937), 421.

60 Ibid, 423, 431 (italics added).

61 Karl Loewenstein, "Militant Democracy and Fundamental Rights, II," *American Political Science Review*, vol. 31, no. 4 (August, 1937), 638, 642, 653 (italics added).

62 For the influence of "militant democracy" in European law, see Gregory H. Fox and George Nolte, "Intolerant Democracies," *Harvard International Law Journal*, vol. 36, no. 1 (Winter, 1995), 1–70; and Carlo Invernizzi Acetti and Ian Zuckerman, "What's Wrong with Militant Democracy," *Political Studies*, vol. 54, no. 15 (2017), 182–199.

63 Arthur Lovejoy, "Communism versus Academic Freedom," *The American Scholar*, vol. 18, no. 3 (Summer, 1949), 334 (italics added to "suicide").

64 *American Communications Assn. v. Douds*, 339 U.S. 382 (1950), 428.

65 *Keyishian v. Board of Regents,* 603–604 for reference to strict scrutiny. A legal irony is that the doctrine of strict scrutiny was developed out of footnote 4, often called the most famous footnote in Supreme Court history, in *United States v. Carolene Products Company* (1938). In *Douds*, Jackson cited this case as the source of the "rational basis" test, which it was. The case protected New Deal economic legislation from judicial review. But in the footnote, Justice Stone expressed anxiety about such a limited conception of judicial review; he suggested that in the future it may be necessary to adopt a different standard, if basic constitutional liberties were threatened by legislation. Jackson ignored the footnote in *Douds*, and by relying on Jackson's opinion in their petition to the Supreme Court, the Regents sounded behind the times in their legal thinking. This is probably why the Supreme Court did not take the case—the court gave no reasons for denying certiorari.

66 Brief for Respondent Angela Y. Davis in Opposition to the Petition for a Writ of Certiorari (October term, 1971), in Cunningham et al., eds., *Regents of the University of California v. Karst*, p. 20 (I note again that pagination in the volume is not continuous; each legal document has its own pagination).

67 On the subject of loyalty oaths for state employees, the Supreme Court soon settled on a moderately conservative position which remains in effect today. In *Cole v. Richardson* (1972), Chief Justice Burger wrote the majority opinion confirming that a state cannot ban employees from membership in any political party, but the opinion upholds the right of the state to require employees to swear allegiance to the U.S. and state constitutions. Today, professors at the University of California must take such an oath—a very faint trace of militant democracy.

68 "Angela Davis at UCLA 10/8/1969," https://www.youtube.com/watch?v=AxCqTEMgZUc. Minutes 27–28, and 32.

69 Ibid, minute 11.

70 Ibid, minute 5.

71 Ibid, minutes 6, 9 (for "institutional racism," a term whose basic meaning, distinct from psychological racism, she explains to the audience).

72 Ibid, minute 4.

73 "Herbert Marcuse and Angela Davis at Berkeley," October 24, 1969, American Archive of Pub-
    lic Broadcasting, https://americanarchive.org/catalog/cpb-aacip_28-7d2q52fm0j. Starting at
    minute 21.

74 Arthur Jensen, "How Much Can We Boost IQ and Scholastic Achievement" in the *Harvard Education
    Review* vol. 39, no. 1 (April, 1969), 79.

75 "On Issues of Academic Freedom in Studies Linking Intelligence and Race," *AAUP Bulletin*, vol.
    60, no. 2 (June, 1974), 153; the AAUP first issued the statement in February, 1974). See also William
    T. Kilgore and Barbara Sullivan, "Academic Values and the Jensen-Shockley Controversy," *The
    Journal of General Education*, vol. 27, no. 3 (Fall, 1975), 177–187, portraying a spectrum of responses
    to race-based research on intelligence.

76 "Herbert Marcuse and Angela Davis at Berkeley," minutes 23, 27.

77 Ibid, minute 15.

78 Ibid, minute 17. See also the UCLA speech, in which Davis discussed Marcuse's *Essay on Liberation*
    (1969): "Angela Davis at UCLA 10/8/1969," starting at 11:30.

79 Marcuse, "Repressive Tolerance," 88. For contemporary criticism of Marcuse's thought on toler-
    ance, see Alisdair MacIntyre, *Herbert Marcuse: An Exposition and a Polemic* (New York: Viking Press,
    1970), 14, 50, 102–103.

80 "AFT," 383, 387.

81 "William F. Smith Elected Board Chairman," *University Bulletin*, vol. 13, no. 37 (June 29, 1970), 197.
    The Regents' report on Davis begins on the same page.

82 "Report of Chancellor Young's Ad Hoc Committee," Addendum A in "AFT," 412.

83 "Report of Chancellor Young's Ad Hoc Committee," 410.

84 Ibid, 411.

85 Ibid.

86 Ibid. The "People's Park" is a reference to conflict over the development of land near UC Berkeley.

87 "AFT," 393.

88 See the AAUP's 1940 "Statement of Principles on Academic Freedom," 6, note 4.

89 Mcauliffe v. New Bedford, 155 Mass. 216, 220.

90 "ATF," 396. In the late 1960s and early 1970s, the AAUP was active in defending professors dis-
    ciplined for extramural speech. See "Academic Freedom and Tenure: The University of Florida,"
    AAUP Bulletin, vol. 56, no. 4 (December, 1970), 405–422 for a particularly complex instance. The
    case centered on a professor who was denied tenure because his speeches advocated student rebellion
    and dismissed the democratic process; his language also allegedly led to the suicide of a graduate
    student.

91 Ibid, 398.

92 Ibid 397.

93 Mark Strasser, "Pickering, Garcetti, and Academic Freedom," *Brooklyn Law Review*, vol. 83, no. 2
    (Winter, 2018), 579–580. See 587–591 for problems in the employee/citizen distinction.

94 For a listing of the Regents who voted on each wide, see William Trombley, "UC Regent Set for
    Firing of Angela Davis," *Los Angeles Times*, May 16, 1970, 23.

95 "Report of the Regents' Committee of the Whole," 198.

96 Ibid, 197–198.

97 Ibid, 200.

98 For example, Michelle Alexander, author of *The New Jim Crow* (2012), recommends Davis
    along with Frederick Douglass, Martin Luther King, and James Baldwin. https://www.nytimes.
    com/2020/06/08/opinion/george-floyd-protests-race.html.

99 See Davis, *Autobiography*, 109–110. where she discusses how reading Marx's *Communist Manifesto*
    struck her like a "bolt of lightning." She determined to quicken the revolutionary process as Marx
    described it.

100 William J. Drummond, "Angela Davis Outlines Her Views on Teaching," *Los Angeles Times*, Octo-
    ber 13, 1969, 26.

101 Ibid.

2 Absolute Meiklejohn

Abstract

Alexander Meiklejohn became the President of Amherst College at an early age. He was fired for his progressive ideas and later fired at the University of Wisconsin for the same reason. In academic exile, he took to the study of law and developed his now-famous "absolutist" theory of the First Amendment. The Supreme Court at first ridiculed his interpretation of free speech but converted to his view in the landmark case of *New York Times v. Sullivan* (1964). Meiklejohn's vision of free speech is not hard to explain—he believed that political speech can never be suppressed—but he also held ideas about academic freedom and liberal education which were anti-libertarian. Influenced by Rousseau, he construed the American college not as a free-speech zone but as a place where students are trained to be good citizens. The students are to be taught, through a required core curriculum, not how to speak freely but how to speak intelligently about political matters. Free speech without liberal education is futile, he believed. The chapter explains Meiklejohn's legal and educational ideals and the ups and downs of their reception in the worlds of law and higher education.

Introduction

On March 28, 1952, at the Annual Meeting of the American Association of University Professors, Alexander Meiklejohn (1872–1962) delivered a lecture entitled "The Teaching of Intellectual Freedom."[1] Meiklejohn had been the President of Amherst College and the director of the University of Wisconsin's Experimental College. He was also a philosopher and champion of civil liberties. In his most recent book prior to the AAUP lecture, *Free Speech and Its Relation to Self-Government* (1948), he argued that the First Amendment prohibits the suppression of political speech of any kind, including communist propaganda. "No one who reads with care the text of the First Amendment can fail to be startled by its absoluteness."[2] In his address to the AAUP, Meiklejohn announced that he would examine academic freedom in its relation to the First Amendment.

> The inquiry which I now venture to present to you is not primarily concerned with the freedom and self-government of the professors of the United States. It is concerned rather with the freedom and self-government of the people of the United States . . . Here, then, is the question which I ask you to consider. What is the relation between the freedom of mind of the professor, as defined by your Association, and the freedom of mind of the people, as defined by the First Amendment?[3]

It was a great question. By suggesting that academic freedom and freedom of speech were linked, Meiklejohn was making a point that seems obvious today. But in 1952, he was swimming against the current.

DOI: 10.4324/9781003052685-3

Established in 1915, the AAUP was dedicated to defending the academic freedom of professors against interventions by university trustees and state legislators. One of the AAUP's founders, the philosopher Arthur Lovejoy of Johns Hopkins University, had resigned from a previous position at Stanford University in 1900 to protest the forced resignation of the economist E.A. Ross whose offense was to oppose the importation of Chinese laborers. This view outraged Jane Stanford, the widow of the university's founder, Leland Stanford, who was also the founder of the Central Pacific Railroad. The Ross case and others like it were the catalysts for the creation of the AAUP, the organization responsible for making academic freedom a core principle in American universities. But what did academic freedom mean for the AAUP at its founding?

The AAUP's 1915 "General Declaration of Principles on Academic Freedom and Academic Tenure," written in part by Lovejoy, defines academic freedom as the license of professors to carry out their "important function," which is

> to deal at first hand, after prolonged and specialized technical training, with the sources of knowledge; and to impart the results of their own and of their fellow-specialists' investigations and reflection, both to students and to the general public, without fear or favor.[4]

This conception of academic freedom had little to do with the First Amendment. Academic freedom, as construed by the AAUP, was a benefit reserved for "specialized" researchers. It was not a constitutional right but an intellectual privilege. In fact, the constitutional right of free speech was not highly developed in 1915. At that time, the First Amendment only applied to the federal government. State legislatures were not restricted by the Amendment. Even after the Supreme Court decided, in 1923, that "Congress shall make no law . . . abridging the freedom of speech" applied to state governments, legal doctrines such as "clear and present danger," which persisted until the 1960s, limited the scope of free speech. In short, it made little sense for the AAUP to hang academic freedom on the hook of the First Amendment.

The AAUP's mission, then, was to articulate a conception of academic freedom which would do *more* to protect the core functions of research and teaching than the First Amendment did to protect the free speech of American citizens in general. The idea of tethering academic freedom to freedom of speech was not on the horizon in 1915. At that time, there was no reason for professors to equate academic freedom with freedom of speech, because freedom of speech did not yet exist in a robust form. Only when First Amendment doctrine developed to the point where professors had something to gain by hanging their liberty on the hook of the First Amendment did the whole issue of how academic freedom relates to freedom of speech become worth thinking about. But Meiklejohn was unique: he foresaw the liberalization of free-speech doctrine in the Supreme Court; he ardently advocated for it, and eventually, his free-speech "absolutism" was embraced by the Court. Thus, he was thinking deeply about how academic freedom and freedom of speech related to each other before the question became current.

Meiklejohn envisioned academic freedom and the First Amendment as sharing a common purpose. His unified theory was based on the idea that the free-speech rights of non-academics, on the one hand, and the academic freedom of professors, on the other hand, emanate from a single source. Both freedom of speech and academic freedom are expressions of "intellectual freedom," which is a prerequisite of democracy—of a community of rational citizens debating matters of public policy. Vibrant self-government, according to Meiklejohn, is based on "the actual intellectual processes by which free men govern a nation."[5] This requires citizens not only to possess the abstract right of free speech but also to have a liberal education.

For the AAUP, academic freedom served to insulate the objective quest for truth inside of the university from the political power of outsiders. Meiklejohn, in contrast, envisioned academic freedom as an instrument with which to prepare young people to extrude into the political process. Likewise, the purpose of a "liberal college" for Meiklejohn is not to promote knowledge for its own sake. It is to prepare future citizens for participation in vigorous debates about public policy. Academic freedom in the university is nothing other than a dress rehearsal for the exercise of free speech in the public sphere. Curiously, the source of academic freedom in Meiklejohn's vision is not anything purely academic; this made his thinking entirely different from the AAUP's pronouncements on academic freedom. *The guiding ideal behind academic freedom for Meiklejohn is not the attainment of scientific truth but the exercise of popular sovereignty.*

In the AAUP address, Meiklejohn said:

> Just as some men make shoes and other men grow food, so it is our business to discover truth in its more intellectualized forms and to make it powerful in the guidance of the life of the community. And since we are thus acting as the agents of the people, they grant to us such of their freedom as is needed in that field of work. In a word, the final justification of our academic freedom is to be found, not in our purposes but in theirs. In the last resort, it is granted, not because we want it or enjoy it, but because those by whom we are commissioned need intellectual leadership in the thinking which a free society must do.[6]

Academic freedom is the right to engage in political debate on campus; it is also a duty to do so. For Meiklejohn, there is a "required education for freedom."[7] Early in his career, Meiklejohn became committed to the idea that liberal education must be based on a core curriculum that promotes students' engagement with complex social and political problems. "The liberal college must endeavor to become the place where mind is made and molded."[8] For the AAUP, academic freedom facilitates the objective pursuit of truth in the disciplines. For Meiklejohn, academic freedom, paradoxically, *compels* one to participate in a structured set of debates which the liberal college configures through its required curriculum.

In Meiklejohn's speculative imagination, an unusually intellectual conception of democracy was tied to a thoroughly political conception of education. Academic freedom is not "a special privilege" of the student or professor; it is the cultivation of the mental faculties "which must be possessed and exercised . . . by every member of a society which is seeking to be self-governed."[9] Meiklejohn offered an impressive synthesis of the First Amendment and academic freedom, but his approach to academic freedom was out of step with his time, i.e., with the AAUP's professional ethos. Also, his reading of the First Amendment was radically out of joint with prevailing legal doctrine. We will see that in *Dennis v. United States* (1951), two justices of the Supreme Court, one of them the chief justice, singled out Meiklejohn's "absolutist" conception of free political speech for scornful criticism. The case upheld criminal penalties for anyone who published or sold material advocating political revolution through violence.

When it came to both academic freedom and free speech, Meiklejohn was swimming against the current. He was, however, accustomed to rejection. He had been fired, in 1923, from the presidency of Amherst College for his socialist opinions. When he afterward became the Director of the Experimental College at the University of Wisconsin, *Time Magazine* lampooned him as "an organ grinder's monkey," a creature who, because he had fallen from grace in the elite academic world, took refuge in a "queer" alternative education program.[10] The Experimental College collapsed in 1932 amid accusations of Bolshevism, indolence, and homosexuality among the students.[11] Meiklejohn went on to start an adult education program in San Francisco, which crumbled after a few years. In 1952, when he spoke to the AAUP, at the age of 80, his failures were widely known. An icon of earnest idealism devoid of practical judgment, he appeared to have no prospects of becoming a person of influence.

Yet, Meiklejohn lived till the age of 92. In his last years, he experienced a remarkable reversal of fortune in terms of the reception of his theory of the First Amendment as affording absolute protection to political speech. Starting in the early 1950s, he began to write exquisitely crafted scholarly articles on the Constitution. He published some of them in leading law journals, such as the *Supreme Court Review*. In 1960, Harry Kalven, Jr., one of the most eminent law professors of the time,[12] wrote a flattering article about Meiklejohn in the *University of Chicago Law Review*. Kalven observed that the philosopher had caught "the contagion of law" and had demonstrated professional expertise through "a major series of essays." In free-speech jurisprudence, Kalven wrote, "what is needed is some fusing of a passion for liberty with a passion for rigorous analysis. And in this, as in so many matters, Mr. Alexander Meiklejohn provides an admirable model."[13]

In 1963, John F. Kennedy selected Meiklejohn to receive the Presidential Medal of Freedom. In 1964, the landmark case of *New York Times v. Sullivan* reversed the Court's previous condemnation of Meiklejohn in *Dennis*. According to Yale Law School professor Akhil Amar:

> In the most celebrated speech case ever decided, the Supreme Court famously proclaims that the First Amendment must be read "against the background of a profound national commitment to the principle that debate on public issues should be uninhibited, robust, and wide-open, and that it may well include, caustic, and sometimes unpleasantly sharp attacks on government and public officials."[14]

Amar adds, "The grand themes of this grand opinion resonate with the First Amendment approach of Alexander Meiklejohn." Richard Epstein of the New York University Law School has described Meiklejohn as "the father of modern First Amendment theory."[15]

Meiklejohn's speech to the AAUP took place just at that time, the early 1950s, when he was making a transition that would enable him to imprint his ideas on American law. Prior to the 1950s, Meiklejohn dabbled in First Amendment theory, but he did not claim to be a master of the artificial reason of the law. In fact, as a champion of the ideal of the broadly educated person, he avoided presenting himself as a specialist of any kind. In the *Liberal College* (1920), he wrote:

> I would define a liberally educated man[16] as one who tries to understand the whole of knowledge as well as one man can. I know full well that every special judgment that he makes will be inadequate. I know the experts have him on the hip, each expert at one point. But yet for human living as a whole, for living as men should live, I'll match a liberally educated man against the field of experts and have no fear that any one of them will beat him.[17]

Meiklejohn added, "It seems to me we need today a Socrates to come again."[18] In *Free Speech and Its Relation to Self-Government* (1948), Meiklejohn wrote, "The book discusses a principle of law. It is written, however, not by a lawyer, but by a teacher."[19] He again pointed to Socrates as the model of inquiry.[20] Meiklejohn's absolutist interpretation of the First Amendment initially lacked rigorous scholarship. Yet, he morphed into a constitutional expert.

This chapter reviews Meiklejohn's whole career, but it differs from other studies of Meiklejohn by highlighting the implications of his late-in-life turn to legal specialization. There are some excellent works about Meiklejohn, but they portray his thought as seamless. The best way to understand Meiklejohn is to begin by appreciating that while he forged a unified philosophy of education and free speech early in his career, this philosophy got no traction in the professional worlds of law and higher education. He achieved influence only by becoming what the Socratic part of his character abhorred: an expert writing in professional journals. There is a tragic element in this sequence because when Meiklejohn adopted the language of legal specialization, he had to set aside components of his philosophy that were not translatable into legalese: notably, his ideas on liberal education. While he gained renown as a First Amendment scholar, he lost his impact as an educational visionary. He achieved only half of his philosophical program.

Meiklejohn's speech to the AAUP in 1952 is one of his last efforts to sustain a vision of democracy (which is to be free and open) interlocking with liberal education (which is to be highly structured). The First Amendment provides the right to speak freely on political matters, while a proper ordering of the college curriculum ensures that young people learn to speak rationally. For Meiklejohn, college is where students are forced to exercise their freedom of speech in relation to carefully chosen readings and structured discussions. The students are not free to ignore their duty to become articulate on political matters. Meiklejohn had explained this paradox in detail in his 1944 essay, "Required Education for Freedom."

> So paradoxical is the nature of freedom that that unless our citizens can understand and feel the necessity which that Amendment expresses, it becomes a dead and meaningless piece of political machinery. To say that men are free to think whatever seems to them valid about democracy does not mean that they are free not to think about it . . . And that vigilance is not, for the liberal college, an elective. It is a democratic requirement.[21]

In the 1952 AAUP speech, he criticized the American academy for promoting freedom of research without promoting "the teaching of intellectual freedom to the people."[22] American colleges, he said, are not preparing students for self-government. "They are doing something else [research], and doing it well. But they are not giving the intellectual leadership in freedom upon which the success of the great experiment in self-government depends."[23] Meiklejohn chastised the AAUP for separating the academic vocation from democratic education.

> Our universities and colleges, whatever else they have accomplished, have failed to meet their deepest obligation . . . We scholars and teachers who have, rightly, demanded intellectual freedom ourselves have not explained either to our pupils or to the community at large the justification of that demand We have seemed to be talking about

a special privilege of our craft rather than about our obligation to that fundamental freedom which must be possessed and exercised, not only by us, but by every member of a society which is seeking to be self-governed.[24]

Today, practically no one believes, or even reflects on the possibility, that the existence of free speech in society depends on choices we make about the college curriculum: that the educational process must not only *protect* free speech but must also *require* that students learn how to apply it to complex political issues.

The Amherst Debacle and Other Failures

Meiklejohn was an idealist in the philosophical sense of the word. He was not an optimist, a believer in progress. Philosophical idealism is the conviction that ideas are more real than things. The world of concepts is more enduring than the social world. The Good can be ignored but never destroyed. When a moral concept clashes with convention, the idealist does not compromise with society. Meiklejohn imbibed this outlook through his study of Plato and Kant, first as a philosophy major at Brown University and then as a graduate student in philosophy at Cornell. Meiklejohn was also a disciple of Rousseau. Eugene H. Perry aptly states that Meiklejohn had an "organic view of freedom" and rejected the "essentially Lockean idea that freedom was a personal right that could be claimed against the group, affirming instead the Rousseauian view that freedom was a right that people worked out in association with each other."[25] Indeed in *Education Between Two Worlds*, Meiklejohn devoted whole chapters to discussing Rousseau. "Human freedom is not freedom from the state. It is freedom in and by the state." In that book, Meiklejohn also defined freedom of speech as a civic right, not a private one.

> Freedom of speech is derived, not from some supposed "Natural Right," but by the necessities of self-government by universal suffrage . . . The guarantee given by the First Amendment is not, then, assured to all speaking. It is assured only to speech which bears, directly or indirectly, upon issues with which voters have to deal—only, therefore, to the consideration of matters of public interest. Private speech, or private interest in speech, on the other hand, has no claim whatever to the protection of the First Amendment.[26]

Meiklejohn's embattled relationship with American society in the first half of the twentieth century resulted from the fact that he thought about democracy like Rousseau, in a nation convinced that it was founded on the ideas of Locke.

Meiklejohn was born in 1872 in England. His parents had immigrated from Scotland so that his father could work in the great textile mills of Lancashire. When Alexander was eight, the family moved to Pawtucket, Rhode Island, a booming textile city. He was an outstanding student, graduating first in high school and at Brown. He was also a superb athlete, excelling in tennis, cricket, and ice hockey. In 1894 he captained the American squad against a Canadian team in the first North American international hockey match. The scholar-athlete rose in meteoric fashion in the elite East coast academic establishment. After receiving a doctorate in philosophy at Cornell, he returned to Brown in 1897 as a professor of philosophy; in 1901, he became dean of the undergraduate college. In 1912, at the age of 40, he became the President of Amherst College, one of the youngest college presidents in America.[27]

Meiklejohn was an inspiring teacher. An Amherst College student recollected:

> In the classroom he was without a rival. No one who took his sophomore course in logic can forget its thrills. . . He would carry the battle to us, testing our comprehension of what had been said, summoning us to debate, challenging us to criticize his thought and our own. There was nothing namby-pamby about his use of the discussion method—no easy going "What do you think Mr. Smith," or "How do you feel Mr. Jones?" Instead, it was: 'How should you think? What ought you to feel? What conclusion have you reached and why?' . . . Meiklejohn had that asset, possessed only by the great teacher, of a sense for the dramatic unity of the teaching hour. On occasions, before the closing bell, a kind of incandescence would descend on us, and the embers of the argument would burst into blazing flame. Afterward we realized that the experience had touched us where we lived.[28]

Meiklejohn failed as a president because he approached administration like teaching. He knew only one role, that of the Socratic master. Like Angela Davis (see the previous chapter), he was supremely self-confident; in rejection, he found confirmation of his critical thinking. It is surely not a coincidence that both Davis and Meiklejohn were highly trained in European philosophy. They excelled at dialectic, at dramatizing how their ideas collided with the prevailing ideas in America, a nation which they regarded as culturally under-developed compared to the ancient Greeks (for Meiklejohn, who adored Plato) and to the modern Europeans (for Davis, who majored in French literature and then studied Critical Theory with Adorno and Marcuse). They drew meaning from dissension. Both were fired from their jobs, and both regained prestige. But in Meiklejohn's case, it took a lot longer.

In June 1923, the Amherst College board of trustees voted to demand Meiklejohn's resignation. The faculty had already voted to do the same. The firing of Meiklejohn was a major news story.[29] Journalists flocked to Amherst. Among them was Walter Lippmann, the nation's leading political columnist. In "The Fall of President Meiklejohn," published in the *New York World*, he wrote,

> From the present student body he elicits a kind of devotion which I have never seen before among college men . . . Amherst has lost a fine educator and a great spiritual leader of youth . . . He did magnificently with students. He failed with the grown-ups.[30]

Meiklejohn's conception of leadership was that the president commands and others follow. Reminiscing on the Amherst experience in his 1952 AAUP speech, he stated that the president should be "the leader of the faculty, using that leadership to give unity and significance to everything which the institution is and does."[31] When he came to Amherst, Meiklejohn quickly signaled that he was in charge by announcing his intention to shake up the curriculum. In his inauguration speech of October 16, 1912, he assaulted the elective system—the system which allowed students to select their field of specialization and the majority of their courses. Prior to Meiklejohn's presidency, Amherst was second only to Harvard, where the elective system had been first introduced by President Charles W. Eliot, in the percentage of courses which students could freely choose.[32] Meiklejohn called the elective system "the belief that all knowledge is so good that all parts of knowledge are equally good." "It is an announcement that they [the faculty] have no guiding principles in their educational practice . . . no genuine grasp on the relations between knowledge and life."[33] For Meikle-john, academic freedom did not include the right of students to choose their courses.

In his early years as President of Amherst, Meiklejohn was able to implement some components of his ideal curriculum, notably a first-year course on Social and Economic Institutions. He wished to add other required courses with titles such as "The Development of Modern Industrialism," "Financial Institutions," "Social Classes," and "The Social Program."[34] The faculty resisted. Indeed, Meiklejohn, the admirer of Socirates, seems to have wanted to produce a collective backlash.

At Sunday chapel, the custom was for the president to give a lesson based on a Biblical reading. Meiklejohn recited poems by Robert Burns. One of the trustees, after receiving a complaint from a student, said, "It is a fine commentary on the situation that a man can have been in college for nearly four years and not know whether his President is an atheist or not." When an alumnus, future US President Calvin Coolidge, then Lieuten-ant Governor of Massachusetts, wished to speak on campus about the need to prepare for entry into World War I, Meiklejohn insisted that the antiwar point of view be rep-resented as well.[35] Meiklejohn organized classes for adults who worked in the mills of Holyoke and Springfield. A trustee who was suspicious of these courses asked Meiklejohn if he would hire a Bolshevik to teach; he responded, "I'd have anyone if he were a good teacher."[36] In his speech at the college's centennial celebration, in 1921, Meiklejohn affirmed that if America is to avoid being "a racial aristocracy," the elite institutions of learning need to welcome students "of other stocks." "And if they do not come, we must go out and bring them in."[37] Meiklejohn was thinking specifically of the need for more Black students. But he also attacked Harvard for its policy of discriminating against Jew-ish applicants.

These were noble positions, but Meiklejohn made no effort to manage the sentiments of those who disagreed with him. He was also a poor manager of finances. He often over-drafted his own salary, and he refused to participate in fundraising. He condescendingly wished the board of trustees well in the centennial fundraising drive. "Go ye, Jasons, shear the alumni, and bring the golden fleece back to campus."[38] A son of one of the trustees commented on Meiklejohn's firing, "To a large extent I think it was unconscious suppres-sion by an alarmed upper class."[39] Against this formulation, one might quibble only with the term "unconscious."

When Meiklejohn resigned in June 1923, he stated,

> Almost invariably, on a current issue, I am against the larger number. That being the case I am willing to take my medicine . . . I don't know where I am to go, but I know that I am to do the same thing again in the same way.[40]

And so he did, except that his tenure in his next leadership position lasted only five years, compared to eleven at Amherst. In 1927 he became the director of the University of Wisconsin's Experimental College. He developed an extensive curriculum focusing on contemporary social problems but again met with resistance. Professors criticized him for not training students in the established disciplines and for allowing his instructors to teach outside of their certified academic specializations. The college also developed a reputation for being a hotbed of loose morals and revolutionary politics.[41] Under pressure from faculty and from the public, the President of the University of Wisconsin, Glenn Frank, who was originally keen on the idea of an alternative college, shut down the ex-periment in 1932.

Championing the Academic Freedom of Communists

Meiklejohn's travails pushed him further westward. He moved to Berkeley and founded an adult education program, the San Francisco School of Social Studies, which opened in 1934 and closed in 1940. During this period, Meiklejohn also became active in the American Civil Liberties Union; he cofounded its Northern California chapter in 1934 and joined the national board of directors in 1940, just in time to take part in a vote about whether communists could serve on the board. He was outvoted. The board expelled the communist Elizabeth Gurley Flynn. Meiklejohn himself was not a communist. He was a member of the League for Industrial Democracy, founded in 1905 by Upton Sinclair, Clarence Darrow, Walter Lippmann, and Jack London. Originally called the Intercollegiate Socialist Society (and renamed in 1921), the group was devoted to spreading socialist ideas in America's universities. Meiklejohn is listed as a vice president in the League's 1935 report.[42]

Defending the free-speech rights of communists was a consistent thread in Meiklejohn's work from the 1930s to his death in 1964. In 1949, he debated the anti-communist philosopher Sidney Hook in the pages of the *New York Times*. Their sparkling exchange focused on the meaning of academic freedom. The context of the debate was the recent dismissal, at the University of Washington, of three professors for being members of the Communist Party. Hook maintained that educators who are communists must swear to the Party that they will engage in propaganda in the classroom. Their commitment to Party ideology outweighs their devotion to the pursuit of truth. Hook drew on the language of the AAUP's 1915 statement on academic freedom to characterize academic inquiry as politically neutral.

Meiklejohn refused to accept Hook's premise that all members of the Communist Party are unthinking beings. He presupposed that all human beings are rational and independent; democracy requires such a presupposition. We must assume, he argued, that the fired professors "do not accept communist beliefs because they are members of the Party. They are members of the Party because they accept Communist beliefs." They are thus no different from people who choose to be Democrats and Republicans. The only real danger to the university, he concluded, "is that lack of faith [in open inquiry] which leads us into the devices and follies of suppression."[43]

Clear and Present Danger

Meiklejohn was on the losing side of the debate about communism and academic freedom, not only because Hook and others effectively linked the concept of academic freedom to political neutrality. The most influential free-speech doctrine of the first half of the twentieth century was stacked against socialism and communism. The doctrine in question construed Congress as a watchdog against radical ideology. In *Schenk v. United States* (1919), Justice Olivier Wendell Holmes declared:

> The question in every case is whether the words used are used in such circumstances and are of such a nature as to create a clear and present danger that they will bring about the substantive evils that Congress has a right to prevent.[44]

Schenck was a member of the Socialist Party and was convicted under the 1917 Espionage Act for publishing pamphlets suggesting that the military draft is a form of servitude in violation of the Thirteenth Amendment. Holmes and the Supreme Court upheld his conviction.

Although Holmes had died in 1935, reverence for his ideas and aphorisms was at a peak when Meiklejohn set out to demolish "clear and present danger" in his 1948 book, *Free Speech and Its Relation to Self-Government*. One sign of the Holmesian cult was *The Mind and Faith of Justice Holmes*, edited by the political scientist Max Lerner in 1943. Lerner wrote, "In Holmes's life there is a wholeness which the New England aristocracy at its best produced." Lerner detected in Holmes "the imprint of a unique personality and of a poetic image."[45] The doctrine of "clear and present danger" was treated as the pinnacle of First Amendment wisdom well into the 1960s.[46] The Supreme Court frequently resorted to "clear and present danger" when evaluating politically controversial speech. Meiklejohn played a key role in discrediting the doctrine, but it was a long battle uphill.

The doctrine of "clear and present danger" was entrenched in academe as well as the courts. The leading academic expert on the First Amendment in the United States from the 1920s to the 1950s was Harvard Law professor Zechariah Chafee, who was a Holmes enthusiast. Chafee was the author of some of the first books on the history of free speech in America, books cited frequently by the Supreme Court. As late as 1955, two years before his death, we can find Chafee uncompromisingly defending "clear and present danger" in testimony to a Senate Sub-Committee on constitutional rights. The sub-committee's charge was to investigate whether the government's loyalty-security programs were violating the free-speech rights of Americans. Chafee stated that in accordance with "clear and present danger," the government was authorized to impose limits on the First Amendment.

> Bad acts are the main crime. Words may be infected when they are closely connected with bad acts. The government does not need to wait until the bad acts begin to be committed.[47]

Chafee was one of two experts on the First Amendment who testified. It is evidence of Meiklejohn's rise as a legal expert in the 1950s that he was the other.

In his prepared statement to the subcommittee, Meiklejohn said:

> Just so far as, at any point, the citizens who are to decide issues are denied acquaintance with information or opinion or doubt or disbelief or criticism which is relevant to those issues, just so far the result must be ill-considered, ill-balanced planning for the general good. It is that mutilation of the thinking process of the community against which the First Amendment is directed . . . Whatever may be the immediate gains and losses, the dangers to our safety arising from political suppression are always greater than the dangers to that safety arising from political freedom.[48]

In direct dialogue with Chafee, Meiklejohn stated:

> You say if the danger is large then you can abridge the freedom of speech and expression generally, which means you are limiting the activity of the thinking process, the attempt to understand it, to find out what the danger is and how to deal with it. I do not get the rationale of the statement.[49]

Meiklejohn had been attacking "clear and present danger" for years. In *Free Speech and Its Relation to Self-Government*, he portrayed Holmes as a "villain" because Holmes took the First Amendment, which said that "Congress shall make no law . . . abridging the freedom of speech" and converted it into an affirmation of the right of Congress to restrict speech.

Lee C. Bollinger, a First Amendment scholar, has written that "no one, until Meiklejohn, had really attacked the intellectual framework" that underlay the doctrine of "clear and present danger."[50] In *Free Speech and Its Relation to Self-Government*, Meiklejohn reprimanded the Supreme Court for endorsing "clear and present danger" and thereby promoting "the break-down of self-government."[51] "May a teacher venture to suggest that the time has come when the court, as teacher, must declare, in unequivocal terms, that no idea may be suppressed because someone in office, or out of office, has judged it to be 'dangerous'?"[52]

Meiklejohn's criticism of "clear and present danger" was provocative enough to earn a response from the Supreme Court. In *Dennis v. United States* (1951), the Court upheld the Smith Act of 1940, which set criminal penalties for anyone who "prints, publishes, edits, issues, circulates, sells, distributes, or publicly displays any written or printed matter advocating, advising, or teaching the duty, necessity, desirability, or propriety of over-throwing or destroying any government in the United States by force or violence." At the trial in District Court, Judge Harold Medina instructed the jury members that they should not focus on how likely the defendants' printed words were to harm the nation. The jurors were to decide instead whether the defendants' words indicated that they would overthrow the government by force if given a chance to do so in the future. An immi-nent threat of violence was not required. When the Supreme Court decided the case, it applied a version of "clear and present danger" devised by judge Learned Hand when the case was heard by the D.C. Circuit Court. According to Hand, if the potential danger is

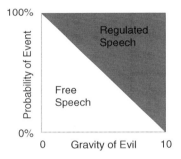

Figure 2.1 The version of "clear and present danger" used in *Dennis v. United States* (1951): "In each case, [courts] must ask whether the gravity of the 'evil,' discounted by its improbability, justifies such invasion of free speech as is necessary to avoid the danger."

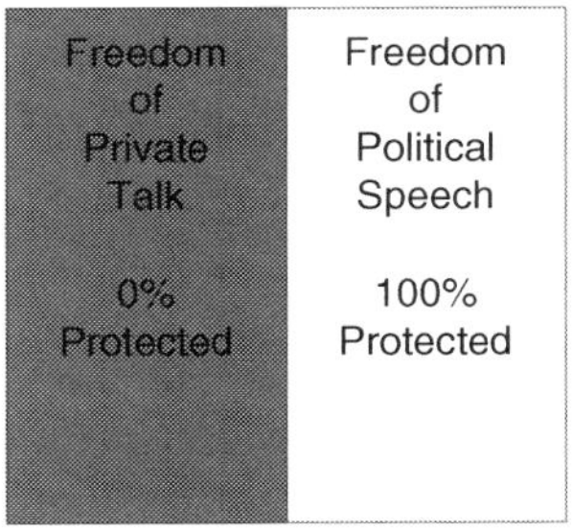

Freedom of Private Talk	Freedom of Political Speech
0% Protected	100% Protected

Figure 2.2 Meiklejohn's understanding of speech under the First Amendment. Private talk falls under the Fifth Amendment. Political speech falls under the First Amendment, where it is absolutely protected. Figures 2.1 and 2.2 adapted from William W. Van Alstyne, *Interpretations of the First Amendment* (Durham: Duke University Press, 1984), 30–31.

great, then the speech can be restricted, even if the probability is small that the danger will occur. Hand wrote, "In each case, [courts] must ask whether the gravity of the 'evil,' discounted by its improbability, justifies such invasion of free speech as is necessary to avoid the danger."[53]

The Hand formulation, affirmed by the Supreme Court in *Dennis*, appears to alter "clear and present danger" by suspending the requirement that the danger be "present." But since it is the *danger* and not the *actual harm* to which Holmes referred, one could reasonably interpret danger to mean the *risk* that harm will occur at any time. Holmes himself had written in the *Common Law* (first pub., 1881), "The possibility of a great danger has the same effect as the probability of a less one, and the law throws the risk of the venture on the person who introduces the peril into the community."[54] A close examination of Holmes's language in *Schenck* shows that he was recycling many of the key terms that he deployed in *The Common Law* when discussing the general principles of torts. One should especially note the presence of the word "liability" in *Schenck*; it is the central concept in tort law and occurs in *The Common Law* hundreds of times. I have highlighted other words that are also frequent in *The Common Law*. Students of law will recognize these terms as staples of tort jurisprudence.

> The question in every case is whether the words used are used in such *circumstances* and are of such a nature as to create a *clear* and present *danger* that they will bring about the substantive evils that Congress has a right to prevent. It is a question of *proximity* and *degree* . . . It seems to be admitted that, if an actual obstruction of the recruiting service were proved, *liability* for words that produced that effect might be enforced.[55]

And here is Holmes in *The Common Law*:

> The cases in which a man is treated as the responsible cause of a given harm, on the one hand, extend beyond those in which his conduct was chosen in actual contemplation of that result, and in which, therefore, he may be said to have chosen to cause that harm . . . The question in each case is whether the actual choice, or, in other words, the actually contemplated result, was near enough to the remoter result complained of to throw the peril of it upon the actor.[56]

Throughout *The Common Law*, Holmes treats torts not as a specialized branch of law but as a source of general principles forming the basis of all law. The basic purpose of law, he argues, is to enable society to function and to provide incentives for avoiding the creation of harms.

The transfer of the logic of torts to the field of First Amendment jurisprudence meant that if the potential harm emanating from the free speech is very grave, then Congress has a right to take preventive action, even if the likelihood that the evil will materialize is slight, and regardless of *when* it will allegedly materialize. This is precisely what Learned Hand was getting it, and it is evident that he too modeled his interpretation of the First Amendment on tort law. In *United States v. Carroll Towing Co.* (1947), the question was whether a towing company had been negligent in its handling of the mooring lines that tied a barge to a pier. The barge came loose in a storm and sank. Hand wrote:

> Since there are occasions when every vessel will break from her moorings, and since, if she does, she becomes a menace to those about her; the owner's duty, as in other

similar situations, to provide against resulting injuries is a function of three variables: (1) The probability that she will break away; (2) the gravity of the resulting injury, if she does; (3) the burden of adequate precautions. Possibly it serves to bring this notion into relief to state it in algebraic terms: if the probability be called P; the injury, L; and the burden, B; liability depends upon whether B is less than L multiplied by P: i.e., whether $B < PL$.[57]

When Meiklejohn affirmed that the right to political speech is "absolute," he was uttering what seemed like an absurdity to the legal community. It was as if he were saying that liability is never attached to speech.

In his majority opinion in *Dennis*, Chief Justice Vinson singled out Meiklejohn's "absolutist" interpretation of the First Amendment for criticism. No wonder, since Meiklejohn rejected the whole idea of balancing free political speech against the risk of harm to others. Vinson wrote:

> Speech is not an absolute, above and beyond control by the legislature when its judgment, subject to review here, is that certain kinds of speech are so undesirable as to warrant criminal sanction. Nothing is more certain in modern society than the principle that there are no absolutes, that a name, a phrase, a standard has meaning only when associated with the considerations which gave birth to the nomenclature . . . To those who would paralyze our Government in the face of impending threats by encasing it in a semantic straitjacket we must reply that all concepts are relative.[58]

Vinson did not mention Meiklejohn by name. But no one else at that time, including Justice Hugo Black, the most libertarian justice on free-speech matters, used the word "absolute" in First Amendment theory. Any doubt about whether "absolute" referred to Meiklejohn was dispelled in Justice Felix Frankfurter's concurring opinion in *Dennis*. Frankfurter described Meiklejohn as an "exponent of the absolutist interpretation of the First Amendment." Frankfurter argued that Meiklejohn's total protection of one type of speech, political speech, inevitably downgraded the constitutional status of other types of speech. "Recognizing that certain forms of speech require regulation, he [Meiklejohn] excludes those forms of expression entirely from the protection accorded by the Amendment."[59]

This was an acute point. In *Free Speech and Its Relation to Self-Government*, Meiklejohn stated that freedom of speech refers to political speech and not "private talk," such as commercial advertising. He argued that private speech does not fall under the First Amendment at all. The First Amendment is "not the guardian of unregulated talkativeness."[60] For Meiklejohn, private discourse is comparable to property, which is referenced in the Fifth Amendment, specifically the clause saying that no person shall "be deprived of life, liberty, or property, without due process of law."

> But this means that, under the Bill of Rights, there are two freedoms, or liberties, of speech, rather than only one. There is a "freedom of speech" which the First Amendment declares to be non-abridgable. But there is also a "liberty of speech" which the Fifth Amendment declares to be abridgable. And for the inquiry in which we are engaged, the distinction between these two, the fact that there are two, is of fundamental importance . . . Individuals have, then, a private right of speech which may on occasion be denied or limited, though such limitations may not be imposed unnecessarily or unequally. So says the Fifth Amendment. But this limited guarantee

of the freedom of a man's wish to speak is radically different in intent from the un-
limited guarantee of the freedom of public discussion, which is given by the First
Amendment.[61]

Meiklejohn's distribution of speech between the First and Fifth Amendments was
unheard of. There were no Supreme Court precedents to support this schema. The word
"speech" occurs in the First Amendment and not in the Fifth, so to categorize non-political
speech as property under the Fifth is a doubtful semantic move. This helps to explain why
Meiklejohn's critique of "clear and present danger" and his "absolutist" theory of political
speech carried no weight with the Court.

Frankfurter drove home the point that since much academic speech is not political, Meiklejohn's theory left professors unprotected by the First Amendment. "Professor Meiklejohn
even suggests that scholarship may now require such subvention and control that it no
longer is entitled to protection by the First Amendment."[62] We are brought once again to
the ambiguous relationship between freedom of speech and academic freedom. Frankfurter
had a soft spot for the teaching and research enterprise. A year after *Dennis*, in *Wiemann v.
Updegraff* (1952), he authored a concurring opinion that contains one of the first discussions
of academic freedom in a Supreme Court case. The case concerned the validity of a loyalty oath prohibiting teachers in Oklahoma from being affiliated "directly or indirectly"
with any group "determined by the United States Attorney General or other authorized
agency of the United States to be a communist front or subversive organization." While
Frankfurter was not against the exclusion of communists from certain areas of employment,
he took exception to anti-communist loyalty oaths in the teaching field.

> It is the special task of teachers to foster those habits of open-mindedness and critical
> inquiry which alone make for responsible citizens, who, in turn, make possible an
> enlightened and effective public opinion. Teachers must fulfill their function by pre-
> cept and practice, by the very atmosphere which they generate; they must be exemplars
> of open-mindedness and free inquiry. They cannot carry out their noble task if the
> conditions for the practice of a responsible and critical mind are denied to them.[63]

Meiklejohn would have agreed with this pronouncement on the freedom of *teaching*. But as
concerns what Frankfurter calls "scholarship," that is, research, Meiklejohn did not accord
the same liberty.

Meiklejohn associated academic freedom with the production of vibrant political debate
in a classroom, not with the pursuit of technical knowledge in a lab. We have already seen
that he considered academic specialization to be inimical to the general education of a
broad-minded citizen. He did not share the AAUP's conception of academic freedom as
a badge of scientific expertise divorced from politics. Meiklejohn argued that academic
research, far from contributing to democracy, can be an instrument of top-down authority.
In *Free Speech and Its Relation to Self-Government*, he raised concern about the growing
reliance of science professors on military grants. Writing about government-sponsored
research to develop atomic and bacteriological weapons, he observed:

> Under present circumstances it is criminally stupid to describe the inquiries of
> [government-funded] scholarship as merely "the disinterested pursuit of knowledge
> for its own sake." Both public and private interests are clearly involved. They subsidize
> much of our scholarship . . . It may be, therefore, that the time has come when the

guarding of human welfare that shall abridge the private desire of the scholar—or of those who subsidize him—to study whatever he may please. It may be that the freedom of the "pursuit of truth" must, in that sense, be abridged. And, if such action were taken with that motivation, the guarantee of the First Amendment would not, in my opinion, have been violated. As I write these words, I am not taking a final stand on the issue which is here suggested. But I am sure that the issue is coming upon us and cannot be evaded.[64]

Frankfurter, it seems, had his eye on this passage when he criticized Meiklejohn in *Dennis.* For Frankfurter, Meiklejohn's vision of an "absolute" right to speak politically sounded repressive of all other forms of communication.

When the Court rejected Meiklejohn, it was building on a foundation of criticism comprised of negative academic reviews of *Free Speech and Its Relation to Self-Government.* In fact, Frankfurter referred readers to Chafee, the Harvard law professor, for a full critique of Meiklejohn. In the *Harvard Law Review,* Chafee stated that there is no historical evidence to suggest that the framers of the Constitution envisioned a distinction between political and private speech. The distinction, he argued, is pure fiction. Chafee, who had taken philosophy classes with Meiklejohn at Brown, cleverly played on the public image of Meiklejohn as an Idealist devoid of common sense.

> At Brown, Mr. Meiklejohn loved to open his logic class by asking: "If I should tell you that I just saw a unicorn running across the campus, how could you prove that I was wrong?" What he has just seen in the First Amendment is a beautiful unicorn.[65]

Nor did Chafee accept the premise, crucial to Meiklejohn's conception of free speech, that the primary aim of the Constitution is to implement self-government. Chafee rejected Meiklejohn's "mystical identification of the rulers with the ruled."[66] He thus dismissed the Rousseauian basis of Meiklejohn's thinking, according to which freedom is the exercise of civic rights, not a bundle of private rights. "Valuable as self-government is," wrote Chafee, "it is in itself only a small part of our lives. That a philosopher should subordinate all other activities to it is indeed surprising."[67]

Finally, Chafee ripped into Meiklejohn for the unlawyerly quality of his thinking. Meiklejohn presented his absolutist theory as a truth hovering above American law. He offered no legal precedents, and he showed no interest in the Constitution other than in the First and Fifth Amendments. Chafee said that Meiklejohn was too concerned with "eternal truth" and should have tried "to stick to the kind of language which lawyers use." Since the First Amendment "is what the Supreme Court says it means," Meiklejohn's philosophy is "useless."[68] Other reviews of the book by legal scholars were equally negative, though not as brilliant.[69]

Meiklejohn and *New York Times v. Sullivan*

The *Dennis* case and Chafee's book knocked Meiklejohn down, but he got up and began a new phase of his career. In the 1950s, he changed his style of writing about the First Amendment. He proved that he could analyze cases and discuss procedural issues on par with law professors and judges. His investigations into free speech appeared *in The Indiana Law Journal, The California Law Review, The Supreme Court Review,* and repeatedly in *The University of Chicago Law Review.* He also published essays containing extensive legal discussions in *The Nation* and the *Harvard Crimson*. The opinion in *New York Times v. Sullivan* (1964), written for a unanimous Court by Justice William H. Brennan, made it official: Meiklejohn was an authority on freedom of speech.

The Court held that a libel judgment rendered under Alabama law violated the First Amendment. Sullivan was the police commissioner of Montgomery. He brought a civil action against the *New York Times* as well as four Alabama clergymen who authored an allegedly defamatory full-page advertisement. The advertisement solicited contributions for "The Committee to Defend Martin Luther King and the Struggle for Freedom in the South." Much of the advertisement consisted of factually disputable comments about the mistreatment by the Montgomery police of Dr. King and Black student protesters. The text, which accused the police (not Sullivan in particular) of brutality and harassment, included some errors of fact: that the police bombed the King home, arrested him seven times on spurious charges, formed a ring around the University of Alabama campus, and padlocked protesting students in a dining hall. At trial, a standard of strict liability was applied. Malicious motives did not have to be in question. It was sufficient to demonstrate that the public accusations were false. A jury awarded $500,000 to Sullivan.

The Supreme Court overturned the verdict. The advertisement was "an expression of grievance and protest on one of the major public issues of our time." The falsity of some of the ad's factual statements did not forfeit its status as protected speech. The Court held that injury to a public official's reputation is not sufficient grounds for repressing speech which is designed to criticize governmental policies and actions.[70]

For a contemporary understanding of the case's importance, we can turn to an article by Harry Kalven, Jr. in the *Supreme Court Review* (1964). According to Kalven, the significance of the case was ambiguous. The Court could interpret its own judgment narrowly or broadly. Understood narrowly, the case's importance was limited to that "pocket" of free-speech cases concerned with the common law tort of libel. The Court was saying that when the criticism of public officials is in question, the common law standard for libelous injury will no longer apply. The plaintiff must prove that the false statements about public officials were made maliciously and with a knowledge of their falseness—a hard standard to meet. In Kalven's words, the Court "was prepared to pay the high price of destroying a considerable part of the common law of defamation."[71]

Under the "larger reading," Kalven pointed out that the effect of the case was to uphold freedom of political speech against *all* incumbrances. There would be no "clear and present danger" test for unorthodox political speech, no matter what kind of harm might ensue from the speech. Kalven supported this interpretation. "If the Court accepts the invitation, it will slowly work out for itself the theory of free speech that Alexander Meiklejohn has been offering us for some fifteen years now." Kalven acknowledged that the broad interpretation would amount to a "revolution of free-speech doctrine," but he suggested that the very idea of democratic self-government required this revolution: "In its rhetoric and sweep, the opinion almost literally incorporated Alexander Meiklejohn's thesis that in a democracy the citizen as ruler is our most important public official."[72]

Kalven was correct to discern Meiklejohn' influence. Brennan did not mention Meiklejohn by name in *New York Times*, but he would later cite Meiklejohn several times in cases that came after. Even more, in an article, "The Supreme Court and the Meiklejohn Interpretation of the First Amendment," published in the *Harvard Law Review* in 1965, Brennan amply acknowledged Meiklejohn's influence in the *New York Times* case. "General acceptance of the educational ideas and practices of this militant champion of freedom may not have been won easily or very soon, but none will deny that his fight over nearly half a century brought substantial victory." Brennan outlined the leading interpretations of the First Amendment that were available to the Court when it decided *New York Times*. He explained how Meiklejohn's understanding of freedom of speech was unique, and how it figured in the Court's decision. Brennan even acknowledged that he drew inspiration from a specific sentence: "The freedom that the First Amendment protects is not, then, an absence of regulation. It is the presence of self-government."[73] The line comes from "The First Amendment is an Absolute," which Meiklejohn published in *The Supreme Court Review* in 1961.[74]

A concurring opinion in *New York Times*, by Hugo Black and William O. Douglas, did mention Meiklejohn. They cited him (and only him) as the authority for the proposition that "an unconditional right to say what one pleases about public affairs is . . . the minimum guarantee of the First Amendment."[75] Kalven noted:

> the [*New York Times*] decision was responsive to the pressures of the day created by the Negro protest movement and thus raises the question so frequently mooted whether the Supreme Court has adhered to neutral principles in reaching its conclusion.

But Kalven added that the Court was "equally compelled to seek high ground in justifying its result."[76] Meiklejohn provided the legal and intellectual high ground needed to justify a shift in the Court's response to civil rights activism.

Meiklejohn was able to supply this high ground because he was self-critical enough to recognize that *Free Speech and Its Relation to its Self-Government* (1948) had not worked. The 1960 reprint of the book, entitled *Political Freedom: The Constitutional Powers of the People*, doubled in size because Meiklejohn included some of the recent articles that he had published. "I now invite the reader to consider attempts made between 1948 and 1958 to widen and deepen the earlier discussion of the First Amendment."[77] What follows is a response to his invitation. Since this involves some technical legal matters, it is worth explaining why it is worth the effort. First, to understand the now well-established constitutional argument that political speech has a special status under the First Amendment, we need to see how Meiklejohn managed to ground it convincingly in legal sources—something he didn't do in *Free Speech and Its Relation to Self-Government*.

Secondly, following Meiklejohn's deep dive into the law will help us understand how his vision of college education—including his vision of a core curriculum—became external to his defense of freedom of speech. Legal arguments differentiated themselves from educational ones in his thought. The result was that his free-speech absolutism became authoritative, while his educational philosophy lost authority. In fact, his defense of free political speech tended to undermine his own curricular philosophy. For if one envisions the campus as a free speech zone, then the professor has a right to engage in one-sided political advocacy in the classroom, rather than overseeing debate among students, as Meiklejohn wished. It is common today to believe that academic freedom means approximately the same thing as free speech. Meiklejohn's conception of academic freedom was a *restrictive* one: it classified some types of research as counter-democratic, and it involved the imposition of a core curriculum. Yet, Meiklejohn's conception of free speech has, over time, subsumed academic freedom, not because courts have held that the two are the same (courts will often defer to universities when it comes to curricular matters) but because of a tendency inside the academy to conflate academic freedom and free speech.

The impact of turning academic freedom into free speech can be observed in the thinning out of the concept of liberal education. For Meiklejohn, liberal education is not the right of students to choose classes and the right of professors to exercise free speech in the classroom, that is, to promote their political agenda. It is a conversation grounded in politically heterogeneous texts and guided by a Socratic instructor. Meiklejohn addressed the question of the professor's role in the classroom as early as 1918, in an *Atlantic Monthly* article, "Freedom in the College." Here he defined academic freedom as a "duty" to promote the mission of the college, which is to educate students for democratic debate. The professor's role is to expose students to competing schools of thought, including unorthodox ideologies, such as socialism, in order to make students aware that a wide universe of plausible choices exists. But "dragging the students by the nose to preconceived conclusions" is "pedagogic sin," he wrote. To the degree that some professors do engage in partisanship, it then becomes incumbent to "make up a college faculty of many advocates, at least one advocate for every important line of popular thought and impulse."[78]

In 1926, Meiklejohn published a short book designed to introduce general readers to philosophy. The editor of the book series wrote, "It is characteristic of Doctor Meiklejohn's method that all of the books recommended in this reading course express views contrary to his own. Here, as elsewhere, he puts the responsibility on the student."[79] Over 30 years later, in the Foreword to *Political Freedom*, Meiklejohn wrote, "[W]hen theories are debated, the teacher's duty is not to give authoritative answers, but rather to clarify questions by challenging their assumptions. He should not seek to end a discussion, but to start it, or to keep it going."[80] The *New York Times* case, though not dealing with academic matters, complicates the question. For if one comprehends the classroom as a locus of free speech, then the professor has an apparent right to engage in political advocacy. And visions of a core curriculum, in which all students must read certain works and professors must teach them in an impartial manner, become difficult to justify, when academic freedom is taken to mean the right to express oneself.

In lieu of an article-by-article summary of the elderly Meiklejohn's legal scholarship, we can observe three primary moves that he made to strengthen his absolutist theory of speech. The first was to bear down closely on the whole text of the Constitution, not just the First Amendment, to support his idea—based on Rousseau rather than Locke—that the Constitution was established to create self-government, The second move was to use both the Constitution and the Federalist papers (which he did not cite at all in *Free Speech and Its Relation to Self-Government*) to argue for a much more restricted conception of Congress's jurisdiction, compared to the ample jurisdiction granted to it by "clear and present danger" (which stated that Congress has a "right" to "prevent" evils). His scholarship in this area was particularly nuanced because he addressed not only the jurisdiction of Congress in its law-making capacity but also the jurisdiction of its fact-finding committees—notably, the House Un-American Activities Committee. The third move was to return to his original stronghold, philosophy, to defend the use of "absolutes" in judicial decisions. These moves catapulted him to the position which Kalven and Brennan accorded him: the most important theorist of the First Amendment since Holmes.

Move 1. Intratextualism

In Free Speech and Its Relation to Self-Government, Meiklejohn's method was almost entirely structural. According to Phillip Bobbitt, structural arguments arise from generalizations about the mode of government that the Constitution as a whole is designed to support.

They are not textual arguments; they do not involve drilling into specific clauses of the Constitution.[81] But the structure—self-government—which Meiklejohn imputed to the Constitution was not what other constitutional experts associated with the text, as we saw in Chafee's review. It was thus necessary for Meiklejohn to supplement the structural argument with a textual argument.

Akhil Amar points out that structural arguments can never stand on their own. Bobbitt considers "structure" and "text" to be separate modes of constitutional interpretation, while Amar suggests that textual arguments must underlie structural ones. For Bobbitt, *McCulloch v. Maryland* is the classic example of a judicial opinion that rests on structural reasoning. But Amar demonstrates that even this opinion hinges on a close reading of the clause which states that Congress has the authority to make "all Laws which shall be necessary and proper for carrying into Execution the foregoing Powers." Since Article 1 does not explicitly grant Congress the right to establish a national bank, this power had to be inferred from the Necessary and Proper Clause. Marshall deployed a clever technique, which Amar calls "intratextualism," for establishing that "necessary" imbues Congress with wide powers. Instead of limiting his analysis to one clause, Marshall examined how the term "necessary" is used in other parts of the Constitution. He found in Article 1 Section 10 that the term "absolutely necessary" occurs in order to set limits on state power:

> No State shall, without the Consent of the Congress, lay any Imposts or Duties on Imports or Exports, except what may be absolutely necessary for executing its inspection Laws.

Marshall reasoned that the word "necessary," when it lacks "absolutely," is meant to endorse a wide latitude for action. Congress can do what is "necessary and proper" means Congress can create a bank if it is a useful way to exercise other commercial functions which are explicit in the Constitution. In this and other ways, Amar shows that Marshall used the constitutional document "as a kind of dictionary or concordance to clarify its own meaning." In his writings post-dating *Free Speech and Its Relation to Self-Government*, Meiklejohn shifted from a structural argument hovering above the Constitution to a densely grounded "intratextual" argument of the kind Amar sees in *McCulloch*.[82]

What exactly did Meiklejohn do? First, he corrected himself. He abandoned the claim that the Fifth Amendment applied to private speech and the First Amendment pertains only to political speech. There was never a textual basis for this argument because the term "speech" does not occur in the Fifth. In none of his articles in the 1950s and 1960s, does the argument appear again. But Meiklejohn did manage to argue that the quintessential, if not the only, form of speech protected by the First Amendment is political speech. He pointed to Article 1, Section 6, the one other place in which the word "speech" occurs in the Constitution: "for any Speech or Debate in either House, they [members of Congress] shall not be questioned in any other Place." This section lends plausibility, Meiklejohn suggested, to the idea that the core type of "speech" protected by the Constitution is political speech.

> The Constitution gives to all "the people" the same protection of freedom which, in Article I, § 6(1) it provides for their legislative agents . . . Just as our agents must be free in their use of delegated powers, so the people must be free in the exercise of their reserved powers.[83]

Meiklejohn refers to members of Congress as "agents" of the people who have "reserved powers." The sovereign people must possess at least as much freedom to speak politically as the members of Congress, who are merely representatives.

The idea of popular sovereignty is itself a governmental structure. But Meiklejohn elicited the structure from the text. He bundled together several parts of the Constitution suggestive of popular sovereignty:

- The Preamble, "*We the people . . .* do ordain this constitution."
- The Tenth Amendment, "The powers not delegated to the United States by the Constitution, nor prohibited by it to the States, are reserved to the States respectively, or to *the people.*"
- Article 1, Section 2, "The House of Representatives shall be composed of members chosen every second year by *the people* of the several States."
- The Seventeenth Amendment, "The Senate of the United States shall be composed of two Senators from each State, elected by *the people* thereof, for six years."[84]

Move 2. Challenging Congressional Jurisdiction

In *Free Speech and Its Relation to Self-Government*, Meiklejohn did not refer to the *Federalist Papers*. The names of Madison and Hamilton do not even occur in the book. In his subsequent work, Meiklejohn deployed the *Federalist Papers* to support the idea that the power of the people underlies the power of Congress. He also demonstrated that the Founders were deeply concerned about the possibility of legislative tyranny. In his Senate testimony, he quoted *Federalist No. 48*. "It is against the enterprising ambition of this department that the people ought to indulge all their jealousy and exhaust all their precautions."[85]

In spite of such passages in the *Federalist Papers*, the Supreme Court, through much of the twentieth century, operated with the belief that Congress is the guardian of the nation's interests. The "clear and present" danger test was premised on the idea that Congress has broad powers to "prevent" evils. It must be remembered that "clear and present danger" originated in an era of judicial deference to legislative authority. As Lerner observed, Holmes had "an inclination to let the legislature have its way." Theodore Roosevelt appointed Holmes to the Supreme Court for this very reason.[86] Progressive judicial thought in the early twentieth century was fundamentally different from what it became later in the civil rights movement. Since *Brown v. Board of Education* (1954), progressive legal thinking construes the Bill of Rights and the Fourteenth Amendment as tools for critically examining federal and state laws. School desegregation, the protection of African American voting rights, the expansion of women's rights and gay rights—these trends have resulted from the "strict scrutiny" of legislation. But Holmes was one of a series of Supreme Court appointees, which included Louis Brandeis and Felix Frankfurter, brought onto the court by presidents in the early twentieth century seeking to limit the scope of judicial review and to expand the capacity of legislatures to impose restrictions on the market.

The central legal doctrine of this school of thinking was the "rational basis" standard of judicial review (discussed in Chapter 1). "Clear and present danger" can be understood as a variant of this standard, for it ultimately legitimated legislative authority. In the first half of the twentieth century, the doctrine of judicial deference to Congress in economic matters bled into the doctrine that courts should defer to Congress on free-speech matters—when an alleged "danger" was present.

Meiklejohn was in a state of shock that judicial doctrine was so favorable to Congress. He realized that he had to prove that "Congress shall make no law . . . abridging the freedom of speech" was part of a pattern in the Constitution, a pattern designed not only to affirm free speech but to restrict the power of Congress. Kalven, who was a keen observer of Meiklejohn's evolution as a legal writer, expressed admiration for the fact that Meiklejohn was able to link his defense of free speech to multiple indications of Congress's limited jurisdiction throughout the whole constitutional text.[87] Meiklejohn set out to prove that even if the First Amendment did not exist, the rest of the Constitution makes it evident that Congress does not have the kind of preventive police power that Holmes ascribed to it.

"The First Amendment and Evils that Congress Has a Right to Prevent" (1951) was Meiklejohn's first substantial legal article; it is a *tour de force* on Congressional jurisdiction. The title is a reference to the last words of the "clear and present danger" test. Meiklejohn stated that the First Amendment, which begins with "Congress shall make no law," is "not unique" as a limitation on Congress. The constitution is saturated with restrictions. Meiklejohn was particularly concerned to show that the Constitution never gives Congress the authority to ensure "national self-preservation." Recent Supreme Court cases, including the *Dennis* case, had frequently used the term "self-preservation" to hold that Congress could limit free expression in the name of national security. Meiklejohn fastened on Article 1, Section 9, which itemizes many limits on Congress: no suspension of habeas corpus, no bills of attainder, no ex post facto laws, and so forth. He noted that the powers of Congress even in times of rebellion and treason are limited.[88]

In another article, "The Balancing of Self-Preservation against Political Freedom," Meiklejohn again underscored that there is no reference to "self-preservation" in the Constitution. Examining the provisions relating to defense, he noted that even the capacity to declare war and to raise armies is delegated to Congress by the people in "precise and guarded" ways. Thus, "No appropriation of money . . . shall be for a longer term than two years." Congress has no authority, says the Constitution, for "the appointment of officers" and "for training [of] the militia."[89]

Meiklejohn observed that the "self-preservation" doctrine stripped the people of a basic right, the right to make a revolution. In "What Does the First Amendment Mean?" (1953), he cited passages in the *Federalist Papers* that endorse not only the right to advocate revolution but the right to engage in actual revolt. "Hamilton goes so far as to declare," Meiklejohn states, "that it is an important advantage of the proposed federal union that it provides an easier and more secure road for revolutionary action than is available in the smaller units of the separate states." Meiklejohn quoted *Federalist No. 28.*

> If the representatives of the people betray their constituents, there is no resource left but in the exertion of that original right of self-defense which is paramount to all positive forms of government, and which against the usurpations of their national rulers, may be exerted with infinitely better prospect of success than against those of the rulers of an individual State . . . The smaller the extent of the territory, the more difficult will it be for the people to form a regular or systematic plan of opposition, and the more easy will it be to defeat their early efforts.[90]

Throughout this article, Meiklejohn argues that the *Dennis* case—in which he had been criticized—is based on a gross misreading of Congressional powers.

There is more. Meiklejohn took on the issue of the jurisdiction of Congress's investigating committees. In his tribute to Meiklejohn, Kalven noted that the House Un–American

Activities Committee, established in 1938, "moved into the McCarthy era apparently without any legal limitations other than those imposed by the privilege against self-incrimination."[91] In "The Barenblatt Opinion" (1960), Meiklejohn argued that it violated the First Amendment to give HUAC the power to intrude into the lives of its so-called "witnesses" and to compel testimony from them. It was one thing for Congress to establish a committee to get a general impression of the scope of communism in American society and another thing entirely to set up a committee to take an inventory of American communists one at a time.

In *Barenblatt v. United States* (1959), the Supreme Court upheld HUAC's investigative powers. The controversy centered on rule 11 of HUAC's charter.

> The Committee on Un-American Activities, as a whole or by subcommittee, is authorized to make from time to time investigations of (1) the extent, character, and objects of un- American propaganda activities in the United States, (2) the diffusion within the United States of subversive and un-American propaganda that is instigated from foreign countries or of a domestic origin and attacks the principle of the form of government as guaranteed by our Constitution, and (3) all other questions in relation thereto that would aid Congress in any necessary remedial legislation.[92]

Meiklejohn argued that the term "investigations" for Congress and its committees means to investigate the contours of a social problem. It does not include the power to compel testimony in a prosecutorial manner from anyone who is suspected of being involved in the problem.[93] Barenblatt was a teacher who refused to answer HUAC's questions about his political beliefs and party affiliations. The novelty of the case is that he invoked the First Amendment rather than the Fifth Amendment. In other words, he refused to answer, not to avoid incriminating himself but because he rejected HUAC's right to inquire at all. Such questions, Barenblatt maintained, violated freedom of speech and association.

Justice Harlan wrote for the Court,

> That Congress has wide power to legislate in the field of Communist activity in this Country, and to conduct appropriate investigations in aid thereof, is hardly debatable. This power rests on the right of self-preservation, 'the ultimate value of any society.'[94]

Meiklejohn argued that asking someone if he is a member of the Communist Party is not inquiring into the person's "activities." He maintained that HUAC could rightfully ask questions such as, "Have you engaged in espionage for an enemy nation?" Or, "Have you incited others to criminal action against the United States?" But it could not force people to profess that they were communists in the absence of any evidence that they had broken the law.

What are the rights of professors who are swept into HUAC's investigations? This was an issue that academic administrators had to confront. Not only was Meiklejohn's defense of First Amendment resistance to HUAC out of favor, but even the Fifth Amendment defense was widely dismissed in academe. The First Amendment challenge was more far-reaching; it questioned the right of HUAC to ask certain questions at all. The Fifth Amendment argument only conferred a right on "witnesses" not to incriminate themselves. Harvard president James B. Conant stated in 1952 that "the invocation of the Fifth Amendment by a faculty member constituted grounds for dismissal."[95] The University's counsel, Oscar Shaw, observed in a letter that "it makes no sense whatsoever" for anybody to plead the

Fifth unless actually engaged in criminal subversive activity. "I thoroughly agree with you," replied the recipient of the letter. It was Chafee, the great defender of "clear and present danger" and critic of Meiklejohn. In January 1953, Chafee co-authored a letter in the *Harvard Crimson* in the form of a memo on the legal issues related to avoiding questions by HUAC. According to the memo, there is no legal right to invoke the Fifth in order to avoid being a witness. The memo was widely read by academic leaders across the country and employed to justify the dismissal of professors who did not cooperate with HUAC.[96] Meiklejohn eviscerated the argument in a response published in the *Crimson*. He pointed out that HUAC too often questioned its "witnesses" about their own beliefs and party affiliations. They were thus turned into defendants, not witnesses, and had a right to invoke the Fifth without penalty.[97]

Move 3. The Vindication of Legal "Absolutes"

In *Dennis,* two justices, Vinson and Frankfurter, derided Meiklejohn for his commitment to "absolute" principles. Vinson wrote:

> Absolute rules would inevitably lead to absolute exceptions, and such exceptions would eventually corrode the rules. The demands of free speech in a democratic society as well as the interest in national security are better served by candid and informed weighing of competing interests, within the confines of the judicial process, than by announcing dogmas too inflexible for the non-Euclidean problems to be solved.[98]

In the field of philosophy, a basic question about any statement concerning the nature of knowledge is whether the statement can stand up to its own standard. Thus, the assertion that all scientific statements must be testable—the verifiability criterion of knowledge—falls on its own sword because it is not itself a testable statement. Likewise, Meiklejohn noted, with regard to "Absolute rules would inevitably lead to absolute exceptions," that such a statement is framed absolutely and "proves itself to be false." Meiklejohn also observed that Supreme Court decisions contain a "flood of absolutes." Even one of his accusers, Frankfurter, deployed absolutes. As Meiklejohn observed, in *McCollum v. Board of Education* (1948), Frankfurter spoke of "the basic constitutional principle of absolute separation" of church and state.[99]

As for Vinson's assertion that modern life contains no space for absolutes, Meiklejohn argued that this confused two different meanings of the word "absolute." Meiklejohn agreed that nothing in the Constitution is absolute in the sense of unchangeable. Any clause can be debated and amended. But while constitutional principles are open to reconsideration, this does not make them "relative." Some of them are absolute in their meaning.[100] The First Amendment says Congress shall make "no" law abridging speech, and no means no—without exceptions.

Conclusion

Long treated as an idealist without practical judgment, Meiklejohn had a profound influence on American free-speech law. In *New York Times v. Sullivan* and subsequent decisions (such as the 1989 *Texas v. Johnson* flag burning case), the Supreme Court has held that political speech is at the core of the First Amendment. The most intriguing question, however, is not whether legal doctrine bears traces of Meiklejohn's influence: it clearly does. The vital matter is whether Meiklejohn's victory in the domain of First Amendment law means that his vision of American education also gained credence. Here, the answer is no. While his idea of free speech has prospered, his vision of liberal education and academic freedom has fallen by the wayside.

I can imagine a reader thinking, "But wait. Aren't free speech and academic freedom the same thing? And don't we want to maximize each?" For Meiklejohn, free speech and academic freedom serve democracy in fundamentally different ways. Free speech is a principle of the democratic public sphere, but under the influence of Rousseau, Meiklejohn believed that one must be educated for freedom, and this process involves compulsion in the form of a required curriculum. Academic freedom is the constitutive principle of universities, whose purpose is to train students to be rational speakers, not just free speakers.

I am not attempting to define what academic freedom *should* mean. I am simply noting that it has meant different things, and the fact that Meiklejohn, a pioneer in free-speech theory, did not view free speech and academic freedom as interchangeable is historically significant. Meiklejohn envisioned the American college as a training ground for civic debate. We should note that he constantly referred to the "liberal college" in his educational writings and never to the "research university." We have seen that he had reservations about the freedom to pursue scientific research in aid of the military. What is not essential for the "liberal education" of students is not covered by academic freedom. And liberal education itself is a "required education for freedom." A core curriculum is needed for the proper cultivation of speech on campus. Without a well-organized college education, Meiklejohn declared in his speech to the AAUP with which I began, "the program of self-government is doomed to futility and disaster."[101]

For Meiklejohn, academic freedom is the basis of an educational process that strives to shape a particular type of person: an informed and articulate democratic citizen. There is something tragic about the fact that today, there are no legal barriers to implementing Meiklejohn's vision of liberal education, but the resolve to do so is missing. Many colleges have "General Education" programs based on the premise that courses taken in the first two years of college should be outside of the student's major. But rarely does General Education focus on introducing all students to political ideas and policy debates. Typically, students are able to choose from a vast menu of General Education options designed to familiarize them with various "disciplines" rather than the leading controversies in democratic theory and practice. Those who propose required core courses run the risk of appearing oppressive to students who think academic freedom means the right to choose their courses, and to professors who think academic freedom means the right to teach what interests them the most. What Meiklejohn envisioned as liberal education now appears to many academics as illiberal.

The majority of American college students are poorly informed about the leading "isms" of modern politics: capitalism, conservatism, libertarianism, socialism, communitarianism, feminism, etc. The triumph of Meiklejohn's legal ideas on free speech has, ironically, helped to assure this political illiteracy. Meiklejohn himself never stopped worrying about the future of higher education.

Can one hundred seventy million people of different racial stocks, of conflicting and changing private interests, of imperfect and impeded communication with one another, learn to think together about the general welfare in such a way that each of them may have a valid sense of responsible sharing in the common enterprise of making and managing a free society? To develop that capacity of mind and will is the primary task of our schools and colleges . . . We Americans lack freedom chiefly because we do not know what it is. And that failure of understanding is not due to a lack of capacity. It is due primarily to a lack of interest in such a reflective or theoretical problem . . . Nothing short of a fundamental transformation of the spirit and method of our national education . . . can fit us for the responsibilities of thinking and deciding which the Constitution lays upon us.[102]

Notes

1 Alexander Meiklejohn, "The Teaching of Intellectual Freedom," *Bulletin of the American Association of University Professors*, vol. 38, no. 1 (Spring, 1952), 10–25.
2 Alexander Meiklejohn, *Free Speech and Its Relation to Self-Government* (New York: Harper, 1948), 17.
3 Meiklejohn, "The Teaching of Intellectual Freedom," 14.
4 "General Declaration of Principles on Academic Freedom and Academic Tenure," in "General Report of the Committee on Academic Freedom and Academic Tenure," *Bulletin of the American Association of University Professors*, vol. 1, no. 1 (December, 1915), 25.
5 Meiklejohn, "The Teaching of Intellectual Freedom," 18.
6 Ibid, 14–15.
7 Alexander Meiklejohn, "Required Education for Freedom," *The American Scholar*, vol. 13, no. 4 (Autumn, 1944), 393–395.
8 Alexander Meiklejohn, *The Liberal College* (Boston: Marshall Jones Company, 1920), 63.
9 Meiklejohn, "The Teaching of Intellectual Freedom," 24.
10 "Athens and Owls," *Time Magazine*, vol. 12, no. 14 (October, 1928), 30–31.
11 Adam R. Nelson, *Education and Democracy: The Meaning of Alexander Meiklejohn* (Madison: University of Wisconsin Press, 2001), 175–190 on criticism of the Experimental College and its demise in 1932.
12 Richard A. Nagareda, "Class Actions in the Administrative State: Kalven and Rosenfeld Revisited," *University of Chicago Law Review*, vol. 75, no. 2 (Spring, 2008), 603–648; Lee Bollinger, "Harry Kalven, The Proust of the First Amendment," *University of Michigan Law Review*, vol. 87, no. 6 (1989), 1576–1583; Vincent Blasi, "Legends of the Legal Academy: Harry Kalven, Jr.", *Journal of Legal Education*, vol. 61, no. 2 (November, 2011), 301–309.
13 Harry Kalven, Jr., "Mr. Alexander Meiklejohn and the Barenblatt Opinion," *University of Chicago Law Review*, vol. 27, no. 2 (Winter 1960), 315, 320, 328. Note that Kalven authored the famous "Report on the University's Role in Political and Social Action," November 11, 1967, which states,

> The mission of the university is the discovery, improvement, and dissemination of knowledge. Its domain of inquiry and scrutiny includes all aspects and all values of society. A university faithful to its mission will provide enduring challenges to social values, policies, practices, and institutions . . . In brief, a good university, like Socrates, will be upsetting.

http://www-news.uchicago.edu/releases/07/pdf/kalverpt.pdf. The influence of Meiklejohn is evident here.
14 Akhil Amar, "Intratextualism," *Harvard Law Review*, vol. 112, no. 4 (February, 1999), 812
15 Richard Epstein, "Was *New York Times v. Sullivan* Wrong?", *University of Chicago Law Review*, vol. 53, no. 3 (1986), 782.
16 About Meiklejohn's use of gendered language, his conception of free speech and of liberal education were tied to his ideal of participatory democracy and the right to vote. Since women had no constitutional right to vote until 1929, his use of "man," at least up to that year, does have overtones of gender exclusion. Meiklejohn was President of Amherst when he wrote *The Liberal College*, and the college was reserved for men. However, Meiklejohn created adult education classes for women at the college (see Nelson, *Education and Democracy*, 100); and in the San Francisco School of Social Studies, which he directed later, 60% of the students were women. Additionally, in his writing after 1929, we can observe a decline in the use of gendered language, though it does not disappear, as some of the quotations in this chapter show. In *What Does America Mean?* (New York: W.W. Norton, 1935), Meiklejohn

speaks often of "men and women," as in "In such a society [a democratic socialist society], men and women could be bound together by the sharing of common purposes, common ideas, which would make them, in some real sense, members of a community." (247) See also "liberal education must be essentially the same for all free men and women." ("Required Education for Freedom, " 395. And *Education between Two Worlds* (New York: Harper, 1942), at 147:

> All members of society must have a liberal education. There shall be one set, and only one set, of schools for all people, whatever their age, whatever their race, whatever their sex, whatever their personal quality, whatever their economic conditions. The first postulate of a democracy is equality of education.

17 Meiklejohn, *The Liberal College*, 75.
18 Ibid, 76.
19 Meiklejohn, *Free Speech*, ix.
20 Ibid, 18–20.
21 Meiklejohn, "Required Education for Freedom," 395.
22 Meiklejohn, "The Teaching of Intellectual Freedom," 22.
23 Ibid, 22.
24 Ibid, 24.
25 Eugene H. Perry, *A Socrates for all Seasons: Alexander Meiklejohn and Deliberative Democracy* (n.p., iUniverse Publishing, 2011), 140. A self-published text, this is nevertheless an excellent work.
26 Meiklejohn, *Education between Two Worlds*, 93–94.
27 For biographical details as well as fine analysis of Meiklejohn's political and educational thought, see Adam R. Nelson, *Education and Democracy: The Meaning of Alexander Meiklejohn, 1872–1964* (Madison: University of Wisconsin Press, 2008).
28 Julius Seelye Bixler, "Alexander Meiklejohn: The Making of the Amherst Mind," *The New England Quarterly*, vol. 47, no. 2 (June, 1974), 182–183.
29 Richard F. Teichgraeber III, "The 'Meiklejohn Affair' Revisited: Amherst and the World in the Early Twentieth Century," in *Amherst in the World*, ed. Martha Saxton (Amherst: Amherst College, 2020), 249–268.
30 Walter Lippmann, "The Fall of President Meiklejohn," reprinted in *Public Persons* (London: Routledge, 2017), 72 (first pub. in *New York World*, June 24, 1923).
31 Meiklejohn, "The Teaching of Intellectual Freedom," 11.
32 Robert Thomas Brennan, "The Making of the Liberal College: Alexander Meiklejohn at Amherst," *History of Education Quarterly*, vol. 28, no. 4 (Winter, 1988), 570.
33 Alexander Meiklejohn, "The Inaugural Address," *Amherst Graduates' Quarterly*, no. 1 (November, 1912), 66 (delivered October 16, 1912).
34 Nelson, *Education and Democracy*, 72.
35 Brennan, "The Making of the Liberal College," 586.
36 Ibid, 588.
37 Cited in ibid, 589. The extraordinary speech, "What Does the College Hope to be During the Next Hundred Years?", given June 21, 1921, and published in *The Amherst Graduates' Quarterly*, August 1921, is online here: https://www.amherst.edu/system/files/media/What_does_the_College_hope_to_be.pdf.
38 Cited by Nelson, *Education and Democracy*, 103.
39 Cited by Lucien Price: *Prophets Unawares: The Romance of an Idea* (New York: The Century Company, 1924), 160. The book is about Meiklejohn's vision of liberal education and his demise at Amherst College. The name of the trustee and his son are not identified.
40 Cited by Brennan, "The Making of the Liberal College," 593.
41 Perry, "A Socrates for All Seasons," 152, 165–166.
42 *League for Industrial Democracy, Thirtieth Anniversary Report* (New York: League for Industrial Democracy, 1935), 7.
43 Alexander Meiklejohn, "Should Communists Be Allowed to Teach?" *New York Times* (March 27, 1949), 66. See also Sidney Hook, "Should Communists Be Permitted to Teach?" *New York Times*, February 27, 1949, 7, 22, 24, 26–28.
44 *Schenck v. United States*, 249 U.S. 47 (1919), 52.
45 Max Lerner, ed., *The Mind and Faith of Justice Holmes* (Boston: Little Brown and Company, 1943), xvii, xlvii.

46 Wallace Mendelson, "Clear and Present Danger: From Schenck to Dennis, *Columbia Law Review*, vol. 52, no. 3 (March, 1952), 313–333; Wallace Mendelson, "Clear and Present Danger: Another Decade," *Texas Law Review*, vol. 39, no. 4 (April, 1961), 449–456; Harry Kalven, Jr. *The Negro and the First Amendment* (Columbus: Ohio State University Press, 1965), contains discussions throughout on the influence of "clear and present danger." See especially the first chapter, "Group Libel, Seditious Libel, and Just Plain Libel," 7–64.

47 "A Survey of the Extent to Which the Rights Guaranteed by the First Amendment are Being Respected and Enforced in the Various Government Loyalty-Security Programs," *Hearings before the Subcommittee on Constitutional Rights of the Committee on the Judiciary United States Senate* (Washington: United States Government Printing Office, 1956), transcript of testimony on November 14, 1955 by Alexander Chafee, 31. Chafee emphasized that "clear and present danger" places some limits on government control of speech, but contra Meiklejohn, whom he repeatedly mentioned in his testimony, Chafee affirmed that it is the government which decides what counts as speech that can be regulated.

48 Ibid, testimony of Meiklejohn, 5–6.

49 Ibid, 77.

50 Lee C. Bollinger, "Free Speech and Intellectual Values," *Yale Law Journal*, vol. 92, no. 3 (January, 1983), 461. Bollinger does not find Meiklejohn's criticism convincing. But Bollinger examines only *Free Speech and Its Relation to Self-Government*, not the more scholarly writings that are a special focus of this chapter.

51 Meiklejohn, *Free Speech and Its Relation to Self-Government*, 68.

52 Ibid, 93.

53 *United States v. Dennis*, 183 F.2d (1950), 212.

54 Oliver Wendell Holmes, *The Common Law* (London: Macmillan, 1882), 155.

55 *Schenck v. United States*, 249 U.S. 47 (1919), 52.

56 Holmes, *The Common Law*, 159.

57 *United States v. Carroll Towing Co.*, 158 F.2d 173 (1947).

58 *Dennis v. United States*, 341 U.S. 508 (1951).

59 Ibid, at 525, note 2.

60 Meiklejohn, *Free Speech and Its Relation to Self-Government*, 25.

61 Ibid, 37–38.

62 *Dennis v. United States*, 525, note 2.

63 Wieman v. Updegraff, 355 U.S. 196 (1952).

64 Meiklejohn, *Free Speech and Its Relation to Self-Government*, 99–100. Readers familiar with Robert C. Post, *Democracy, Expertise, and Academic Freedom: A First Amendment Jurisprudence for the Modern State* (New Haven: Yale University Press, 2013) will note similarities with Meiklejohn (whom Post amply cites). But a difference is that only Meiklejohn draws the hard conclusion which follows from defining academic freedom in relationship to democracy: it means that much that is deemed academic in the modern university is not covered by academic freedom. Post does not consider whether a considerable segment of scientific research is outside the bounds of education in the service of democratic citizenship.

65 Zechariah Chafee, "Review of Free Speech and Its Relation to Self-Government by Alexander Meiklejohn," *Harvard Law Review*, vol. 62, no. 5 (March, 1949), 896.

66 Ibid, 896, footnote.

67 Ibid, 900.

68 Ibid, 894–895.

69 E.g., Osmond K. Fraenkel, review of Meiklejohn, *Free Speech and Its Relation to Self-Government*, in *Law and Contemporary Problems*. vol. 14, no. 1 (Winter, 1949), 167–169; John Courtney Murray, review of the same, *Georgetown Law Review*, vol. 37 (May, 1949), 654–662.

70 *New York Times v. Sullivan,* 376 U.S. 270–271.

71 Harry Kalven Jr., "The New York Times Case: A Note on the Central Meaning of the First Amendment," *Supreme Court Review*, vol. 1964 (1964), 204–205, 209.

72 Ibid, 205, 209, 221.

73 William J. Brennan, Jr., "The Supreme Court and the Meiklejohn Interpretation of the First Amendment," *Harvard Law Review*, vol. 79, no. 1 (November 1965), 1, 18.

74 Alexander Meiklejohn, "The First Amendment is an Absolute," *The Supreme Court Review*, vol. 1961 (1961), 252.

75 *New York Times v. Sullivan,* 376 U.S. 297.

76 Kalven, "The New York Times Case," 193–194.

77 Alexander Meiklejohn, *Political Freedom: The Constitutional Powers of the People* (New York: Galaxy, 1965; first pub. 1960), 95.

78 Alexander Meiklejohn, "Freedom in the College," *The Atlantic Monthly*, January 1918, 84, 87–88.

79 Anonymous Preface to Alexander Meiklejohn, *Philosophy* (Chicago: American Library Association, 1926), 8.

80 Meiklejohn, *Political Freedom*, xii–xiii.

81 Phillip Bobbitt, *Constitutional Fate* (Oxford: Oxford University Press, 1984), esp. 74.

82 Akhil Amar, "Intratextualism," *Harvard Law Review*, vol. 112, no. 4 (February, 1999), 748, 758. Amar also praises Meiklejohn's intratextual analysis of free speech: 816, note 266.

83 Alexander Meiklejohn, "The First Amendment is an Absolute," 256.

84 The text in which Meiklejohn does the most to amalgamate references to "the people" is Ibid. But see also his "What Does the First Amendment Mean?" *University of Chicago Law Review,* vol. 20, no. 3 (Spring, 1953), 461–479.

85 Meiklejohn, testimony in "A Survey of the Extent to Which the Rights Guaranteed by the First Amendment are Being Respected," 4.

86 Lerner, *The Mind and Faith of Justice Holmes*, xxxiii.

87 Kalven, "Mr. Alexander Meiklejohn," 320.

88 Alexander Meiklejohn, "The First Amendment and Evils that Congress Has a Right to Prevent," *Indiana Law Journal*, vol. 26, no. 4 (1951), 486.

89 Alexander Meiklejohn, "The Balancing of Self-Preservation against Political Freedom," *California Law Review*, vol. 49, no. 1 (March, 1961), 10–11, discussing article I, section 8.

90 Alexander Meiklejohn, "What Does the First Amendment Mean?" 467.

91 Kalven, "Mr. Alexander Meiklejohn," 316.

92 Alexander Meiklejohn, "The Barenblatt Opinion," *University of Chicago Law Review*, vol. 27, no. 2 (Winter, 1960), 329 (citing rule 11).

93 Ibid, 332.

94 *Barenblatt v. United States*, 360 U.S. 128 (1959), citing Dennis v. United States, 341 U.S. 509.

95 Ellen Schrecker, *No Ivory Tower: McCarthyism and the Universities* (New York: Oxford University Press, 1986), 183.

96 Ibid, 184–187.

97 William M. Beecher, "Educator Attacks Chafee-Sutherland Doctrine," followed by Meiklejohn's letter, The Harvard Crimson, February 25, 1954: https://www.thecrimson.com/article/1954/2/25/educator-attacks-chafee-sutherland-doctrine-pone-year/.

98 Dennis v. United States, 341 U.S. 524–525.

99 Meiklejohn. "What Does the First Amendment Mean?" 474–475.

100 Ibid; see also Meiklejohn, "The First Amendment and Evils that Congress Has a Right to Prevent," 490–491.

101 Meikeljohn, "The Teaching of Intellectual Freedom," 22; see also 24.

102 Meiklejohn, *Political Freedom*, 160–161.

3 Indoctrination

From Lovejoy to Foucault by Way of Black Studies

Abstract

What constitutes indoctrination in the classroom? Does a professor have a free-speech right to turn a college course into a forum for political activism? If there is such a free-speech right, is it limited by the professional duties implicit in the concept of academic freedom? This chapter, and the next one, map out debates over these questions, from the founding of the American Association of University Professors in 1915 to the present. The founders of the AAUP warned against classroom indoctrination and created what I call an "anti-political orthodoxy." This chapter includes an account of the formation of Black Studies departments and other developments in higher education that created cracks in this orthodoxy.

Introduction

In the autumn of 2016, the University of Massachusetts, where I work, undertook a Campus Climate Survey "to help the university better understand the challenges of creating a respectful and inclusive campus environment."[1] The survey posed questions designed to determine the scope of bias on the UMass campus; 38% of the university's 21,687 undergraduate students participated. A 50-page report assessing the results appeared in April 2018.

From an idealistic viewpoint, the purpose of "climate" surveys is to give students a voice: a chance to reveal patterns of exclusion and to enable campus leaders to frame new policies that will deter bigotry. From a cynical perspective, the function of "climate" surveys is the opposite: to *deprive* students of a voice, that is, to preempt public outbursts of anger, to convert a potential campus disturbance into a body of academic data that experts can control: in sum, to avoid the kind of uprisings that occurred in 2015 at the University of Missouri, where anti-racist protesters brought about the resignations of the President and Chancellor.

From any perspective, however, the UMass survey results were surprising. "Climate" reports are a by-product of educational progressivism; they are typically meant to uncover discrimination based on race, gender, and sexual orientation. The term climate in education traces to Roberta M. Hall and Bernice R. Sandler, authors of "The Classroom Climate: A Chilly One for Women?" (1982).[2] Sandler was a key figure in creating Title IX of the Higher Education Amendments of 1972 (prohibiting sex-based discrimination in educational institutions receiving federal funds). Since the 1990s, a profusion of "climate" studies has appeared in education journals.[3] Some representative titles are:

- "Assessing Campus Climate for Gays, Lesbians, and Bisexuals at Two Institutions" (*Journal of College Student Development*, 1997)

DOI: 10.4324/9781003052685-4

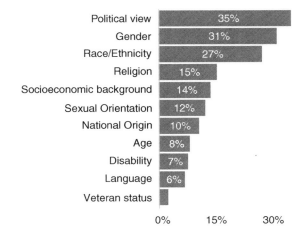

Figure 3.1 Perceived basis of being singled out unfairly by instructors.

- "Nine Themes in Campus Racial Climates and Implications for Institutional Transformation" (*New Directions for Student Services*, 2007)
- "LGBT Campus Climate: The Good and the Very Bad" (*Diversity and Democracy*, 2012)
- "Am I Welcome Here: Campus Climate and Psychological Well-Being Among Students of Color" (*Journal of Student Affairs Research*, 2021).

The 2018 report summarizing the UMass climate survey was unusual, for it highlighted a type of bias that is generally omitted from the "climate" literature: political bias. A section of the report is about "Negative Remarks Related to Social Identity." Participants indicated how often they experienced insulting comments in a variety of settings: social media, campus residence halls, dining facilities, sports, public spaces outdoors, and in class. The results indicated that the leading basis of negative remarks was "Political View," with "Racial/Ethnic" identity in second place. Another section focused on the perception of unfair treatment by instructors in the classroom; 35% of the students who reported being targeted unfairly by an instructor indicated that the abuse occurred on the basis of their political views.[4]

The report states:

> Isolation and hostility . . . surfaced when instructors or peers assumed that the entire class shares a liberal political orientation; in these cases, moderate, conservative, or non-liberal students can feel invisible. In addition, students described situations where faculty did not moderate discussions in a neutral way.

The report then lists a series of comments made by students, including, "Multiple professors I have this semester OPENLY MOCK individuals for not subscribing to the same liberal ideology that they do." After the quotations, the report sums up, "There was a perception expressed that the university's strong liberal bias hinders political diversity."[5]

The social scientist in charge of the report was Joya Misra, a professor of Sociology and Public Policy at UMass. On a university web page, Misra describes her work as follows:

> Her research and teaching primarily focus on social inequality, including inequalities by gender and gender identity, race, class, ethnicity, sexuality, nationality, citizenship,

parenthood status, and educational level. She considers how policies may work to both reinforce and lessen inequalities; her aim is to create more equitable societies and workplaces.[6]

The data generated in the climate survey made it difficult to ignore political bias, and Misra deserves credit for giving weight to this type of discrimination when it did not figure in her own research agenda. In a section called Recommendations for Change, the report states:

> Students note that they are being asked to be tolerant of students whose identities differ from theirs, but their own political identify is not tolerated. They argue that creating a truly inclusive campus requires open discourse on politics . . . Undergraduate students emphasize the importance of helping students develop their thoughts by exposing them to a wide variety of perspectives. Some students called for greater neutrality, asking faculty not to disclose their political leanings or attempt to influence or critique students' perspectives.[7]

Yet, there are no action items in the report. Misra and her team frame no suggestions about how to mitigate political bias in the classroom: no training sessions about ideological diversity for professors, no creation of a reporting mechanism for abused students, no suggestion that professors can be disciplined, as they can be for gender-based and racial bias, and no proposal to avoid hiring professors who have a track record of bringing political zeal into the classroom. The report amply dramatizes the pervasiveness of political bigotry in teaching, but the reader is left hanging without any way to solve the problem.

An explanation for why universities hesitate to impose restrictions on teaching is this: any limits on the content of instruction would appear to violate the professor's academic freedom. However, defining academic freedom as the freedom to engage in politics in the classroom is a recent innovation. Although the argument that academic inquiry ought to be political arose in the late1960s, it was only around 2005 that the American Association of University Professors (AAUP) began to go out on a limb to defend political advocacy inside the classroom. Since its founding in 1915, the AAUP has played a vital role in defining and protecting academic freedom. We will see that throughout most of its history, the AAUP upheld a distinction between academic inquiry and political activism.

The present chapter, and the next one, examine the debate about academic freedom and classroom professionalism from 1915 to the present. The two chapters provide an account of the debates, over the past 100 years, about what constitutes acceptable teaching within the limits of academic freedom. I must confess that I began the inquiry with the belief that political activism in the classroom is evil. But the arguments for the other side, which I came across in my research, have convinced me that this is an unresolvable issue. It is not so much that impartiality is impossible to achieve; I have already suggested, in the Introduction, that impartiality is possible. The problem is that the modern university has made an irrevocable decision to include disciplines that are openly political in their orientation. Salient examples are Black Studies and Women's Studies, but there are others, such as Environmental Studies, which are political without being about identity politics. Once the university consecrates such fields, it can no longer hold up theoretical physics or analytical philosophy as paradigmatic of all "academic" investigation.

This chapter and the next one aim to prove that a significant change in the meaning of academic freedom has occurred. The debate about what is unacceptable "indoctrination" and what is acceptable "advocacy" in the classroom is an excellent way to measure how the idea of academic freedom has morphed over time. This particular question—the role of politics in the classroom—is also a meta-question: it subsumes other questions. The debate over teaching has required the contestants to argue about the definition of knowledge, objectivity, university, and democracy.

The AAUP's landmark 1915 "General Declaration of Principles on Academic Freedom and Academic Tenure" spoke against "taking unfair advantage of the student's immaturity by indoctrinating him with the teacher's own opinions."[8] The freedom of the academic to teach and to conduct research was conditional upon the obligation to refrain from political activism in these activities. The founders of the AAUP were concerned that if universities were perceived by the outside world as centers of political activism, then legislators and the general public would feel entitled to interfere in the workings of the university. Professors are not elected. In a democratic polity, they are not sovereign. If universities declare teaching and research to be political in nature, then it is reasonable to conclude that these activities fall under the jurisdiction of the democratic process. In the early twentieth century, as we will see, elected governmental officials often intervened precisely because they presumed that the university is political. The AAUP, whose primary mission was to prevent the firing of academics by non-academic agents, promoted the image of university professors as unbiased experts—as professionals whose disciplinary commitments were purely scholarly and not political in nature.

I shall call this "the anti-political orthodoxy": the insistence that there can be no academic freedom of professors, no autonomy of the university, without a separation of politics and academics. The orthodoxy continues to have adherents, but this chapter shows how it came to be doubted; the next chapter shows how the AAUP itself abandoned the orthodoxy. I do not provide a history of how American professors actually taught. When I say, for example, that the anti-political orthodoxy was unquestioned before the 1960s, I do not mean that all professors kept political bias out of the classroom. I mean that no widely publicized theory of academic freedom yet existed to consecrate political activism in the classroom. Likewise, to say that today, we are in a period of post-orthodoxy does not mean that most universities are like UMass Amherst in terms of the "climate" in the classroom. It means that the concept of academic freedom no longer provides a firm basis for reining in professors who choose to see themselves as political activists behind a lectern.

Weber on the Separation of Academics and Politics

Max Weber was one of the greatest thinkers ever to address the question of the relationship between academic inquiry and political commitment. He was certainly the greatest to have supported the anti-political orthodoxy. Yet, Weber seems to have had little impact on the debate in the United States. His writings, such as the *Protestant Reformation and the Spirit of Capitalism* and *Economy and Society*, became canonical in the social sciences.[9] But his denunciation of professors who bring politics into the classroom is not referenced in any American text on the meaning of academic freedom that I have encountered, with the exception of the very recent writings of Stanley Fish, who is a leading defender today of the anti-political orthodoxy.[10] I include Weber because the remarkable depth of his reflections helps us to discern imperfections in the way that Lovejoy and other Americans framed the anti-political orthodoxy. I wish to suggest that one reason the orthodoxy cracked in the 1960s and beyond is that it was never articulated with the kind of intellectual power which Weber brought to it.

In 1917, Weber delivered a speech in Munich entitled "Wissenschaft als Beruf," usually translated as "Science as a Vocation." The German word *Wissenschaft* does not refer uniquely to natural science; it can refer to scholarship of all kinds. Likewise, the word *Wissenschaftler* can mean a scientist or an academic. A better translation, then, is "The Academic Vocation," or "The Academic Calling." But I refer to the speech as "Science as a Vocation" because that is what it is usually called. A good deal of the speech, which was published in 1919, consists of a scolding of professors who preach from the lectern. Weber said:

> To take a practical political stand is one thing, and to analyze political structures and party positions is another. When speaking in a political meeting about democracy, one does not hide one's personal standpoint; indeed, to come out clearly and take a stand is one's damned duty. The words one uses in such a meeting are not means of scientific analysis but means of canvassing votes and winning over others. They are not plow-shares to loosen the soil of contemplative thought; they are swords against the enemies: Such words are weapons. It would be an outrage, however, to use words in this fashion in a lecture or in the lecture-room.[11]

One can discern a rage, restrained by biblical metaphor (swords and plow-shares), which gives the speech an emotional power that we will not find in early twentieth-century discussions of academic freedom in the United States. Weber's speech is an impassioned effort to sum up his anguished philosophy: to explain what it means to be an academic in a secularized society that lacks a transcendent value system, or what Weber famously called a "disenchanted" society.[12] The concept of disenchantment makes "Science as a Vocation" more than a commentary on the limits of academic freedom. The text expresses Weber's existential philosophy and his exploration of the structure of decision-making in a relativistic universe.

For Weber, there is no universal morality, but there is professional integrity. To be a responsible person means to recognize the special duties associated with one's calling. "In any profession, the task as such has its claims and must be performed in accordance with its own inherent laws."[13] Being a politician and being an academic are entirely different practices; hence, political and academic discourse should always be distinguished from each other. Weber, who edited an important German social scientific journal, suggested that a scholarly article can include political exhortations, but the author must not write as if the political prescriptions logically result from the academic findings. Political claims must be framed as personal reflections, as supplements to one's academic conclusions.

> There is and remains—and *this* is what matters to us—an eternal, unbridgeable difference as to whether an argument is aimed at our feelings and our capacity for embracing with enthusiasm concrete practical goals . . . *or* finally, [whether it is aimed] at our ability and need to *order* empirical reality *intellectually* in a manner that claims *validity* as empirical truth.[14]

Weber did very little teaching. He wrote about pedagogy because he construed the classroom, unlike the published text, which has room for political commentary, as a purely academic space. *Hence, he regarded a professor's conduct in the classroom as the true test of academic integrity.*

What makes the classroom different from the published article? It is the presence of students, who are dependent on the professor to a degree that readers of an academic text are not dependent on the author. It is a relationship of power. In "Science as a Vocation," he stated:

> In the lecture-room we stand opposite our audience, and it has to remain silent. I deem it irresponsible to exploit the circumstance that for the sake of their career the students have to attend a teacher's course while there is nobody present to oppose him with criticism. The task of the teacher is to serve the students with his knowledge and scientific experience and not to imprint upon them his personal political views.[15]

As W.G. Runciman observed, "Weber was very properly concerned, in his writings on method, to attack the lecture-room moralists whose social science is no more than a gloss of counterfeit objectivity used to disguise their sermons and prejudices."[16]

Weber's German contemporaries did not miss the point. Critics understood that Weber conceived of the modern individual as one who must compartmentalize political passion and not pretend that academic discourse can justify it. Responding to the speech, Erich von Kahler wrote that the core of Weber's address was the proposition that "politics has no place in the lecture-room." But Kahler rejected Weber's call for self-restraint and role division. A traditional humanist, Kahler identified with the ancient and medieval philosophies that offered a synthesis of truth and goodness. The role of professors is to represent the "wholly undivided, living unity growing within ourselves."[17] Reviewing an anthology containing Kahler's response, and other responses to Weber's speech, Peter Baehr, a sociologist, observes:

> What particularly disturbed Weber's audience was his argument that modern life consists of a number of orders or spheres—the economic, political, aesthetic, erotic, ethical, scientific among them—each of which is governed by its own immanent, distinctive principles. One had to choose between, and within, these dissonant spheres, or hold them in tension; they could not be reconciled or transcended.[18]

From this perspective, modern life is fractured. The introduction of political advocacy in the classroom, the quintessential academic space, is for Weber a "childish"[19] expression of nostalgia for an all-embracing *Weltanschauung*.

But what Weber dramatized particularly well, and what American advocates of political neutrality in the classroom never expressed as effectively, was the pathos of his own argument: the *painfulness* of keeping facts and value judgments separate. Weber had considerable potential as a political leader. He sacrificed it for the academic vocation, which means that he accepted a split between his capacity to change the world and his job to understand it. To have an academic "vocation" or calling means that one is called *away* from the righteous conviction that one's own values are truthful above all competing value systems. Weber gives this point special force in "Science as a Vocation when he quotes with approval these words from Tolstoy, "Science is meaningless because it gives no answer to our question, the only question important to us: 'What shall we do and how shall we live?'"[20]

Weber's intention, when he insisted on the fact/value distinction, was not to trivialize moral or political commitment. He meant to ennoble the subjective choices we make by highlighting their lack of rationality. We are free beings because we can engage in logically unforced decision-making. To suggest that moral and political choices are academically predetermined robs the human image of the element of freedom. To affirm that values are scientifically grounded also removes the awareness of tragedy in decision-making. When we make an important moral or political choice (to be a Catholic, to be a socialist, to join the military, to make being a parent our priority in life, etc.), we also close off other options for the good life. The very choices that give our life meaning also restrict the scope of our life's meaning. There is no value that subsumes all others; there are multiple "gods"[21] and "irreconcilably antagonistic values"[22] that compete for our attention. For Weber, an academic is one who bears a particular responsibility for sustaining this tragic consciousness.

Lovejoy and His Mutations, 1915–1950

Arthur Lovejoy's vision of academic life was much like Weber's. But Lovejoy writings on academic freedom, though influential in his era, never attained the depth of "Science as a Vocation." In fact, Lovejoy's thought on academic freedom lacked the power even of his own philosophical writings on other topics. The comparison with Weber allows us to see that the popularization of the concept of academic freedom in the United States was so closely tied to an organization, the AAUP (which Lovejoy co-founded), that the discourse of academic freedom acquired a bureaucratic tone. The impersonal character of the anti-political orthodoxy put it at a disadvantage when, starting in the 1960s, politically impassioned intellectuals began to reject it.

Lovejoy was born in 1873. His mother died of a drug overdose, possibly suicide, when he was an infant. His father abandoned his medical career and became a minister. Against his father's hope, Arthur did not pursue a clerical career; he pursued philosophy. His scholarly writings, even when addressing theological topics, were impeccably neutral. Lewis Feuer has observed that "in philosophy, history, and social theory Lovejoy was probably the least ideological of American thinkers" of his generation.[23] One of Lovejoy's first publications was "The Buddhistic Technical Terms *Upādāna* and *Upadeśa*" (1898); other early articles were "Religion and the Time Process" (1902) and "The Origins of Ethical Inwardness in Jewish Thought" (1907). An expert at mapping out old and unfamiliar ideas, Lovejoy refrained from declaring any system to be true above others.

In the early twentieth century in England and the United States, philosophy was becoming a highly technical discipline; the analytical impulse tended to separate the discussion of logical issues from the discussion of the history of philosophy. But Lovejoy, who founded the *Journal of the History of Ideas* in 1940, was also a leading commentator on the contemporary analytical scene. He did not take sides. He focused on itemizing the differences among competing schools of philosophy. He was also skillful in eliciting ambiguities from a given theory in order to demonstrate that it harbored mutually exclusive claims: a kind of deconstructionism *avant la lettre*. This approach is evident from the very titles of essays such as "The Thirteen Pragmatisms" (1908), "On the Discrimination of Romanticisms" (1924), and "Morris's Six Theories of Mind" (1933).

In 1916–1917, Lovejoy served as President of the American Philosophical Association. In his presidential address, "Conditions of Progress in Philosophical Inquiry," he portrayed the philosopher as the opposite of one who "proselytizes." Lovejoy suggested that philosophy has reached a permanent stage of non-consensus. In philosophy, progress will not take the form of a resolution of the major questions. Progress will lie in a clearer understanding of how different answers to a given question compare to each other. Against "uniformitarianism" Lovejoy upholds the principle "that mere diversity . . . is worth taking pains to conserve." The overlap with Weber is most striking when Lovejoy inveighs against the notion that the professor's role is to "edify" others.

> An eagerness to serve the spiritual needs of one's generation is a generous and noble thing; but it is a very different thing from an eagerness to probe an intricate logical

problem to its obscurest elements and its nicest distinctions . . . To this day, however, there still attaches to the current conception of the office of the teacher of philosophy much of this paradoxical duality . . .

Lovejoy acknowledges that every person is entitled to have "working hypotheses about the world and human life that transcend any present possibility of proof." However,

the two types of mental process are distinct . . . the ends of edification and of rigorous inquiry are not . . . to be sought by the same means, nor, as a rule, at the hands of the same persons.

The job of the philosophy professor is to inform others of the "multiplicity" of viewpoints with regard to any particular problem. The record of philosophy is "kaleidoscopic," and the discipline needs to teach its material in an "undogmatic and non-partisan" manner.[24]

Lovejoy was one of the primary authors of the AAUP's 1915 "General Declaration of Principles on Academic Freedom and Academic Tenure."[25] John Karl Wilson, the author of a doctoral thesis on the history of academic freedom, describes Lovejoy as "the most powerful influence in creating the AAUP and influencing its early approach to academic freedom."[26] Lovejoy's concern with academic freedom originated when he was a philosophy professor at Stanford. In 1900, Jane Stanford, the widow of the university's founder, fired the economist Edward A. Ross for articles and speeches criticizing the employment of Chinese laborers in the railroad industry, which was the basis of the Stanford fortune. Jane Stanford also tried to place a total ban on faculty political activity.[27]

Lovejoy resigned in protest. After several visiting professorships at different institutions, he took a permanent position at Johns Hopkins in 1910. Some accounts of the Ross affair simplify the controversy by portraying Ross as a liberal critic of the railroad barons who exploited cheap foreign labor. But Ross couched his arguments in racist terms. He declared in 1900 that "the Aryan race" was committing "race suicide" by allowing poor Asians to proliferate.[28] According to Wilson, "Jane Stanford defended the Chinese against racism, including an effort in 1891 by Stanford students to ban Chinese workers from Stanford's cafeterias." He adds, however, that her concern for Chinese people did not "extend to the conditions of those workers who suffered tremendous exploitation and loss of life helping to make her family more wealthy."[29]

In 1915, a professor at the University of Utah was fired for helping to defend the labor activist and songwriter Joe Hill against the charge of murder. President Kingsbury, under pressure from the governor and board of regents, also fired four professors for criticizing the university administration and expressing progressive political views (in one case, the professor promoted his views in class). Seventeen professors resigned from the university to protest the dismissals. The events at Utah, and similar firings at the University of Colorado, inspired Lovejoy to join with Columbia University economist, Edward R.A. Seligman, to create the AAUP. Their goal, as described by Thomas Haskell, was to carve out "professional autonomy and collegial self-governance" for academics.[30]

The 1915 "Declaration" establishes the right of professors to regulate their own activities, free of control from trustees and legislators. The key section of the document is entitled "The Nature of the Academic Calling." Academics are defined as those who "deal at first hand, after prolonged and specialized technical training, with the sources of knowledge." Their function is "to impart the results of their own and their fellow-specialists' investigations and reflection, both to students and to the general public, without fear or favor."

Professors are "trained for, and dedicated to, the quest for truth," and the ideas that they express are to be their own conclusions, "not echoes of the opinions of the lay public, or of the individuals who endow or manage universities." The "disinterestedness and impartiality of their inquiries" elevate university professors above political partisanship.[31]

In addition to rejecting the competency of governors, legislators, and trustees in academic matters, the "Declaration" displays a general mistrust of public opinion in the spirit of Alexis de Tocqueville and John Stuart Mill's critique of conformity in democratic societies. This is a feature of the "Declaration" that has rarely been observed.

> The tendency of modern democracy is for men to think alike, to feel alike, and to speak alike. Any departure from the conventional standards is apt to be regarded with suspicion. Public opinion is at once the chief safeguard of a democracy, and the chief menace to the real liberty of the individual. It almost seems as if the danger of despotism cannot be wholly averted under any form of government. In a political autocracy there is no effective public opinion, and all are subject to the tyranny of the ruler; in a democracy there is political freedom, but there is likely to be a tyranny of public opinion.[32]

The university is to be a "refuge" from "the tyranny of public opinion."[33]

> It should be an intellectual experiment station, where new ideas may germinate and where their fruit, though still distasteful to the community as a whole, may be allowed to ripen until finally, perchance, it may become a part of the accepted intellectual food of the nation or of the world. Not less is it a distinctive duty of the university to be the conservator of all genuine elements of value in the past thought and life of mankind which are not in the fashion of the moment . . . the university is, indeed, likely always to exercise a certain form of conservative influence. For by its nature it is committed to the principle that knowledge should precede action, to the caution (by no mean synonymous with intellectual timidity) which is an essential part of the scientific method, to a sense of the complexity of social problems.[34]

The emphasis on "complexity" is consistent with Lovejoy's philosophical pluralism. One can also see traces of his historical relativism (that past ideas are as valid as present ones) in this stricture against "indoctrinating" students:

> Since there are no rights without corresponding duties, the considerations heretofore set down with respect to the freedom of the academic teacher entail certain correlative obligations. The claim to freedom of teaching is made in the interest of the integrity and progress of scientific inquiry; it is, therefore, only those who carry on their work in the temper of the scientific inquirer who may justly assert this claim . . . The university teacher, in giving instruction upon controversial matters . . . should, in dealing with such subjects, set forth justly, without suppression or innuendo, the divergent opinions of other investigators; *he should cause his students to become familiar with the best published expressions of the great historic types of doctrine upon the questions at hand he should*, above all, remember that his business is not to provide his students ready-made conclusions, but to train them to think for themselves . . . The teacher ought also to be especially on his guard against taking unfair advantage of the student's immaturity by *indoctrinating* him with the teacher's own opinions before the student has had an opportunity fairly to examine other opinions upon the matters in question . . .[35]

One weakness in the argument against "indoctrinating" students is that it hinges on the assumption that there is a set of academic topics deemed to be "controversial" and upon which there is no right interpretation; but for some unstated reason, this kind of subject matter is still considered sufficiently academic to include in university courses. Why not leave out questions that have no answers? Or rather, what makes such questions academic and not theological? The "Declaration" provides no basis for distinguishing what is "controversial" from what is outside the bounds of academic inquiry altogether.

The best answer to any theoretical criticism of the "Declaration" is that it was an effective response to early twentieth-century intrusions into the academy, such as the firing of professors in Utah. It is also important to recognize that the distinction between academics and politics was widely accepted in the early twentieth century; the framing of this distinction in the "Declaration" is moderate in comparison to other formulations from the era. John H. Wigmore drove a much wider wedge between academics and politics. Wigmore was a law professor at Northwestern University and the president of the AAUP from 1916 to 1917. In December of 1916, he published an article in *The Nation* in which he argued that academics should steer clear of politics entirely in order to avoid tarnishing the image of universities as politically neutral. According to Wigmore, scholars who write editorials outside the field of their academic appointment or become involved in political campaigns off-campus forfeit their academic freedom. The academic is not to engage "in partisan action as a citizen."[36] Wigmore considered academic freedom a trade-off. All academic endeavors, including academic errors made in good faith, are immune from punishment; but to gain this protection, the scholar must give up freedom of political speech. Academics who violate this code should be punished by the university's trustees.

A week later, Lovejoy replied. The 1915 "Declaration" had emphasized the professor's freedom of "extra-mural utterance." "It is clearly not proper that they should be prohibited from lending their active support to organized movements which they believe to be in the public interest."[37] Curiously, Lovejoy accepted Wigmore's principle that academics should avoid being prominent in electoral politics.[38] His primary point in response to Wigmore was procedural, that only the faculty should have the power to decide if a professor's political speech is unprofessional. Lovejoy argued that if administrators and trustees are allowed to fire an academic for pursuing politics off-campus, they might fire everyone whose politics they do not like.[39] Wigmore's answer appeared right after Lovejoy's. A professor who "goes on the stump of partisan politics," he wrote, inevitably brings the name of the university into the conflict. The university then "ceases to stand apart as a disinterested cloister of truth-seekers." The professor must sacrifice a portion of "civic liberty" to obtain academic freedom. Wigmore was open to the idea that the faculty should police itself, but he did not think that "such a system of well-ordered self-discipline" currently existed. [40]

Wigmore's insistence that the professor must sacrifice free speech off-campus will strike many people today as bizarre. Why should a professor have to relinquish any basic constitutional liberties to gain the benefit of academic freedom? But as a law professor, Wigmore would have known that employment contracts could include a waiving of civil liberties. The Massachusetts Supreme Court case of *McAuliffe v. Mayor of New Bedford* illustrates this principle. The case concerned a police officer who was fired after violating a municipal regulation providing that no officer was allowed to give aid to a political campaign. Oliver Wendell Holmes stated, "The petitioner may have a constitutional right to talk politics, but he has no constitutional right to be a policeman."[41] In other words, refraining from political activity could be made a condition of employment. Wigmore simply applied this logic to the professoriate.

Lovejoy's defense of the professoriate was tepid, for he focused on *how* professors should be punished and barely challenged Wigmore on *whether or not* they should be punished for political activity outside the university. Either he was never fully on board with the liberal ideas in the "Declaration" about extra-mural utterances or he was drifting to a more conservative position. Lovejoy was Chairman of the AAUP committee that issued a "Report on Academic Freedom in Wartime" early in 1918. The report declares that the freedom of extramural utterance applies only in time of peace. It states that academics who advocate resistance to compulsory military service should be fired, as should professors who argue that war in general is immoral. The report belies the ivory-tower conception of the university delineated in the "Declaration," where academics are portrayed as motivated by the "disinterested" pursuit of truth.

The 1918 report refers to the vital *political* function of academics. American colleges and universities

> have trained a body of youth who, in this time of the testing of our national fibre, have with the rarest exceptions manifested a splendid and self-devoting loyalty to the cause of their country, in which they have learned to recognize also the cause of humanity and justice and human freedom. And, on the material side of our national effort, it is evident that the United States could have played no considerable or creditable part in a struggle in which the utilization of exact scientific knowledge is the fundamental prerequisite to success, had it not been for the work of American men of science during the past quarter-century, and had the government not been able to draw from our institutions of higher learning a great corps of trained experts, ready and eager to do their part in the nation's service.[42]

In March 1918, the editors of the *The Nation* issued a statement rebuking the AAUP for its report. In "The Professors in Battle Array," the editors condemned the proposition that university authorities can fire academics for political speech that is not prohibited by law.

> We must criticise this position which in our view jeopards [sic] the very conception of the university . . . The essence of university life is freedom to think, freedom to differ . . . The fundamental error in the committee's position, as we see it, lies in the apparent assumption that a state of war fundamentally changes the work of a university . . . We hold that it exists for the discovery and proclamation of the truth, not for propaganda purposes, no matter how righteous the propaganda.[43]

Lovejoy responded: "Freedom, academic or other, is not an absolute and all-sufficient end in itself, to be pursued at the sacrifice of all other human interests. It is in the main a means to ulterior ends." Lovejoy defines those "ends" as "the progressive discovery of truth" and "the development of diverse types of personality." Since Lovejoy regarded the Central Powers as a threat to the ideal of an open society, he considered the war to be a defense of the university and academic freedom.

> The American college, if it maintained the kind of neutrality, with respect to the present struggle, would, in fact, be not merely tolerating but facilitating the efforts of those who would repeat in America the achievement of the Lenins and the Trotzskys in Russia. In such a case, the college cannot escape the hard necessities of the situation. It must either be . . . an accomplice in activities which, if successful, would bring about

the defeat and the dishonor of the republic and do immeasurable injury to the cause of freedom throughout the world; or else it must determine that it will not give countenance and aid to those who, upon a fair trial, are clearly proved to be engaged in such activities—whether or not they have already come within the reach of the law.[44]

Lovejoy was conceding that open-ended intellectual inquiry ultimately rests on a political foundation, liberal democracy. Whatever threatens liberal democracy, threatens academic freedom.

For decades, Lovejoy continued to be highly regarded as an authority on academic freedom. One of the most important collaborative academic projects of the early twentieth century was *The Encyclopaedia of the Social Sciences*. Its 15 volumes began to appear in 1930, and its goal was to provide a comprehensive synthesis of human affairs based on the findings of social scientists throughout the world. The project was edited by Edwin R.A. Seligman, the Columbia University economist who co-founded the AAUP with Lovejoy. Lovejoy was an editorial consultant for the *Encyclopaedia*, and he wrote its entry on "Academic Freedom."[45]

As in the "Declaration," Lovejoy emphasized that academic freedom entails the duty to avoid partisanship in the classroom:

> They [students] are entitled to learn the contemporary situation in each science, the range and diversity of opinion among specialists in it . . . The same rights of the student . . . demand of the university teacher, in his function of instruction as distinct from investigation and publication, special care to avoid the exclusive or one-sided presentation of his personal views on questions upon which there is no agreement among experts. He is not entitled to take advantage of his position to impose his beliefs dogmatically upon his students; the nature of his office requires that alternative opinions be fairly expounded, and that the student be encouraged and trained to reach his own conclusions.[46]

Lovejoy's *Encyclopaedia* article contains one feature which distinguishes it from the 1915 "Declaration": a discussion of the theory of evolution. He notes that Arkansas, Mississippi, and Tennessee had banned the teaching of evolution in public schools and universities, on the grounds that the state should be "neutral" on matters impacting religion.

Lovejoy wrote:

> A state may, in short, have a university or do without. But it cannot have one . . . if it excludes, under a misconception of the principle of neutrality, both a large part of the subject matter of science and also the method of free inquiry and free expression, which is necessary to the functioning of this type of social institution.

Lovejoy observed that the three southern legislatures assumed that to teach the theory of evolution is necessarily to violate neutrality. He then analyzed the various meanings of the word "teach." It can mean to state the arguments which compose a theory, to indicate the prevailing opinion of experts with regard to the theory, to express the teacher's own opinion on the theory, and finally "to inculcate it dogmatically or to proselytize in behalf of it." According to Lovejoy, laws prohibiting the teaching of evolution in the last sense are compatible with academic freedom, but laws prohibiting the teaching of evolution in any of the other senses violate academic freedom.[47]

In 1949, Lovejoy published an influential essay, "Communism Versus Academic Freedom" in *The American Scholar*. His thesis was that members of the American Communist Party should not be admitted to university faculties. Lovejoy based his exclusion on the concept of academic freedom. Since professors are to be independent "investigators," they cannot be the spokespersons for ideologically driven organizations. In communist societies, according to Lovejoy, the universities are subordinate to the government's ideology. Members of the Communist Party swear to uphold the party line; their teaching does not flow "from the free pursuit of knowledge." Lovejoy stated that all departments of economics and political science should provide exposure to the writings of Marx and other theorists of communism; and members of the Communist Party should be invited to campus to speak to students. But he was against hiring communist professors because of the probability that they would practice indoctrination.[48]

In the 1960s, the Supreme Court ruled that university employers cannot make assumptions about what an individual believes, based on the sole fact of membership in a political party (see Chapter 1). But in 1949, Lovejoy's position was not barred by constitutional law. Lovejoy wrote:

> It will perhaps be objected that the exclusion of Communist teachers would itself be a restriction upon freedom of opinion and of teaching . . . and that it is self-contradictory to argue for the restriction of freedom in the name of freedom . . . The believer in the indispensability of freedom, whether academic or political, is not thereby committed to the conclusion that it is his duty to facilitate its destruction, by placing its enemies in strategic positions of power, prestige, or influence . . . the conception of freedom is not one which implies the legitimacy and inevitability of its own suicide . . . there is *one* kind of freedom which is inadmissible—the freedom to destroy freedom.[49]

Lovejoy's conception of freedom resonated in the theory of "militant democracy" articulated by Karl Loewenstein. The German-born political scientist who emigrated to the United States in 1933 explained how fascist parties in Europe took advantage of democratic liberties, such as freedom of speech, in order to subvert democracy.[50] Militant democracy meant that free societies must protect themselves against the abuse of freedom. Loewenstein faulted the European democracies for their "legalistic self-complacency and suicidal lethargy."[51] West Germany's post-war constitution, the "Basic Law," which was ratified in 1949, the year in which Lovejoy published "Communism versus Academic Freedom," incorporated the principle of militant democracy. The Basic Law, which is now the constitution of a united Germany, does not afford freedom of speech to those who oppose the democratic order. The Basic Law also permits the Constitutional Court to ban extremist political parties. The Communist Party of Germany has been banned in Germany since 1956.[52]

The US Supreme Court never banned the American Communist Party, but it did permit states to prohibit the hiring of Party members in public institutions. My aim is not to defend Lovejoy's position but to suggest that his anti-communism had broad resonance in his time. In June 1949, the Regents of the University of California required professors to take an oath of loyalty to the US Constitution and to swear that they were not members of the Communist Party. The faculty protested but not necessarily because they believed that Party members should be eligible to teach. The faculty resented being singled out for a loyalty test: California public employees in general were not required to take an oath. On

March 13, 1950, the University of California Faculty Senate surveyed the professors of all campuses in the California state system on two questions; 90% of the faculty responded. The first question asked whether one supported or opposed the oath requirement. The faculty voted 89% against the loyalty oath. The second question was whether communists were fit or unfit to teach at the university. As background to the question, the Faculty Senate included an extract from Lovejoy's "Communism Versus Academic Freedom" and a contrary statement composed by the AAUP. The AAUP statement against a ban on hiring communist professors included this passage:

> If a teacher, as an individual, should advocate the forcible overthrow of the government or should incite others to do so; if he should use his classes as a forum for communism, or otherwise abuse his relationship with his students for that purpose; if his thinking should show more than normal bias or be so uncritical as to evidence professional unfitness, these are the charges that should be brought against him. If these charges should be established by evidence adduced at a hearing, the teacher should be dismissed because of his acts of disloyalty or because of professional unfitness, and not because he is a Communist. So long as the Communist Party in the United States is a legal party, affiliation with that party in and of itself should not be regarded as a justifiable reason for exclusion from the academic profession.

79% of the faculty respondents chose Lovejoy's position.[53]

Attempting to make sense of why so many professors favored barring communists, the historian Bob Blauner suggested that it must have been "the climate of fear sweeping the nation."[54] He asserts that the "hysteria" promoted by Senator Joseph McCarthy had infected the professoriate. This is speculation and does not consider the possibility that Lovejoy's academic argument may have resonated powerfully among the faculty. The faculty certainly did not hesitate to oppose the loyalty oath (question 1). But opposing the oath did not mean supporting the hiring of communists. In fact, faculty opposition to the oath was dispelled in October 1950, not by abolishing the oath but by generalizing it through the Levering Act mandating a loyalty oath for all state employees. The stigma of being singled out for a loyalty test then disappeared.

None of this means that Lovejoy's position on communism was "correct." We are examining the historical conditions of plausibility for his argument, not its truth status. One of the principles that made Lovejoy's case for the exclusion of communists thinkable was the concept of academic freedom, which Lovejoy himself had played a leading role in defining. Once one posited a distinction between academic inquiry and political activism, the question concerning Communist Party members was simply whether they could be presumed to be more committed to the second rather than the first. Lovejoy recognized that not all Party members adhered to the Party orthodoxy, but he considered it "a question, not of certainty, but of probability," that Party members would practice classroom indoctrination. "And estimates of probability, based not on definitions but on experience, should, where grave dangers are involved, be the guide of policy."[55] Finally, Even the AAUP, when it opposed the exclusion of communists merely for being Party members, conceded that a communist is unfit to be in the classroom

> if he should use his classes as a forum for communism, or otherwise abuse his relationship with his students for that purpose; if his thinking should show more than normal bias or be so uncritical as to evidence professional unfitness.

While the exclusion of communists was a matter of debate, the exclusion of those who used the classroom for political propaganda was not questioned.

Black Studies and Academic Freedom

The 1960s brought to the discussion of academic freedom more than a repudiation of the anti-communism of the 1950s. The very notions of academic inquiry and knowledge began to shift. Prior to the 1960s, no school of thought in the United States offered a head-on critique of the basic distinction between academics and politics. This is not to say that professors always kept their political orientation a secret in the classroom. What was missing was a *theory* that legitimized political advocacy in the classroom.

As we encounter new conceptions of the teacher's role in the classroom, we can observe that they are tied to different conceptions not only of the academy but of democracy. Alexander Meiklejohn, we have seen, had a procedural image of what "freedom" means in a democracy. Citizens are free when they can speak in an unencumbered way about matters of public policy. Freedom does not lie in any particular result of public deliberation. Democratic freedom may even result in the repudiation of democracy. The creation of Black Studies (and other "studies" programs in the 1960s and 1970s) stemmed from a different assumption: freedom means transforming American society in a particular way. Freedom means expanding freedom, especially for minority groups. The formation of Black Studies and other activist disciplines is a crucial moment in the history of academic freedom in the United States, for nothing has done more to change the meaning of academic freedom than the modification of the disciplinary landscape.

Before turning to the Black Studies movement, it is necessary to say a few words about why other radical movements in the 1960s do not receive much attention in this chapter. Apart from the fact that some omissions always need to be made, I am not convinced that the usual candidates for inclusion have as much importance for the history of academic freedom as Black radicalism had. The 1964 Free Speech Movement (FSM) at Berkeley and the Students for a Democratic Society (SDS), founded in 1962, are often treated as iconic of campus radicalism in the 1960s. But if one reviews the speeches and writings of Mario Savio, the student leader of the FSM, or the SDS's famous Port Huron Statement, one finds scant evidence to suggest that the students envisaged fundamental changes in how we define academic knowledge. It is true that FSM and SDS ridiculed research-oriented professors who kept aloof from students. But FSM was principally a struggle by students to gain the right to engage in political protest on the campus's public squares. They also wished to create political clubs and to have the right to set up tables to distribute political literature.[56] The idea was to create political free-speech zones on campus. The university quickly yielded to the demands of Berkeley students in 1964. While FSM and SDS played an important role in politicizing the atmosphere on American college campuses, the claims made by these predominantly white student organizations involved no fundamental rethinking of the university's disciplinary map or the concepts of academic inquiry and freedom.

In *The Black Revolution on Campus*, Martha Biondi makes a strong case that histories of protest in the 1960s often place too much emphasis on white student activists against the Vietnam War, and not enough emphasis on the agitation of Black student protesters to transform the American university. "Most crucially, Black students demanded a role in the definition and production of scholarly knowledge."[57] Black student activism exploded across the country in 1968. A major goal was, as Biondi says, "the incorporation of Black studies in American higher education." She also notes, "the early Black studies movement advanced ideas that have had significant influence in American and African American intellectual life. It emphasized interdisciplinary study, questioned notions of objectivity, destabilized metanarratives, and interrogated prevailing methodologies."[58]

I seek to confirm Biondi's claims but with a caveat. With terms like "destabilized metanarratives" Biondi is not using the language of Black students and professors in the 1960s. She is using a language of the 1980s, a language associated with the popularization of French postmodernist theory in the United States. The critique of academic objectivity by Black intellectuals in the 1960s was trenchant, but French theory added a level of complexity to the argument. It took the arrival of French theory in the United States to deepen the intuitions of the founders of Black Studies programs and to spread the critique of academic objectivity into "white" disciplines like English.

The first Black Studies program was established at Merritt College, a two-year public college in Oakland, in 1968. Bobby Seale and Huey Newton, future leaders of the Black Panther Party, were involved; as students, they had called for the creation of Black history courses in 1965–1966.[59] San Francisco State College, the second institution to create Black Studies, has garnered more scholarly attention because violent student protests took place. In November 1969, the Black Student Union called a strike. Confrontations between students and the San Francisco Tactical Squad occurred repeatedly over five months and led to nearly 800 arrests. On March 20, 1969, the administration agreed to create a new School of Ethnic Studies that would include programs in Black Studies, Chicano Studies, and other group studies.[60]

The philosophy underlying the Black Studies movement had a Black nationalist, antiintegrationist character. Jimmy Garrett, a student leader at San Francisco State, wrote, "We are no longer striving for an integrated society. Those days are gone. We are struggling for self-determination. Self-determination for our black lives; self-determination for our black communities; and self-determination for black education."[61] The Black Student Union, when demanding the creation of a Black Studies department, declared, "We, the Black students at San Francisco State . . . feel that it is detrimental to us as Black human beings to be controlled by racists, who have absolute power over determining what we should learn."[62]

The sociologist Nathan Hare was the leading faculty member in the creation of Black Studies at San Francisco State. In his "Conceptual Proposal for Black Studies," Hare spoke of the need for "a black educational renaissance."[63] He referred to the ideal of "integration" as "an irony of recorded history." Integration has been "used in the second half of this century to hold the black race down just as segregation was so instigated in the first half." Integration elevates individual members of the group while failing to alter the lot of the group as a whole. Integration "weakens the collective thrust which the group might otherwise master."[64] In a section called "Redefinition of Standards," Hare questioned academic requirements that have the impact of excluding underprivileged students. He included the use of footnotes, comprehensive written exams, oral exams, language requirements, and the doctorate as a prerequisite for university teaching. He also rejected the requirement to publish.

> Never mind the fact that articles outside the liberal-moderate perspective have slim chances of seeing the light of day in "objective" scholarly journals. More ludicrous is the fact that the black historian in adhering to the tradition of "footnoting," is

placed in the unenviable position of having to footnote white slavemaster historians or historians published by a slaveholding society in order to document his work on the slavery era.[65]

In another publication, "Questions and Answers about Black Studies," Hare challenged "the naive notion that traditional education is value-free."[66] He argued that the established academic system simply did not work for students who were not from "white suburbia." He wished to carve out a space in which black youth could develop "a sense of pride or self, of collective destiny, a sense of pastness as a springboard in the quest for a new and better future." Hare described his vision as "pragmatic"—to prepare Black students to develop "socio-economic skills" and "community involvement." One of his guiding pedagogical principles was to involve students in the community. For example, students in a Black history course "would have as a requirement some participation in panel discussions for younger children in church basements or elementary and junior high schools. A class project might be the establishment of a black history club."[67]

Another major figure in the Black Studies movement was Charles V. Hamilton, who co-authored *Black Power: The Politics of Liberation* with Stokely Carmichael in 1967. Hamilton spent most of his career at Columbia University but promoted the ideal of a "black university" as a model for the historically black colleges such as Morehouse and Spellman. In "A Re-Examination of Goals," published in the *Negro Digest*, he called for "a black college revolutionary in its purposes, revolutionary in its procedures, revolutionary in its goals."

> I propose a black college that would *deliberately* strive to inculcate a sense of racial *pride and anger* and concern in its students. I propose a black college where one of the criteria for graduating *summa cum laude* would be the demonstrated militancy of the candidate . . . I propose a black college whose faculty and administrators would be on fire with the desire to eradicate human injustice. A college whose faculty and administrators would reject the shibboleths of "objectivity" and "aloofness," because they would know that these are merely synonymous for "passivity" and "irrelevancy."[68]

Rejection of the distinction between academics and politics is also striking in the thought of Vincent Harding, a historian and civil rights leader. In "Statement of Purpose" (1969), which he composed for the new Institute of the Black World Martin Luther King, Jr. Memorial Center in Atlanta, Harding repeatedly described the institution's mission as a "struggle." He envisioned it as "a gathering of black intellectuals who are convinced that the gifts of their minds are meant to be fully used in the service of the black community. It is therefore an experiment with scholarship in the context of struggle." The Institute will encourage black artists "searching for an aesthetic which will contribute to the struggle for the minds and hearts of our people." It will promote public policy studies "committed to the struggle of that [the Black] community for self-determination." It will strive to prepare a cadre of young men and women "precisely trained in the scholarship of the black experience and fully committed to the struggles of the black world."[69]

In another article that serves as a manifesto for Black history, Harding wrote:

> It is impossible, of course, to speak of the "intellectual" pilgrimage toward blackness without mentioning the political one . . . As is the case with the intellectuals of any

hard-pressed and colonized people, black intellectuals in American have had their inner lives inextricably bound up with the life of the "outer" struggles of our people.[70]

Congruent with Harding's vision was "Black Studies: A Political Perspective" (1969), by Mike Thelwell, who became the director of UMass Amherst's new department of Afro-American Studies in 1970. Thelwell proclaimed that

> an effective black studies faculty must be recruited from the handful of academics who have a particular radical stance towards the reevaluation of the treatment of the black experience in their own disciplines, and from among the ranks of active black intellectuals with experience in the political and cultural battlefronts of this country and the Third World.[71]

According to Thelwell, the American university is "an overwhelmingly white institution, which was conceived, created, structured and operated so as to service an oppressive social order." The American university was founded on the assumption that "the educational needs, both psychological and practical of the black student [are] identical with the white." Thelwell spoke of the "fallacy of an integrated society"[72] Much of his article is a response to critics of Black Studies within the black intellectual community, critics who continued to uphold the ideal of integration and opposed black nationalism. Taking on the voice of such critics, Thelwell wrote:

> It [Black Studies] creates a false dichotomy, smacks of separatism, not to say black racism, creates a serious problem of standards and violates the concept of academic *objectivity*. Also, what assurances will we have that what will take place within that autonomous entity will be *education* and not indoctrination?[73]

Thelwell replied to his imagined interlocutor:

> All of these questions are predicated on the assumption of a culturally homogeneous society, the myth of scholarly objectivity, a rejection of history, the denial of conflicting class interests within society, and differing perceptions of necessities by the black and white community.[74]

Continuing his critique of academic neutrality:

> Scholarly objectivity is a delusion that liberals (of both races) may subscribe to. Black people and perceptive whites know better. The fact is that the intellectual establishment distinguishes itself by its slavish acceptance of the role assigned to it by the power-brokers of the society. It has always been the willing servant of wealth and power, and the research done in the physical sciences, the humanities, and social sciences has been, with very few honorable exceptions, in service to established power.[75]

One of the most sophisticated critiques of disciplinary objectivity was framed by the psychologist Cedric Clark (later Syed Malik Khatib). "Black Studies ought also to involve itself deeply and systematically with philosophical pursuits, particularly the philosophy of knowledge itself, or *epistemology*."[76] Clark was the Chairman of Black Studies at San Francisco State from 1979 to 1982. He drew on Thomas Kuhn's *The Structure of Scientific*

Revolutions (1962) to suggest that academic theories are rooted in "paradigms" which bring certain questions into focus while excluding others. Clark held that no academic theory is "value free."[77] He suggested that the "Newtonian conception of space and time" made psychologists reluctant to acknowledge that slavery had long-lasting effects on the mindset of Black people.

> The point is that "long in the past" and "recent" are highly misleading terms when we recognize that space and time are not absolute but relative. In other words, in terms of a relative universe, the occurrence of slavery might be as near in succession as the time it took you to finish reading this sentence. Time and space are not absolute, but infinite.

According to Clark, slavery is the "dominant experiential aspect of black Americans." Black Studies will be based on the philosophical principle that

> *all knowledge is rooted in social relations, particularly as these are determined by racial classifications.* In other words, what the individual perceives as "truth" or "valid knowledge" is a function of the racial group he belongs to—particularly when he is studying race-related phenomena.[78]

The ideas propagated by advocates for Black Studies did not go uncontested within the progressive Black community. Biondi notes that some Black academics were turned off by the militancy of students who wished to decide who was eligible to teach Black Studies. At times, students wished to screen out candidates with white spouses.

> An interracial couple did not exemplify the idea of Black people coming together that animated much of the Black Power movements, and some [students] felt that marriages of Black men to white women, in particular, constituted a race-based rejection of African American women.[79]

At Columbia, Black students protested when the white historian Eric Foner (now regarded as one of the leading progressive historians of his generation) was hired to teach a course in Black history.[80] The black historian John Blassingame of Yale University was particularly outspoken against the screening of faculty candidates based on whether they had the "right shade of 'blackness'" and "the right ideological leanings."[81]

The sharpest critique of Black Studies was a text that receives only a brief mention by Biondi: an anthology edited by Bayard Rustin, *Black Studies: Myths and Realities* (1969). The volume contains contributions from some leading Black intellectuals and civil rights leaders, including Kenneth B. Clark, whose work in child psychology (with his wife Mamie Phipps Clark) helped convince the Supreme Court *in Brown v. Board of Education* (1954) to ban racial segregation in public schools. In May 1969, Clark quit the Board of Trustees of Antioch College decrying its "racially organized and exclusionary" Afro-American Studies Institute.[82] His letter of resignation is included in the volume edited by Rustin. Another contributor, Roy Wilkins, was Executive Director of the National Association for the Advancement of Colored People from 1964 to 1977. Rustin himself organized the March on Washington in 1963, and he was head of the AFL-CIO's A. Philip Randolph Institute, which promoted the integration of formerly all-white unions.

Rustin saw Black Studies as "a pretext for separatism"[83] and a repudiation of Martin Luther King, Jr.'s mission to achieve integration.

Is black studies an educational program or a forum for ideological indoctrination? . . . Is it a means to achieve psychological identity and strength, or is it intended to provide a false and sheltered sense of security, the fragility of which would be revealed by even the slightest exposure to reality?[84]

According to Rustin,

it can only be self-defeating for blacks to reject the traditional college curriculum and concentrate their energies upon the study of black culture. They will render themselves incapable of competing for jobs against individuals who have mastered the difficult intellectual skills that are required in our modern economy.

Finally, there is the fear that the educational function of black studies will be subordinated to political and ideological goals. Many young Negroes hope to use black studies programs to train cadres of ghetto organizers. Others want to totally re-write black history, substituting new myths and distortions for the old, eliminating those aspects of black history that are uncomplimentary, exalting those that support their political persuasion, and, if necessary, creating events that have no existence outside of their own myth-engendering imaginations.[85]

One contributor, Martin Kilson, a political scientist and the first black full professor at Harvard, echoed Rustin's concern about a lack of "scholarly detachment."[86] "Most of today's militant advocates of Afro-American studies," he claimed, have rejected "objectivity and self-detachment . . . they demand that Afro-American studies serve explicit ideological ends—namely, the glorification of the black experience in America and Africa" "[I]t is not the function of colleges to train ideological and political organizers of whatever persuasion."[87]

The only white contributor to the book was the eminent Yale historian of the American South, C. Vann Woodward, whose book, *The Strange Career of Jim Crow* was "the historical Bible of the civil rights movement," according to Martin Luther King, Jr.[88] Woodward's essay in Rustin's volume, "Clio with Soul," had earlier appeared in 1969 in the *Journal of American History*. Like Rustin, Woodward was concerned that Black radicalism was undermining the ideal of integration—including the integrative ideal of the discipline of history. "Either black history is an essential part of American history and must be included by all American historians, or it is unessential and can be segregated and left to black historians."[89] Woodward's plea was against the balkanization of Black history and Black Studies. But there is more. Woodward provocatively questioned assumptions about identity.

. . . so far as their culture is concerned, all Americans are part Negro. Some are more so than others, of course, but the essential qualification is not color or race. When I said "all Americans," unlike Crevecoeur, I included Afro-Americans. They are part Negro too, but only part. So far as their culture is concerned, they are more American than Afro by far and more alien in Africa than they are at home, as virtually all pilgrims to Africa have discovered.

In this way, he attempted to prevent disciplinary fragmentation.

Women's Studies programs, founded around the same time as Black Studies, were premised on a similar ethos of political struggle. But the formation Women's Studies meant that an academic discipline representing the interests of the majority of the population was now positioned against the anti-political orthodoxy. A good sense of the founding spirit can be gained by reading Roberta Salper, a co-organizer of the first Women's Studies department, created at San Diego State University in 1970. In an article of 1971, published in the New Left magazine *Ramparts* (edited by David Horowitz, who would later become a militant critic of Women' Studies departments), Salper wrote, "Like Black Studies, Women's Studies owes its existence to pressures from a political movement centered outside the campus."[90] Describing Women's Studies as the "academic arm" of the broader-based Women's Liberation Movement, she opposed the idea of "courses safely nested within the ivy halls" that will not "radically change anyone."[91] In short, she rejected the separation of academics and politics.

Salper was so concerned about the need to maintain a political edge in Women's Studies that she warned against the tendency of feminist professors and students to sink into a "soft sisterhood" (i.e., a support group) that has "no objective relationship to the rest of society."[92] What makes her essay more than a simple denunciation of patriarchy is her insistence on the twofold threat to Women's Studies: the threat from conservatives who wish to depoliticize all academic programs, and the threat from some feminists who would turn Women's Studies into group therapy. "The cultural celebration of sisterhood can be a crucial stepping-stone to radical political action, but not if culture becomes a surrogate for political development, and if our movement cannot criticize its own illusions."[93]

The Postmodernist Overlay

The popularization in the 1970s and 1980s of radical French theory, often called "postmodernism"—though this term was not wielded by most of the French theorists in question—deepened the critique of the anti-political orthodoxy and spread this critique into older disciplines. The most iconic French thinker was Michel Foucault, whose impact was by no means a flash in the pan. In 2007, he was still the most highly cited author of books in the humanities and social sciences.[94]

No summary will be adequate, but it is worth highlighting the profound incursions made by postmodernism into the idea of academic objectivity. We have seen that Lovejoy's epistemology, strictly speaking, was not a defense of objectivity in the sense of every major question having one scientific or scholarly answer. Rather, Lovejoy believed that professors should teach the leading controversies in their fields. However, he and the other founders of the AAUP did portray the academy as separate from politics. What made Foucault's thought relevant to the debate about academic freedom was his insistence that academic discourse is intrinsically political. Academic "discourses" are "regimes" which organize "power" relations. It is not that Foucault refuted pre-existing conceptions of the relationship between academics and politics; rather, he originated a new way of talking about this relationship. The term politics, in particular, denotes something utterly different in Foucault and in the anti-political orthodoxy. For Lovejoy and Weber, politics refers to current political parties and the questions that they struggle over. A professor who editorializes in class along party lines—say, by defending a component in the platform of the Republican Party—is behaving unprofessionally. But teaching a class on Great Books of the West is not. For Foucault, all forms of academic classification (such as "Great") serve to legitimize distinctions between what is normal and abnormal, valued and valueless, in human life; he considered politics to be the imposition of any frame of reference that tends to produce one type of person rather than another. This kind of politics is indeed very difficult, perhaps impossible, to avoid. The effect of Foucault's work has been to make proponents of the anti-political orthodoxy appear to be "conservative," that is, unwilling to criticize power in all its forms, and insensitive to the existence of power other than that related to the state.

The term academic freedom does not figure in Foucault's writings, as far as I know. Curiously Foucault had esteem for the structure of American universities. In one interview he even suggested that the American university was an exception to his critique of the hegemonic role of academic discourse in modern life.

> If I were younger, I would have immigrated to the US: I see possibilities. You don't have a homogeneous intellectual and cultural life. As a foreigner, I don't have to be integrated. There is no pressure on me. There are a lot of great universities, all with very different interests.[95]

Evidently, he found the decentralized American university system profoundly different from the centralized and hierarchical education system in France, which served as his model for what "discipline" means.

But Foucault's admiration of America as an open space is not what he is known for. He is known for redefining and expanding the meaning of power and politics. In *The Order of Things: An Archaeology of the Human Sciences* (published in English, 1970), Foucault argued that what it means to know something has changed profoundly from the Renaissance to the present. There is more than one modern "episteme" or way of thinking about truth. Knowledge does not accumulate across time in a linear fashion. Instead, each era has epistemological assumptions which limit what kind of sentences can be accepted as candidates for truthful discourse. "Episteme" is similar to Kuhn's "paradigm" (referenced by Cedric Clark), but Foucault did more to relativize knowledge. In Kuhn, the decision to move from one paradigm to another is done consciously, as scientists decide to focus on "anomalies" in a previous paradigm: unexplained phenomena that do not fit into the dominant scientific paradigm. Though Kuhn is ambiguous on what constitutes "progress" in science, he did not give up on the idea. While a new paradigm focuses on previously unexplained facts, it does not focus only on those facts; rather, a strong new paradigm tries to subsume most of what was previously known.

> First, the new candidate must seem to resolve some outstanding and generally recognized problem that can be met in no other way. Second, the new paradigm must promise to preserve a relatively large part of the concrete problem solving ability that has accrued to science through its predecessors.[96]

Kuhn suggested that if one examined leading scientific theories in a field without knowing in advance what order they appeared in, one could construct a chronology on the basis of each theory's scope.[97]

Not so with Foucault. According to him, changes in the "episteme" occur without people realizing it. In *The Order of Things* (first published in English in 1970), as in the *The Archaeology of Knowledge*, he discussed how the epistemes, or rules of discourse, operate beneath consciousness and limit the boundaries of thought. This emphasis on the unconscious has two important corollaries.

First, it means that the critical scholarship inspired by Foucault is meant to be applied to scholarship itself. Critical scholarship is supposed to unveil assumptions and biases that even the top practitioners of the disciplines are not aware of. This is similar to the Marxist criticism of "false consciousness,"[98] though, given the relativistic atmosphere of Foucault's thought, what is in question is not so much the falseness of the disciplines as their failure to recognize their particular presuppositions. The proper subject of the academic disciplines is nothing other than the academic disciplines themselves! For example, in English, the history of how the professoriate has fashioned the distinction between "great" and "low" literature. Of course, not every discipline has embarked on a critical reconstruction of its own history; but the objective status of many disciplines has been brought into question by professors in these same disciplines.

The second corollary is that the nature of power must be reimagined in knowledge-based terms. Power for Foucault is not restricted to, and is not even primarily, state power. Real power since the eighteenth century is the explosion of techniques for achieving the control of populations. The techniques are embedded in the academic disciplines whose net effect is to control behavior by defining what constitutes health and normality. The power of the sovereign—the threat of death or torture—takes a backseat to rules based on scientific knowledge.

As noted above, for Weber and Lovejoy, the claim that "everything is political" would have been meaningless. In contrast, for Foucault, politics is not a realm outside of claims to truth. Power is to be found wherever such claims are made. In "Truth and Power," one of Foucault's most popular interviews, the French theorist dramatized the "need to cut off the King's head"—to extract the state and the problem of sovereignty from political theory. He spoke of "the politics of the scientific statement," how power circulates "among scientific statements," and the "internal regime of power" in modern science. For example, the discipline of psychiatry articulates "the mental normalization of individuals" and its opposite, the conditions of institutionalization for mental illness. "[E]ffects of truth are produced within discourses which in themselves are neither true nor false." Foucault thus applies a series of political metaphors (such as "politics" itself and "regime") in order to construe the disciplines of knowledge as sources of power. Everything in a culture that tends to reproduce the culture is now deemed to be "political."[99]

Opponents of French theory have questioned its extreme relativism. Some of them have also suggested that American followers of Foucault added a political agenda that Foucault himself did not promote. Paul Adam Rosenberg uses the term "Anglophone postmodernism" to refer to the fusion of abstract French theory and American concerns with race and gender identity.[100] François Cusset, in *French Theory*, makes a similar point. He states that French theory

> was to pave the way in the United States for minority theories . . . If Derrida or Foucault deconstructed the concept of *objectivity*, the Americans would draw on those theories not for a reflection on the figural power of language or on discursive constructions, but for a more concrete political conclusion that *objectivity* is synonymous with "subjectivity of the white male." What they developed was an entirely unexpected link between literary theory and the political Left.[101]

The problem with Cusset's interpretation is that it ascribes too many after-effects to French theory. Leftist identity politics did not emanate from French theory; this political orientation preceded French theory, which merely provided a new platform that widened its influence. Nevertheless, there is some irony in what Rosenberg calls "Anglophone postmodernism." Irony in the fact that Foucault, Derrida, and other French theorists became more influential in the United States than in France. Irony, too, in the fact that American academic life, in spite of its alleged power structure, was open and flexible enough to accommodate the creation of Black Studies, Women's Studies, and Postmodernism.

The formation of Black Studies and Women's Studies introduced a major crack in the anti-political orthodoxy. French theory deepened the fissure, but as noted above, Foucault did not fasten on the idea of academic freedom. The implications of his work for the meaning of academic freedom and political advocacy in the classroom were debated in the 1990s, which is where the next chapter continues.

Notes

1 University of Massachusetts Campus Climate Survey Undergraduate Report, April 2018, p. 2. https://www.umass.edu/diversity/sites/default/files/inline-files/undergraduate.pdf.
2 Pub. as a report by the Association of American Colleges, Washington, DC, February, 1982. https://eric.ed.gov/?id=ED215628.
3 There is no critical scholarship on the spectacular rise of "climate" as a category in higher education. But an explanation for the popularity of this discourse can be found in Julie A. Reuben, *The Making of the Modern University* (Chicago: University of Chicago Press, 1996). Reuben traces the massive growth, in the 1990s, of the "Student Life" sector of administration in American universities: professional (non-faculty) academic advisors, psychological service staff, diversity officers, etc. Student Life administrators are dedicated to creating a "climate"—as distinct from a curriculum—that is conducive to "student success," especially for minority students. I imply no judgment here. The reader who thinks that singling out "climate" for genealogical analysis implies a conservative viewpoint should consider that some critics of the "neo-liberal" university regard diversity and inclusion as a discourse that functions to legitimate capitalist hegemony. Brandi Lawless, "Neoliberal Multiculturalism on College Campuses," *Communication Teacher* (2021), print publication forthcoming: DOI: 10.1080/17404622.2021.1923768. My primary point is simply that "climate" reports rarely take on the question of political bias among faculty members. In the rare cases in which they do, as at UMass, they do not lead to policy changes. This chapter seeks to explain why.
4 University of Massachusetts Campus Climate Survey, 14.
5 Ibid, 41–42.
6 https://blogs.umass.edu/misra.
7 University of Massachusetts Campus Climate Survey, 50.
8 "General Declaration of Principles on Academic Freedom and Academic Tenure," in "General Report of the Committee on Academic Freedom and Tenure," *Indiana Law Journal*, vol. 91, no. 1 (Winter, 2015; first pub. 1915), 67.
9 A 1997 survey of members of the International Sociological Association to identify the ten most influential books for sociologists placed Weber's *Economy and Society* first and *The Protestant Ethic* fourth. https://www.isa-sociology.org/en/about-isa/history-of-isa/books-of-the-xx-century.
10 Stanley Fish, *Versions of Academic Freedom: From Professionalism to Revolution* (Chicago: University of Chicago Press, 2014), 31–32. Fish is discussed in the next chapter.
11 Max Weber, "Science as a Vocation," in *From Max Weber: Essays in Sociology*, ed. H. H. Gerth and C. Wright Mills (New York: Oxford University Press, 1946; first pub. 1919), 145–146. For background on the original speech and publication in German, see Max Weber, *Collected Methodological Writings*, ed. Hans Henrik Bruun and Sam Whimster (London: Routledge, 2012), 353.
12 Weber discusses "disenchantment" in *Science as a Vocation*, 139.
13 Max Weber, "The Meaning of 'Value Freedom' in the Sociological and Economic Sciences," in Max Weber: *Collected Methodological Writings*, ed. Hans Henrik Bruun and Sam Whimster, 307 (first pub. 1917). This essay also contains arguments against bringing politics into the classroom; see 310.
14 Max Weber, "The 'Objectivity' of Knowledge in Social Science and Social Policy," in Ibid, 105; published in 1904, when Weber became coeditor of the *Archiv für Soziaalwissenschaft und Sozialpolitik*. (Italics in original.)
15 Peter Breiner, "Science and Partisanship in Max Weber," in *Scientific Statesmanship, Governance, and the History of Political Philosophy*, ed. Kyriakos N. Demetriou and Antis Loizides (New York: Routledge, 2015), 242, 257.
16 W. G. Runciman, *Social Science and Political Theory* (Cambridge: Cambridge University Press. 1971; first pub. 1963), 156.

17 Erich von Kahler, "The Vocation of Science," in *Max Weber's 'Science as a Vocation'*, eds. Peter Lassman and Irving Velody (London: Unwin Hyman, 1988), 43.

18 Peter Baehr, reviewing several books on Max Weber and writing specifically about Lassman et al., Max Weber's "Science as a Vocation," *The British Journal of Sociology*, vol. 43, no. 1 (March, 1992), 142.

19 Weber, "Science as a Vocation," 136, 142–143.

20 Ibid, 143. For extended criticism of Weber's stark separation of academic discourse and valuation, see Runciman, *Social Science and Political Theory*, 156–175.

21 Ibid, 148.

22 Weber, "The Meaning of Value Freedom," *Collected Methodological Writings*, 315.

23 Lewis Feuer, "Arthur O Lovejoy," in *International Encyclopedia of the Social Sciences*, ed. David L. Sills, vol. 18 (New York: Macmillan, 1979), 468.

24 Arthur Lovejoy, "On Some Conditions of Progress in Philosophical Inquiry," *The Philosophic Review*, vol. 26, no. 2 (March 1917), 128, 134, 137, 148, 160.

25 Thomas Haskell, "Justifying the Rights of Academic Freedom in the Era of 'Power/Knowledge,'" in *The Future of Academic Freedom*, ed. Louis Menand (Chicago: University of Chicago Press, 1996), 67.

26 John Karl Wilson, "A History of Academic Freedom in America" (Ph.D. Thesis, Illinois State University, 2014), 101. In later writings, cited in other chapters of this book, the author goes by the name of John K. Wilson.

27 Haskell, "Justifying the Rights of Academic Freedom," 49.

28 Wilson, *A History of Academic Freedom*, 99–100 (quoting Ross).

29 Ibid, 100.

30 Haskell, "Justifying the Rights of Academic Freedom," 54.

31 "General Declaration of Principles on Academic Freedom and Academic Tenure," 25, 30.

32 Ibid, 31–32.

33 Ibid, 32.

34 Ibid.

35 Ibid, 35; italics added.

36 John H. Wigmore, "Academic Freedom of Utterance," *The Nation*, vol. 103, no. 2684 (December 7, 1916), 539.

37 "General Declaration of Principles on Academic Freedom and Academic Tenure," 20, 37.

38 Arthur O. Lovejoy, "Academic Freedom," *The Nation*, vol. 103, no. 2685 (December 14, 1916), 561.

39 Lovejoy, "Academic Freedom," 561.

40 John. H, Wigmore, "To the Editor of the *Nation*" (responding to Lovejoy), *The Nation*, vol. 103, no. 2685 (December 14, 2016), 562.

41 McAuliffe v. Mayor of New Bedford, 155 Mass. 216 (1892), 216.

42 Arthur O. Lovejoy et al., "Report of Committee on Academic Freedom in Wartime," *Bulletin of the American Association of University Professors*, vol. 4, no. 2/3 (February–March 1918), 30.

43 "The Professors in Battle Array," *The Nation*, vol. 106, no. 2749 (March 7, 1918), 255.

44 Arthur O. Lovejoy, "Academic Freedom in War Time," *The Nation*, vol. 106, no. 2753 (April 4, 1918), 402 for quotations in the previous paragraph as well.

45 Arthur O. Lovejoy, "Academic Freedom," in *Encyclopaedia of the Social Sciences*, ed. Edwin R. A. Seligman (New York: Macmillan, 1930), 384.

46 Ibid, 385.

47 Ibid, 385–386. See also Arthur O. Lovejoy, "Anti-Evolution Laws and the Principle of Religious Neutrality," *Bulletin of the American Association of University Professors*, vol. 15, no. 4 (April 1929), 307–314.

48 Arthur O. Lovejoy, "Communism versus Academic Freedom," *The American Scholar*, vol. 18, no. 3 (Summer, 1949), 335–336.

49 Ibid, 334.

50 Karl Loewenstein, "Militant Democracy and Fundamental Rights," published in two parts in *The American Political Science Review*, vol. 31, no. 3 (June 1937), 417–432 and vol. 31, no. 4 (August 1937), 638–658.

51 Loewenstein, "Militant Democracy" (Jun, 1937), 431.

52 In the German Basic Law, see especially article 18, "Whoever abuses the freedom of expression . . . in order to combat the free democratic basic order shall forfeit these basic rights." On the banning of the German Communist Party, see Paul Franz, "Unconstitutional and Outlawed Political Parties: A

German-American Comparison," *Boston College International and Comparative Law Review*, vol. 5, no 1 (1982), 51–89.

53 For the text of the ballot, see "Letter, March 13, 1950: Memorandum on Proposition 1 and Proposition 2," Online Archive of California, https://oac.cdlib.org/view?docId=hb0199p04j&brand=oac4&doc. view=entire_text. For the results, see Bob Blauner, *Resisting McCarthyism: To Sign or Not to Sign California's Loyalty Oath* (Stanford: Stanford University Press, 2009), 108; and "The Loyalty Oath at the University of California: A Report on Events, 1949–1958," in the Free Speech Movement Archives, https://www.fsm-a.org/stacks/AP_files/APLoyaltyOath.html. The AAUP statement on the ballot is an extract from "Academic Freedom and Tenure: Report of Committee A for 1948," *Bulletin of the American Association of University Professors*, vol. 35, no. 1 (Spring, 1949), 49–65 (see esp. 56).

54 Blauner, *Resisting McCarthyism*, 108.

55 Arthur O. Lovejoy, "Rejoinder to Lowe," *The Journal of Philosophy*, vol. 49, no. 4 (February, 1952), 112; responding to criticism, by Victor Lowe, of Lovejoy and Sidney Hook for assuming that Party members subscribe to all Party orthodoxies: Victor Lowe, "In Defense of Individualistic Empiricism: A Reply to Messrs. Lovejoy and Hook," *The Journal of Philosophy*, vol. 49, no. 4 (February, 1952), 100–111.

56 Hal Draper, *Berkeley, The New Student Revolt* (Alameda, CA: Center for Socialist History, 1965), 20–25, 30–35, 94.

57 Martha Biondi, *The Black Revolution on Campus* (Berkeley: University of California Press, 2012), 2–3.

58 Ibid, 174–175.

59 Ibid, 41.

60 Ibid, 43–73, for detailed account of events at San Francisco State.

61 Cited in ibid, 45.

62 Ibid, 56.

63 Nathan Hare, "Conceptual Proposal for Black Studies," in *Shut it Down! A College on Crisis, San Francisco State College, October, 1968-April 1969, A Report to the National Commission on the Causes and Prevention of Violence*, ed. William Orrick Jr. (Washington, DC: U.S. Government Printing Office, 1969), Appendix 4, 160.

64 Ibid, 161.

65 Ibid, 161–162.

66 Nathan Hare, "Questions and Answers about Black Studies," *The Massachusetts Review*, vol. 10, no. 4 (Autumn, 1969), 732.

67 Ibid, 727, 732.

68 Charles V. Hamilton, "A Re-Examination of Goals," *Negro Digest* (September, 1967), 6–8.

69 Vincent Harding, "The Institute of the Black World Marin Luther King, Jr. Memorial Center: Statement of Purpose and Program," *The Massachusetts Review*, vol. 10, no. 4 (Autumn, 1969), 713–715.

70 Vincent Harding, "Beyond Chaos: Black History and the Search for the New Land", in *Historians on History*, ed. John Tosh (London: Pearson, 2nd edition, 2008), 119; Harding's text was first published in 1970.

71 Mike Thelwell, "Black Studies: A Political Perspective," *The Massachusetts Review*, vol. 10, no. 4 (Autumn, 1969), 711.

72 Ibid, 708.

73 Ibid, 709 (italics in original).

74 Ibid.

75 Ibid.

76 Cedric Clark, "Blacks Studies or the Study of Black People?" in *Black Psychology*, ed. Reginald L. Jones (New York: Harper and Row, 1972), 11 (italics in original).

77 Ibid, 5.

78 Ibid, 12. All italics are in the original.

79 Biondi, *The Black Revolution*, 187.

80 Ibid, 186.

81 Ibid.

82 Peter Khiss, "Clark Scores 'Separatism' at Antioch," *New York Times* (May 23, 1969), 29.

83 Bayard Rustin, "Introduction," in *Black Studies: Myths and Realities*, ed. Bayard Rustin (New York: A. Phillip Randolph Educational Fund, 1969), 6.

84 Ibid, 5.

85 Ibid, 6–7.
86 Martin Kilson, "Realism in Afro-American Studies," in *Black Studies*, ed. Rustin, 10.
87 Ibid, 10–12.
88 Stephen J. Whitfield, review of *The Letters of C. Vann Woodward*, ed. Michael O'Brien in *Southern Cultures* (vol. 21, no 4; Winter, 2015), 121.
89 C. Vann Woodward, "Clio with Soul," in *Black Studies*, ed. Rustin, 27 (Rustin also quotes this passage in his "Introduction," 6).
90 Roberta Salper, "Women's Studies," *Ramparts*, vol. 10, no. 6 (December, 1971), 57.
91 Ibid.
92 Ibid, 60.
93 Ibid.
94 Reuters Ranking 2009 (based on data from 2007), http://www.eoht.info/page/Humanities% 20citation%20ranking.
95 Rex Martin, interview with Michel Foucault, October 25, 1982, in L. H. Martin et al., *Technologies of the Self: A Seminar with Michel Foucault* (London: Tavistock, 1988), 13.
96 Thomas S. Kuhn, *Structure of Scientific Revolutions* (Chicago: University of Chicago Press, 1970; 2nd enlarged edition), 168.
97 Ibid, 205–206.
98 On "unmasking" discourses in modern Western thought and the persistence of Marxist ideas even in post-Marxist thought, see Peter Baehr, *The Unmasking Style in Social Theory* (New York: Routledge, 2019).
99 Michel Foucault, "Truth and Power" in Foucault, *Power/Knowledge: Selected Interviews and Other Writings 1972-1977*, ed. Colin Gordon (New York: Pantheon Books, 1980; first pub. 1972), 112, 116, 118, 121.
100 Paul Adam Rosenberg, "The Pattern of Large-Scale History: Hegel's System and Its Political Transformations in Marx and Postmodernism" (doctoral thesis, King's College, Cambridge University, 2001), 4.
101 François Cusset, *French Theory: How Foucault, Derrida, Deleuze, & Co. Transformed the Intellectual Life of the United States* (Minneapolis: University of Minnesota Press, 2008), 131; see also 154.

4 Eminent Conversions

1990s–Present

Abstract

This chapter brings the debate about the place of political activism in the university, and particularly in the classroom, up to the present. It focuses on the polarization of debate in the twenty-first century. I suggest that the unmeasured hostility between right (standing against political activism on campus) and left (standing for political activism) has been fueled by the personal experience of certain academics who underwent profound conversions in their ideologies. In purging themselves of their past views, these converts have contributed to the rhetoric of denunciation which is now characteristic of American academic life. The chapter examines the Ward Churchill controversy and the controversy over the Academic Bill of Rights sponsored by David Horowitz as examples of polarization. The chapter also reveals how an organization, the AAUP, converted from the "anti-political orthodoxy" to a politically radical position.

Introduction: Two Conversions

> What else is this life about but vanishing? We come and go as strangers. We disappear even in advance of our deaths. Do we ever know ourselves? I can remember swearing as a youth of twenty that I would never become the man I eventually was at forty. Who could be more surprised at the way my life turned out than I? David Horowitz, *Radical Son* (1997)[1]

By the 1990s, the traditional conception of academic freedom, which I have called "the anti-political orthodoxy," was no longer in sync with theoretical currents, broadly denoted as "postmodern," in the humanities and social sciences. The orthodoxy rested on a distinction between what is academic and what is political. This distinction was not as simple-minded as critics of "objectivity" sometimes claim it to be. Arthur O. Lovejoy, who co-founded the AAUP in 1915, considered the major problems of philosophy to be unresolvable; he promoted a style of teaching and scholarship that mapped out competing responses to questions that did not admit final answers. The AAUP's 1915 "General Declaration of Principles on Academic Freedom and Academic Tenure" did not speak of "objectivity." It did use the words "impartial" and "disinterested," and it endorsed a style of teaching based on intellectual pluralism.

> The university teacher, in giving instruction upon controversial matters, while he is under no obligation to hide his own opinion under a mountain of equivocal verbiage, should, if he is fit for his position, be a person of a fair and judicial mind; he should, in

DOI: 10.4324/9781003052685-5

dealing with such subjects, set forth justly, without suppression or innuendo, the divergent opinions of other investigators; he should cause his students to become familiar with the best published expressions of the great historic types of doctrine upon the questions at issue; and he should, above all, remember that his business is not to provide his students with ready-made conclusions, but to train them to think for themselves, and to provide them access to those materials which they need if they are to think intelligently.[2]

Lovejoy and other founders of the AAUP never asserted that academic knowledge is absolute. However, this does not mean that the postmodernist critique of academic neutrality is off the mark. For there is a problem that Lovejoy and the founders of the AAUP did not reflect upon, a problem that would become central in the twenty-first-century debate about what constitutes classroom indoctrination.

The problem stems from the fact that the disciplines tend to generate mutually exclusive conceptions of what constitutes a proven proposition. What is considered an established truth in one discipline or subdiscipline can be viewed as a matter of ongoing controversy in another. Granted that students should be taught the controversies in given a field, but who decides what is controversial and what is settled? What should happen when scholars in a specific field do not consider a proposition (such as "Western societies are patriarchal") controversial, when scholars outside the field regard it as debatable?

In our century, the AAUP has adopted the view that truth is what the members of a particular discipline or subdiscipline say it is; hence, as the AAUP explained in a report called "Freedom in the Classroom" (2007), "It is not indoctrination for professors to expect students to comprehend ideas and apply knowledge that is accepted within a relevant discipline."[3] This parochial epistemology is based on the argument that (a) there are no generic academic standards and (b) each discipline and subdiscipline should be trusted to create its own standard for what counts as true.

The goal of this chapter is to demonstrate how this view became institutionalized in the AAUP and why it was strategically valuable for the AAUP to take such a position in the context of what the organization's leaders perceived as attacks on academic freedom. I also highlight some cases in which leading participants in the contest over the meaning of truth and academic freedom radically changed their viewpoint. It is one thing to map out an intellectual debate and to suggest that each side has compelling arguments. This I have tried to do throughout the present book. But it deepens our understanding if we can observe shifts in the thinking of specific figures, as we already did with Lovejoy in the previous chapter. Conversions help us grasp the thin borders between apparently opposite ideas.

David Horowitz was a leading intellectual of the New Left in the 1960s and 1970s. In *Corporations and the Cold War* (1969), he wrote:

> There are two principal ways . . . by which corporate ideology comes to prevail in the larger political realm. In the first place, it does so through the corporate (and upper class) control of the means of communication and the means of production of ideas and ideology (the mass media, the foundations, the universities, etc.).[4]

Horowitz spectacularly shifted to the far right in the early 1980s. In his memoir, *Radical Son* (1996), he wrote:

> The situation in the universities was appalling . . . Marxism had produced the bloodiest and most oppressive regimes in human history—but after the fall, as one wit

commented, more Marxists could be found on the faculties of American colleges than in the entire former Communist bloc . . . Radical politics had become the intellectual currency of academic thought.

Horowitz went on to lead a campaign, beginning in 2003, to convince state legislatures to implement an "Academic Bill of Rights" (ABOR) designed to protect students against indoctrinating professors. For him, the notion that each discipline has the right to determine what counts as truth was as horrendous as capitalism had been to him before. This chapter aims to demonstrate that the debate about academic freedom in the twenty-first century has been profoundly altered by Horowitz's Manichean rhetoric, which is a point of continuity between his communist and post-communist identities.

But Horowitz and other conservatives are not solely responsible for the polarization of debate about academic freedom. A mimetic process can be observed between the right and the left in this regard. Consider the case of Cary Nelson, author of *Manifesto of a Tenured Radical* (1997), and President of the AAUP, 2006–2012. Nelson saw the world through the lens of postmodernism tinged with Marxism. He attributed the major problems in higher education to capitalism and the "corporatization" of the university.[5] Nelson, who was Horowitz's chief adversary during the ABOR campaign, defended the right of professors to engage in political advocacy in the classroom. Under his leadership, the AAUP took the position that it is not indoctrination for professors to promote political ideas upon which there is a consensus in the discipline. For Nelson, disciplines are "the only real models for organizing faculty we have." And "disciplinary consensus" is the basis for "what students have to comprehend and apply."[6]

Yet, Nelson later modified his position. The shift became apparent around the time Nelson ceased being President of the AAUP. His chief political passion had been anti-capitalism; it now became opposition to anti-Zionism. In a 2017 pamphlet denouncing the influence of the Boycott, Divestment, Sanctions (BDS) movement in multiple academic disciplines, he wrote:

> There is too much evidence of the political corruption of academic disciplines . . . To ignore the issue, moreover, will be to watch the problem rapidly get worse . . . Some disciplines no longer promote self-critical intellectual reflection The time to confront these trends is now.[7]

Nelson was decrying the very disciplines, such as Women's Studies, that Horowitz had indicted for being politically rather than academically oriented. As with Horowitz, Nelson's Manichean rhetoric remained constant, even as his ideological enemy changed. The discussion of academic freedom in our century bears traces everywhere of the language of denunciation. To make such an argument, it is helpful to illustrate what it means to debate academic freedom in a less thoroughly polarized atmosphere. The 1990s is often portrayed in terms of the academic "Culture Wars," but at least as concerns the issue of whether political advocacy belongs in the classroom, academic freedom was discussed in a collegial manner.

Before ABOR: The 1990s

Disputes over Horowitz's ABOR transformed the whole field of debate about academic freedom. With legislation under consideration, the stakes were high; the quality of thought became correspondingly low. But low compared to what? The 1990s was a period of intensive theoretical reflection and disagreement about the meaning of academic freedom, including its implications for the classroom. Debate flourished because, with no threat of legislative control hanging over their heads, academics with different viewpoints engaged each other in a tolerant manner. The participants in the debate were amenable to leaving the debate open-ended, inconclusive. Defenders of the anti-political orthodoxy were of course concerned about the growth of campus radicalism. But they had the satisfaction of knowing that the AAUP leadership was still committed to the principles of 1915. Leftists who believed that teaching should seek to bring about political change knew that their views were contrary to the mainstream conception of academic freedom, but disciplines such as Black Studies and Women's Studies were plainly here to stay; postmodernism was transforming some of the older disciplines, such as English, as well. In sum, the 1990s, known as a period of "Culture Wars," was in fact a time of relative peace in the academy. Everyone could air their views with nuance and without paranoia (which is not the case today). What follows is a selective tour of those views.

William W. Van Alstyne was the leading legal expert on academic freedom in the late twentieth century. As an author of several books on the First Amendment, he was particularly well qualified to assess the constitutional status of academic freedom. He was also a major figure in the AAUP. He first became involved in 1965, when he testified on the AAUP's behalf against an attempt by legislators in North Carolina to enact a "speaker ban" that would have prevented Communists from being guest lecturers at state universities. He became General Counsel of the AAUP (1969–1970) and its President (1974–1976). His signature publication on academic freedom was "Academic Freedom and the First Amendment in the Supreme Court of the United States: An Unhurried Historical Review" (1990).

The word "unhurried" signals that this is a very long article. "Unhurried" also suggests that the article aims to be a nuanced exploration of its topic, which is the incorporation of academic freedom into Supreme Court jurisprudence. The erudition displayed in this article does not lend itself to a simple left/right classification. Van Alstyne's conception of academic freedom, to be sure, was a traditional one: he upheld the separation of academics and politics as a precondition of academic freedom; in short, he defended the anti-political orthodoxy.

In "Unhurried Review," he gave the concrete example of choosing a textbook for a course. Academic freedom implies the liberty of a professor to choose the textbook but only if the choice is made on academic grounds: because it is the most comprehensive, the most lucid, etc. But suppose the professor chooses for a different reason:

> Perhaps because the publisher had opposed the war in Vietnam and the faculty, or a majority of the faculty, also opposed the war in Vietnam. Perhaps because the publisher had contributed money to a prolife organization or, conversely, to Planned Parenthood, and, again, the faculty also favored that social cause. Perhaps because the author is one's nephew-or niece. The range of nonprofessional (and also of unprofessional) reasons is nearly inexhaustible.[8]

In such cases, political authorities outside the university would be justified in canceling the instructor's choice and prescribing a textbook of *their* choice.

Though traditional in his outlook, Van Alstyne argued that academic freedom is not only a professional value associated with the university but is also a subset of freedom of speech under the First Amendment; this argument is uncharacteristic of those who support the anti-political orthodoxy.[9] Intuitively, anyone wishing to distinguish sharply between academic inquiry and political advocacy would not wish to claim that the First Amendment subsumes academic freedom. As we saw in the chapter of this book on Meiklejohn, freedom of speech, since the Civil Rights Movement and *New York Times v. Sullivan* (1964), means that *political* speech enjoys special protection under the Constitution. If academic freedom is a form of free speech, and free speech in turn means uninhibited political speech, why should the First Amendment not cover the selection of a textbook for political reasons? This is why Stanley Fish, author of *Save the World on Your Own Time* (2012), upholding the separation of academics and politics, insists that academic freedom is unrelated to the First Amendment.[10] Van Alstyne's originality was that he assembled the Court's scattered dicta on academic freedom in order to nestle academic freedom inside of the First Amendment

He notes that when the AAUP was founded in 1915, free speech was not a robust constitutional value. The incorporation of the First Amendment against the states had yet to occur. The idea of academic freedom in the early twentieth century

> developed largely without benefit of the first amendment . . . in response to the vacuum of doctrine associated with the first amendment as hard law . . . the AAUP sought to gain some purchase *against* the law by pressing forward with the idea of the university as an institution necessarily characterized by academic freedom, in other words, in which academic freedom is inseparable from academic work.[11]

Van Alstyne does not trace the incorporation of the First Amendment against the states, starting in the 1920s. That story is too well known among law professors for him to include it. (I review incorporation and its relevance for academic freedom, in Chapter 2.) Van Alstyne focuses on how the justices of the Court, starting in the 1950s, began to use the term "academic freedom" in cases dealing with the free-speech rights of teachers vis-à-vis repressive state laws. Justice William O. Douglas was the first to use the term, in *Adler v. Board of Education* (1952). At issue was a New York law providing for the removal from public employment of anyone advocating the use of violence to overthrow the US government as well as anyone belonging to a group listed as subversive. The Court's majority sustained the law. In dissent, Douglas, as Van Alstyne says, "drew on the first amendment to shelter academic freedom."[12] Douglas declared that if the state did not wish to "raise havoc with academic freedom," it should limit itself to outlawing actions which endanger public safety. "There can be no real academic freedom" in an atmosphere in which teachers are spying on each other to discover subversive words or party affiliations.[13]

Van Alstyne suggests that starting with *Adler,* the Court began to identify academic freedom as a subcategory of free speech. But he also underscored the point that academic freedom, even when wrapped up as a constitutional right, still hinged on the distinction between academics and politics. Van Alstyne presumes something which Douglas did not actually make explicit, that if a teacher advocated violent revolution not outside the school but *in the classroom*, the First Amendment and academic freedom would not apply. In Van Alstyne's interpretation, Douglas's dissent went no further than the protection of the teacher's extramural speech.

One shortcoming of "Unhurried Review" is that, while the author is thorough in his coverage of Supreme Court cases that mention academic freedom, he does not acknowledge the birth, since the 1960s, of the new academic disciplines, such as Black Studies and Women's Studies, which promote politicized teaching. The article is weak in its presumption of a professional consensus that there is a fundamental difference between academic inquiry and political activism. Van Alstyne writes as if the Supreme Court has modified its doctrines over the decades and the academy has not. Thus, in spite of its erudition, his article does not confront some major issues.

The highest level of engagement with the question of how to define the boundary between academic and political activity is to be found not in stand-alone articles but in two anthologies in which competing perspectives are juxtaposed. The two anthologies from the 1990s to which I now turn reflect an effort to avoid polarization and recognize the legitimacy of intellectual difference.

Of the two, the more impressive is *Advocacy in the Classroom: Problems and Possibilities*, edited by Patricia Meyer Spacks (1996). Spacks was a University of Virginia English professor who served as President of the Modern Language Association and President of the American Academy of Arts and Sciences. The book was based on a conference sponsored by several leading academic organizations, including the AAUP, the American Council of Learned Societies, and the American Philosophical Association.[14]

The majority of the book's 39 contributors uphold the anti-political orthodoxy, but there are salient exceptions; moreover, the arguments both for and against political advocacy in the classroom are made by authors of diverse political commitments. There is no left-right fault line in this collection. Myles Brand, the President of Indiana University, opens the volume with a paper that defends the orthodoxy but tempers its application in practice. Here he sounds like the 1915 "Declaration."

> There are constraints on advocacy that result from one's professional obligations. To abridge these constraints is to exceed advocacy and undertake proselytizing . . . The faculty member's part of the obligation is to advocate within the bounds of a contextualized account [of disagreements in the field]; the institution's part of the obligation is to offer the student a balanced approach . . . Proselytizing attempts to remove this decision from the student; it substitutes the judgment of the teacher for that of the student.[15]

According to Brand, "The student ought to have the benefit of learning alternative positions. Some alternatives can be garnered from assigned readings. But that is not sufficient. The student should have available alternatives presented in a manner that permits exploration and debate."[16] Brand recommends that "the entire campus curriculum should be reviewed periodically" for ideological balance, and he notes that "such reviews rarely occur."[17]

When he served as the President of the University of Oregon, Brand had to respond to an incident in which an instructor, in a writing course for first-year law students, used class time to state that he was gay and to advocate for gay rights. The instructor condemned Supreme Court decisions that did not uphold gay rights, and he assigned readings that were not on the common syllabus for the sections of the course. The law school dean, described by Brand as "conservative," notified the instructor that his contract would not be renewed. Members of the campus and the local gay community protested. Brand stepped in and reappointed the instructor for a year. However, he did not reappoint the dean.[18] Brand's judgment was that the instructor "failed to fulfill his professional obligation," but this was by no means a firing offence, unless the instructor repeatedly engaged in proselytism after being warned not to do so.[19]

Another contributor to the Spacks volume, Michael Olivas, was General Counsel to the AAUP when the conference took place. He argues, "academic freedom does not give carte blanche to professors."[20] Olivas attempts to dispel the notion that academic freedom is another name for the free-speech rights of professors. In the university, academics are governed by professional standards which limit their speech. "Faculty should be entitled to special consideration only in pursuing academic endeavors (hence 'academic' freedom), such as in the laboratory, library, or classroom. Extending the protection of academic freedom to extra-academic speech in this light is unprincipled."[21] Olivas references the 1915 "Declaration" to support his argument[22]; he also adduces *Cohen. v. San Bernardino Valley College* (1995), a federal case in California concerning an English and Film Studies professor who read articles from *Playboy* and *Hustler* in class. Cohen expressed what some students regarded as unmeasured enthusiasm for pornography. In the wake of student complaints, a Faculty Grievance Committee required Cohen to attend a sexual harassment seminar and provide a syllabus for each of his courses to prospective students by certain deadlines. Cohen sued, claiming that his rights to academic freedom and free speech were violated.

The court declined to hold that the college's disciplining of Cohen violated "general notions of academic freedom under the First Amendment." The judicial opinion contains a "pro and con" analysis that is a good model of non-Manichean thinking. In other words, while Olivas cites the case to support the anti-political orthodoxy, the reader is also exposed to non-binary thinking and could choose to disagree with the court—on the basis of the court's own words.

> In fairness, the Court must note that there is evidence in the record that Cohen's teaching style is effective for at least some students . . . there is the danger that the most sensitive and the most easily offended students will be given veto power over class content and methodology . . . Colleges and universities, as well as the courts, must avoid a tyranny of mediocrity, in which all discourse is made bland enough to suit the tastes of all students.

The Court continued:

> However, colleges and universities must have the power to require professors to effectively educate all segments of the student population . . . If colleges and universities lack that power, each classroom becomes a separate fiefdom in which the educational process is subject to professorial whim . . . [T]he public employer must be able to achieve its mission and avoid disruption of the workplace. Within the educational context, the university's mission is to effectively educate students.[23]

The court cited several prior cases to back up the proposition that a public employer can censor the speech of its employees, when the speech disrupts the functioning of the organization. Some of these precedents involved public educational institutions. Thus, the reader learns that while the First Amendment is designed principally to protect the speech of individuals against governmental regulation, free speech does not always trump a public employer's interest in restricting the speech of employees on the job.

Another contributor to the Spacks volume was Nadine Strossen, who was President of the American Civil Liberties Union when the volume was published. Of course, the ACLU is the leading American foundation devoted to the protection of free speech. Yet, Strossen's position on classroom politics is consistent with the anti-political orthodoxy; she recognizes that professionalism is an important factor in the classroom. Her essay is thus a prime example of intellectual fluidity in the Spacks volume.

Strossen cites an ACLU policy guide:

> In the classroom, a teacher should promote an atmosphere of free inquiry. This should include discussion of controversial issues without the assumption that they are settled in advance or that there is only one "right" answer in matters of dispute. Such discussion

should include presentation of divergent opinions and doctrines, past and present, on a given subject.[24]

Strossen condemns classroom "indoctrination" as a kind of "totalitarianism." The right of teachers to express themselves is curbed by the right of students to be exposed to diverse ideas in a non-repressive environment.[25] Unlike Van Alstyne, Strossen does not consider academic freedom to be inscribed in the First Amendment. She states that references to academic freedom in Supreme Court cases are mere dicta and not part of the legal holdings; hence, the Court's occasional paeans to academic freedom are not binding.[26]

Many other essays in the Spacks volume provide variations on the anti-political orthodoxy. It is evident that in the 1990s, vigorous opposition to activism in the classroom was not perceived as inherently "right wing,"—as it often is today. A particularly interesting example is the paper by Jeffrey Wallen, a literary scholar at Hampshire College. Founded in 1970, Hampshire is a progressive college with no academic departments; every student designs an interdisciplinary "concentration." Wallen notes that almost everyone at Hampshire is on the Left. He does not exclude himself from this generalization, and he has no record of publicly supporting conservative political causes. But he argues that classroom advocacy fosters intolerance and hampers dialogue. Advocacy "shuts down opposing viewpoints" and tends to "insulate the students from any examination of their presuppositions and convictions." Constantly focusing on the need for social change, Wallen states, precludes open inquiry about the fundamental question of what kind of change is worth pursuing: what does social justice mean?[27]

The Brown University philosopher and poet, Felicia Ackerman, makes a similar point in her contribution to the volume. She criticizes Women's Studies departments for being ideologically homogeneous. Women's Studies departments were founded on the assumption that the courses in other academic departments are informed by biased male perspectives. Even if that were true in the 1970s, Ackerman argues, it is surely not true now. The challenge today is the opposite.

> If no instructor in women's studies is supposed to be negative or even neutral about certain core feminist claims, where will students hear these claims discussed by instructors other than their adherents? Are they discussed much in non-women's studies courses at all?[28]

Within the Spacks volume, a critical response to Ackerman comes from Helen Moglen, a professor of English and Women's Studies at the University of California, Santa Cruz. In "Unveiling the Myth of Neutrality: Advocacy in the Feminist Classroom," she rejects the "dichotomy" between advocacy and professionalism. She suggests that professors are "responsible for modeling the difficult skills of advocacy for their students." As a professor, one teaches students how to defend their ideas by campaigning for one's own. The "openly political classroom" is the best preparation for students who are destined to live in a competitive democratic society. To be a feminist, she concedes, is "inevitably" to be an advocate for women and to advance "women-centered" knowledge. Moglen still rejects "indoctrination," which occurs when teachers impose their agenda on students whom they treat as passive. But the real threat to democracy, she states, is posed by those who claim that advocacy in the classroom is intrinsically unprofessional.[29]

The most cogent criticism of the anti-political orthodoxy in the Spacks volume is by Michael Bérubé, an English professor at Pennsylvania State University. During Nelson's presidency of the AAUP (2006–2012), Bérubé would become a member of the AAUP's Executive Committee and of its Committee A on Academic Freedom. At the time the Spacks volume appeared, however, his views were contrary to those of the AAUP, which are represented by Brand, Olivas, and Strossen. As we will see, Nelson's leadership of the AAUP was a turning point because he declared the 1915 "Declaration" to be outdated. In the Spacks volume, Bérubé wrote:

> . . . the surest way to trap yourself inside a narrow, parochial, "subjective" view of the world is to believe that you have transcended all merely subjective worldviews. Indeed, the reason hermeneutics demand of us that we theorize our own historical and epistemological positions is that if we *fail* to do so, if we attribute to ourselves the Archimedean point beyond history and "interest," we will almost certainly lapse into dogmatism and intransigence.[30]

Of course, this is debatable. But Bérubé gives his argument, in favor of activism, real bite through concrete examples. He suggests that many academic fields not only permit but require political advocacy as an integral part of professional conduct. What makes his point acute is that he does not illustrate it by using leftist programs such as Black Studies or Women's Studies; he uses conventional fields. He discusses Stephen Meyer, a political scientist at MIT and a conservation commissioner in Massachusetts. In 1995, Meyer criticized proposed revisions of the 1972 Clean Water Act as harmful to the environment He blamed scientists who considered themselves above the fray of politics and who withheld their own critical thoughts on the proposed revisions. Bérubé suggests that it was appropriate for Meyer to bring his criticism—both of the legislative amendments and of the narrow professionalism of scientists who kept their distance from public controversy—into his scholarship and teaching. Bérubé argues that there is nothing unprofessional about Meyer criticizing scientists who pay no attention to the social ramifications of their work. Bérubé asks, too, are not professors of Education who focus on education for the disabled supposed to be advocates for the needs of students with disabilities? If a bill were pending which would cut funding for special education, are professors in this field supposed to refrain from criticizing it in the presence of students?[31]

Louis Menand, who was an English professor at CUNY (and is now at Harvard) bridges some of the differences between Bérubé and the defenders of the anti-political orthodoxy. He suggests that "advocacy" is a vague term and that constructing a volume on this subject "was a bad idea." He states that a math professor who lectures on why we should emulate the moral life of the Victorians is obviously not covered by academic freedom. But such off-topic preaching almost never occurs, he suggests. As for professors who share their point of view on matters relating to the course, this is what professors ought to do: the job of professors is to profess. "That's what academic freedom is all about . . . My interpretation is better than your interpretation." As an example, Menand refers to a professor teaching that *Heart of Darkness* is a racist novel, which not only says something about the novel but also implies that racism is bad, which is a political and moral principle.[32]

> The accusation that professors who emphasize the political implications of the books they teach are not really professors but are "advocates" is an invitation to authorities external to the university to intervene in the university's own legitimate intellectual

activity. It is an extremely dangerous rhetorical position to take, and that is why I am so concerned to find it adopted, in however a constructive a spirit, by the organizers of this volume.[33]

Menand states that professors on the left need to "tolerate a diversity of opinions and encourage criticism and debate within the classroom." There must be no "political orthodoxy" in the classroom. But he claims that a spirit of skepticism and self-questioning is already characteristic of the professoriate. When professors do overstep the limits, "the good sense of college students" recognizes it. If they find the professor's take disagreeable, "they advise their friends to register for someone else's course."[34]

When these words were published, in 1996, a volume entitled *The Future of Academic Freedom,* edited by Menand, was in press. Like the Spacks volume, the Menand anthology illustrates debate at a high level. I shall forego a detailed summary of the nine essays in this book, in the interest of moving forward to the twenty-first century. Menand's volume is essentially a mirror image of the Spacks volume. The majority of contributions are postmodernist in spirit; they dismiss concerns about political bias in academe. Questioning whether there is even a need to link academic freedom to an ideal of political neutrality, most of the authors deny that there are any inherent problems associated with freeing up professors to pursue their political commitments within the academy. However, a lengthy contribution by the Rice University historian, Thomas Haskell, takes an opposing stance. Haskell's chapter comes right after the chapter by Richard Rorty, who takes a postmodernist position. The Rorty-Haskell exchange exposes the reader to high-level debate about truth and academic freedom.

Rorty's argument, in a nutshell, is that academic freedom is a professional value, and no professional norm is dependent on a specific conception of truth. In Rorty's language, there is no "correspondence" between a given professional value and a specific epistemology. This accords with his belief that the theory of knowledge should be abolished as a branch of philosophical inquiry. It is an inconclusive subject and nothing practical depends on its findings. By way of an analogy, Rorty states that belief in God is not a necessary precondition for having a good character.

Curiously, Rorty concedes that in practice, if not in logic, the disappearance of belief in God does affect behavior. "But in the long run it may make a lot of difference whether a society is regulated by the members' fear of nonhuman sanctions or by secular sentiments of pride."[35] It is not clear how this helps his argument that a theory of truth is not needed to sustain a commitment to academic freedom. Additionally, Rorty does not acknowledge that criticizing epistemology as inconclusive is nothing new. Rorty attacks believers in "objectivity" who allegedly ground the idea of academic freedom in the possibility of absolute knowledge. But as Haskell points out, the founders of the AAUP, like Lovejoy and John Dewey, were pragmatists and skeptics. "[T]he founders of the modern university were not wedded to a naive correspondence theory of truth and made important concessions to truth's historicity, to its conventionality, and occasionally even to its cultural variability."[36] They could be described as postmodernists, except the conclusions they drew from the fact that human knowledge is limited were the opposite of postmodernists: instead of encouraging political activism, the authors of the "Declaration" called for political self-restraint. The very concept of a university that enjoys academic freedom, that is immune from control by elected officials, is contingent on the claim that academic inquiry is different from political activism. "The central thrust of the 1915 report was . . . to put forth a strong claim for the corporate authority of professional [academic] communities."[37] Positing the apolitical character of academic investigation is not a result of believing in objectivity; it is a result of believing in the university's independence.

In a long review of the Menand volume, entitled "Can Academic Freedom Survive Postmodernism?" David Rabban rightly observed that the Rorty-Haskell exchange is the most intellectually elevated segment of the book, and he devoted his review to suggesting that Haskell got the better of the argument.[38] Rabban was General Counsel of the AAUP, 1998–2006. His review is one more piece of evidence that the AAUP held to the anti-political orthodoxy prior to Nelson's presidency. But the larger point, at this stage of my argument, is that the Menand volume, like the Spacks volume, is a theater of high-level debate about academic freedom. The two anthologies reveal a kind of academic culture in which one brings together opposing opinions into a collage, enabling readers to comprehend each "shape," or argument, through contrast.

I, David Horowitz

In 2003, David Horowitz set out to transform American higher education by convincing state legislatures to impose an Academic Bill of Rights (ABOR) on public universities. By 2006, the legislatures in 23 states were considering passing laws requiring public universities to implement the ABOR.[39] The ABOR became one of the hottest controversies in American higher education. By the end of 2006, it was the topic of 73 articles in *Inside Higher Education*.[40]

Horowitz's campaign differed from previous assertions of the anti-political orthodoxy in two ways. The first was his strong emphasis on the academic freedom of students. Professorial self-restraint, he argued, was not merely a professional obligation; it was part of a student's right to learn, and universities must codify this right. The second was Horowitz's appeal to state legislatures. In *Indoctrination U: The Left's War Against Academic Freedom,* he wrote:

> I had no recourse but to take the issue to state legislatures, if only to rouse public opinion on the matter . . . My purpose was not to urge legislators to micromanage state universities, but to gain leverage that might help the university administrators enforce academic guidelines that were already in place.[41]

Horowitz's gift for sensationalizing a problem, for inscribing it in a good-versus-evil framework, was a key ingredient in the ABOR movement. At the same time, Horowitz's image proved to be a liability, as he well knew. "I was aware that my public persona contributed to the problem," he wrote, in reference to militant opposition to the ABOR by the professors' union in the state of New York.[42] The head of the union had declared, "The Academic Bill of Rights is nothing more than a quota system for political extremists so they can deliver their right-wing political sermons in the classroom."[43]

We are starting to get a taste of the rhetoric of denunciation in the ABOR debate. The union head's comment is not an entirely accurate characterization of the ABOR, for the text of the ABOR is framed, as we will see, in a politically neutral manner. Likewise, Graham Larkin, a Stanford Art History professor and Vice President of the California branch of the AAUP, described Horowitz in *Inside Higher Education* as a "liar extraordinaire and author of the incomparable bullshitting manual *The Art of Political War and Other Radical Pursuits.*"

> He believes you should drown your political opponents in a steady stream of bullshit, emanating every day from newspapers, TV and radio programs, as well as lavishly

funded smear sites and blogs. He also thinks you should go on college lecture circuits where you can use incendiary rhetoric to turn civilized venues into the Jerry Springer show, and then descend into fits of indignant self-pity when someone responds with a pie to your face.[44]

Though Horowitz claimed to be demonized unfairly by the left, he was a provocateur himself, as can be seen in the titles of some of his books: *The Professors: The 101 Most Dangerous Academics in America* (2007); *One Party-Classroom: How Radical Professors at America's Top Colleges Indoctrinate Students and Undermine Our Democracy* (2009). Moreover, while the text of the ABOR is difficult to link to any specific political ideology, Horowitz wrote so many books and articles discharging political hatred against the left that one can hardly fault critics for portraying the ABOR as part of a conservative crusade.

Horowitz infused into the ABOR debate a passion for self-vindication: a narcissism that is evident in the pervasiveness of the word "I" in everything he wrote about the ABOR. Chapter 1 *of Reforming Our Universities: The Campaign for an Academic Bill of Rights* is typical. Horowitz's "proof" that the American academy is corrupted by leftist indoctrination is his own experience: notably, what he learned during his visits as a guest speaker to American campuses. Often what he construes as political bias is nothing other than faculty members expressing their dislike for him. At the University of Hawaii in Honolulu, his speech was boycotted by many faculty members; he cites this as evidence of the close-mindedness of professors in general.[45] He writes that he was once asked how many times his campus speeches were disrupted. His reply to this contrived demand for more autobiography is a block quotation—Horowitz quoting himself—that is more than a page long, and each of the 14 sentences begins with the word "I."[46]

Horowitz has had a large impact on public debate about academic freedom in the twenty-first century. His passion for confession and denunciation has helped to polarize higher education. At the source of his preoccupation with auto-justification is his anguished conversion from communist to conservative, a conversion that seems to have never achieved psychological closure.

He was born in 1939 to a Jewish family in Forest Hills, New York. His parents were high school teachers who became communists in the 1920s. The father was fired in 1951 for refusing to swear, in accordance with the 1940 Feinberg Law, that he was not a Communist Party member. The mother accepted early retirement. Horowitz became devoted to revolutionary socialism in his teens. After studying English at Columbia, he enrolled in the graduate English program at Berkeley where, as he says in his memoir, *Radical Son,* he fell in with a group of "red diaper babies."[47] In June 1962, he co-organized one of the first student demonstrations against the Vietnam War. Horowitz dropped out of the doctoral program. He spent several years in England, where he became friendly with leading socialist intellectuals such as Bertrand Russell, Isaac Deutscher, and Ralph Miliband. He returned to Berkeley in 1968 to become the editor of *Ramparts*, one of the New Left's most successful magazines. He established his own name as a New Left thinker with several books, including *Empire and Revolution: A Radical Interpretation of Contemporary History* (1969) and *The Free World Colossus* (1971). The latter, providing a litany of America's imperialist misdeeds, became popular in the growing anti–Vietnam War movement.

Horowitz had a special interest in racial inequality. At Columbia, he had joined the campus branch of the NAACP. As editor of *Ramparts*, he cultivated relations with the Black Panther Party, becoming a confidant of Huey Newton and a successful fundraiser for the Party. The turning point in Horowitz's political and emotional life occurred when

Betty Van Patter was murdered in December 1974. Horowitz had recommended her to Newton as a bookkeeper. Her killer was never identified by the police. Horowitz was certain that Newton ordered her killing after she discovered financial irregularities in the Panthers' records. Horowitz reports that Van Patter's death changed his life by making him doubt his leftist commitments and sending him into an "internal free fall."[48] His comrades on the left, who viewed the Panthers as icons of revolution, refused to acknowledge any of the group's criminal activities. Horowitz felt isolated. It took him ten years till he embraced conservatism and the Republican Party. In between, that is, in the late 1970s and early 1980s, he felt "out of order" and surrounded by "outer darkness."[49] He drank heavily, was prone to serious auto accidents, and his marriage fell apart. In *Radical Son*, he speaks repeatedly of his fear of being killed by the Panthers, or by other leftists whom he had attacked in print.[50] He describes himself as "the most hated ex-radical of my generation."[51]

The Text of the ABOR

The text of the Academic Bill of Rights is brief, at 1,100 words. It consists of two sections. In the first, "The Mission of the University," Horowitz affirms that the central purposes of a university are "the pursuit of truth," "the study and reasoned criticism of intellectual traditions," and "the teaching and general development of students to help them become creative individuals and productive citizens of a pluralistic democracy." In the second section, "Academic Freedom," Horowitz states:

> Academic freedom and intellectual diversity are indispensable to the American university . . . This means that no political, ideological, or religious orthodoxy will be imposed on professors and researchers through the hiring or tenure or termination process, or through any other administrative means by the academic institution. Nor shall legislatures impose any such orthodoxy through their control of the university budget.

The main purpose of the ABOR, however, is to affirm the academic freedom of students, not professors. Academic freedom "means the protection of students . . . from the imposition of any orthodoxy of a political, religious or ideological nature." The following is the crux of the document as a "Bill of Rights" for students.

> Students will be graded solely on the basis of their reasoned answers and appropriate knowledge of the subjects and disciplines they study, not on the basis of their political or religious beliefs.
> Curricula and reading lists in the humanities and social sciences should reflect the uncertainty and unsettled character of all human knowledge in these areas by providing students with dissenting sources and viewpoints where appropriate. While teachers are and should be free to pursue their own findings and perspectives in presenting their views, they should consider and make their students aware of other viewpoints.
> Academic disciplines should welcome a diversity of approaches to unsettled questions.
> Exposing students to the spectrum of significant scholarly viewpoints on the subjects examined in their courses is a major responsibility of faculty. Faculty will not use their courses for the purpose of political, ideological, religious, or anti-religious indoctrination.[52]

Nowhere in the ABOR is it suggested that universities should hire conservative professors, or that it is better to espouse conservative ideas in the classroom than radical ideas. Whatever ulterior aspirations Horowitz may have had to promote right-wing ideology, the document is impeccably neutral.

Throughout the ABOR controversy, critics maintained that the problem Horowitz was attacking—the use of the classroom to promote partisan politics—was not real; that it was a fabrication of the extreme Right. Here we confront a knotted set of problems, not only in the ABOR controversy but in higher education in general. Providing credit-based courses and degrees is the only thing that distinguishes universities from other institutions. Yet, the assessment of teaching in American universities is one of the least professionalized features of academic life. The reality is that we don't know how widespread and flagrant political activism in the classroom is. The only commonly used instrument of assessment, the student evaluation form, generally does not ask students directly if the professor overstepped professional limits. And even if it did, students are not necessarily able to distinguish Socratic questioning from one-sided advocacy. Gerald Graff captured the ambiance of research universities when he observed that teaching is generally a "solo activity" enacted in "a self-contained" space. We are "screened from our colleagues' classrooms." Graff suggests that one reason for this is "our fear of what we might hear in them if we were not." Graff goes so far as to suggest that the classroom tends to

> shelter us from the criticism of our assumptions to which we would risk exposing ourselves if our courses were in dialogue. We tell our students we want them to disagree with us, yet we send them the very opposite message when we let our classroom walls separate us from the disagreement of our colleagues.[53]

In spite of the difficulty of measuring the scope of the problem, it seems unreasonable to say that the problem is only a figment of the right's imagination. In *The Academic Bill of Rights Debate*, a volume pitched against Horowitz, one article purports to prove statistically that there is no indoctrination problem. Fenwick and Zipp report that in response to a survey, "only" 19% of faculty members said that influencing the political structure through their teaching is "very important" to them.[54] This hardly disproves Horowitz's argument.

On the other hand, Horowitz did exaggerate. He fueled misrepresentation. *One-Party Classroom: How Radical Professors Indoctrinate Students and Undermine Our Democracy,* opens with a portrait of Bettina Aptheker, a member of the American Communist Party's central committee in the 1970s. Horowitz quotes Aptheker's memoir in which she says she pursued an academic career after a Party member told her, "It's your revolutionary duty."[55] She became the first Women's Studies professor at the University of California, Santa Cruz and, according to Horowitz, built the entire department on her agenda, eventually giving it the more radical name of Feminist Studies and hiring faculty such as Angela Davis. Horowitz then asserts that Aptheker's "career is a metaphor for the political trends that have reshaped America's liberal arts classrooms over the past generation."[56] He goes on to assert that there are 10,000 college classes nationwide whose primary purpose is not to educate students but to train them in left-wing ideologies and political agendas. "The students who pass through these courses are numbered in the millions."[57]

Apart from the dubious statistical claims made here and elsewhere, two other flaws characterize Horowitz's books about indoctrination. The first is that Horowitz never considers conservative indoctrination in the classroom. The second is that some of the cases he presents work against his argument because the professors in question were reprimanded, fired, or denied tenure, revealing that some universities have procedures for dealing with the abuse of classroom authority—thus making legislation unnecessary. The chapter of *One-Party Classroom* on Columbia, entitled "Uptown Madrassa," focuses on charges of antisemitism made by students against certain professors in Middle Eastern Studies at Columbia University. Horowitz does not mention that Columbia President Lee Bollinger implemented new rules that allowed students to file grievances against professors who present their political opinions in an overbearing manner.

> Conduct that is grievable under these obligations may include, among other things: failure to show appropriate respect in an instructional setting for the rights of others to hold opinions differing from their own; misuse of faculty authority within an instructional setting to pressure students into supporting a political or social cause; and conduct in the classroom or another instructional setting that adversely affects the learning environment.[58]

The policy is still on the books at Columbia. It is currently included not only in the undergraduate bulletin but also in the bulletin of several graduate divisions.

Ward Churchill: A Denial of Complexity at All Levels

In One-Party Classroom, a chapter about the University of Colorado at Boulder is called "Ward Churchill U." Horowitz's treatment of the facts in the Churchill case is distorted by his ideological fervor. But the coverage of this complex case by others is hardly more sophisticated. The Churchill case is an index of the general degradation of the discussion of academic freedom in our time. Not only Horowitz but other participants in the Churchill controversy failed to register the fundamental ambiguities in the meaning of plagiarism, free speech, employer discrimination, and academic freedom.

Horowitz argued that Churchill, who was fired for allegedly committing plagiarism and falsifying evidence, was an example of academic life out of control at the University of Colorado and throughout the academy. Churchill, a tenured professor and Chair of the Department of Ethnic Studies, was dismissed from the University of Colorado in 2007, having been found guilty of fraudulent practices in writings arguing that the US government was complicit in the genocide of Native Americans. One set of issues concerns whether he really engaged in academic fraud. Another question concerns the fact that he was singled out for an investigation. If one is chosen for an investigation for discriminatory reasons (e.g., on account of one's race or one's political associations), are the findings of the investigation binding?

Throughout the controversy, no one denied that an investigation took place only because Churchill had incurred anger by calling victims of the terrorist attack on the World Trade Center "little Eichmanns" (after the Nazi Adolf Eichmann). Churchill's essay, "Some People Push Back: On the Justice of Roosting Chickens," appeared a day after 9/11, in *Dark Night Field Notes*, an electronic journal dedicated to the struggle for the liberation of indigenous peoples. Responding to media descriptions of the victims as innocent civilians, Churchill tried to underscore the complicity of those killed in the foreign policy of a colonialist government.

> True enough, they were civilians of a sort. But innocent? Gimme a break. They formed a technocratic corps at the very heart of America's global financial empire—the "mighty

engine of profit" to which the military dimension of U.S. policy has always been enslaved—and they did so both willingly and knowingly. Recourse to "ignorance"—a derivative, after all, of the word "ignore"—counts as less than an excuse among this relatively well-educated elite. To the extent that any of them were unaware of the costs and consequences to others of what they were involved in—and in many cases excelling at—it was because of their absolute refusal to see. More likely, it was because they were too busy braying, incessantly and self-importantly, into their cell phones, arranging power lunches and stock transactions, each of which translated, conveniently out of sight, mind, and smelling distance, into the starved and rotting flesh of infants. If there was a better, more effective, or in fact any other way of visiting some penalty befitting their participation upon the little Eichmanns inhabiting the sterile sanctuary of the twin towers, I'd be really interested in hearing about it.[59]

This is obviously a gross simplification of the identity of those who died. Yet, the essay elicited no outcry when published. Several years later, Churchill was invited to speak at Hamilton College. The essay caught the attention of some faculty members. On the day Churchill was scheduled to speak, February 3, 2005, *The O'Reilly Factor*, the top-rated staple of Fox News, ran a segment in which Bill O'Reilly characterized Churchill as "insane." Politicians and media commentators urged the university to fire Churchill. But his political commentary, expressed off-campus and not reflecting in any direct manner his performance as a professor, was protected by the Supreme Court's First Amendment doctrine and by the policies of the AAUP.

The AAUP's 1915 "Declaration" referred to a professor's "freedom of extramural utterance and action."[60] The AAUP's 1940 "Statement on Academic Freedom and Tenure" was less liberal, calling upon academics to exercise restraint in their off-campus discourse. By the time of the Churchill case, however, Supreme Court doctrine prohibited public employers from requiring employees to sacrifice their constitutional right to express themselves as citizens off the job.[61] In 1965, the AAUP itself "clarified" (in reality, revised) the 1940 document by stating that "a faculty member's expression of opinion as a citizen cannot constitute grounds for dismissal unless it clearly demonstrates the faculty member's unfitness to serve. Extramural utterances rarely bear on the faculty member's fitness for continuing service."[62]

Even though Colorado Governor Bill Owens demanded that Churchill be fired, the professor of Ethnic Studies was clearly on safe ground. His enemies had to find a different reason to fire him. In response to charges by some scholars in Native American history, notably John LaVelle of the University of New Mexico, that Churchill's work was severely flawed, the university regents formed an Investigative Committee (IC) to examine Churchill's published work. On May 16, 2006, the IC submitted its findings in a 124-page report to the university's Standing Committee on Research Methods (SCRM). The majority of the SCRM recommended dismissal, though only one member of the IC did. Of the other IC members, two recommended a suspension without pay for two years, and two recommended a suspension without pay for five years.[63] The president of the university, Hank Brown, advised the Regents to dismiss Churchill, and they voted 8–1 to fire him on July 25, 2007.

None of the IC members were specialists in Native American history. At the outset, the IC's report concedes that its existence is due to a political backlash against Churchill's "little Eichmanns" essay. "Thus, the Committee is troubled by the origins of, and skeptical concerning the motives for, the current investigation." "Nevertheless, serious claims of academic misconduct have been lodged and they require full investigation."[64] To justify overlooking the motives leading to its own existence, the IC proposed the following comparison.

> To use an analogy, a motorist who is stopped and ticketed for speeding because the police officer was offended by the contents of her bumper sticker, and who otherwise would have been sent away with a warning, is still guilty of speeding, even if the officer's motive for punishing the speeder was the offense taken to the speeder's exercise of her right to free speech. No court would consider the improper motive of the police officer to constitute a defense to speeding, however protected by legal free speech guarantees the contents of the bumper sticker might be.[65]

One wonders what the IC would have said about punishing speeders who had been stopped on account of their race—a natural hypothetical to consider, given that Churchill purported to be a Native American. At the time of the IC's investigation, the ACLU regarded racial profiling as a violation of the Fourteenth Amendment's Equal Protection Clause.[66] To present the bumper sticker analogy as if it plainly justifies the IC's inquiry is also illogical, for the IC could not have known before its investigation that Churchill was "speeding," i.e., that he committed academic fraud.

Putting aside analogies, the basic issue is whether an employee can be disciplined for making mistakes which have been uncovered through an inquiry undertaken for a discriminatory reason. Two transgressions collide here: the transgression of the employee and that of the employer. Is society better served by punishing the employee who broke a rule, or by preventing the employer from arbitrarily targeting employees for investigation? Commentators on the Churchill case have taken sides without recognizing that the question is in fact a very hard one.

On the charges of plagiarism and falsifying evidence, the IC concluded that Churchill misleadingly stated that certain scholars agreed with his claim that English settlers, and later the US army, deliberately infected Native Americans with smallpox. The IC also found that he had "ghost written" articles, i.e., written articles under names other than his own, and then cited them in his publications to support his arguments. Finally, the IC found that Churchill plagiarized the work of Fay G. Cohen of Dalhousie University. (Churchill, in contrast, claimed that he himself had ghost-written the parts of Cohen's article that he recycled!)

Diametrically opposed were the findings of the Colorado branch of the AAUP in its "Report on the Termination of Ward Churchill." If the IC's report was twisted by its eagerness to overlook the political motivation behind the investigation of Churchill, the Colorado's AAUP's report (henceforth, CAR), is distorted by its resolve not to acknowledge any academic wrongdoing on Churchill's part. The committee that issued CAR consisted of three members, only one of which was a tenure-track professor. Concerning the "little Eichmann" essay, CAR says:

> His thesis was similar in concept to Pat Robertson's statement that 9/11 was God's retribution for Americans' toleration of gays. In other words, both implied that Americans had a collective responsibility for actions that supposedly motivated the attackers. Yet Pat Robertson's career and reputation were not destroyed.[67]

CAR, finding that allegations of plagiarism and fabrication of evidence were false, goes so far as to call the members of the IC "academic frauds."[68] CAR also recommended "that faculty in search of employment consider a position at the University of Colorado only as a last resort because of the University of Colorado's indifference to the ideals of academic freedom."[69]

Churchill filed a civil lawsuit against the Board of Regents for wrongful termination and violation of his freedom of speech. In March 2009, a jury returned a verdict that Churchill was fired not because of his supposed research misconduct but in retaliation for the exercise of his First Amendment rights. The jury was under the impression that the judge would reinstate Churchill at the university. Churchill had indicated that he sought nothing else, no monetary damages. Hence, the jury awarded him $1, the minimum required by law. Things turned in an even more bizarre direction when the judge refused to reinstate Churchill; in fact, the judge vacated the jury's verdict by applying the legal principle that the Regents enjoyed immunity from being sued. The Colorado Supreme Court upheld the principle that the Regents are similar to judges, who enjoy "absolute immunity," which must be upheld in order to avoid an avalanche of suits by disgruntled litigants against judges. The Court reasoned that the Regents are a "quasi-judicial" body because they sometimes decide whether or not to punish university employees. The Court thus endowed the regents with something called "quasi-judicial absolute immunity."[70]

However, when briefly considering the merits of Churchill's claim that he was wrongfully terminated, the Court conceded that he may well have been justified in believing that the creation of the IC was a pretext to punish him for his constitutionally protected speech in the "little Eichmanns" essay. The Court provided the relevant precedent in the Colorado case law, *Lawley v. Department of Higher Education* (2001), to support the argument that even when an employee merits demotion or dismissal, the action is invalid if the employee was singled out capriciously. The Colorado Supreme Court made this concession to Churchill only to highlight that he might have been reinstated if he had protested his firing in a special grievance procedure—not a civil trial—under the Colorado Rules of Civil Procedure. This was, however, too little too late. As the Court well knew, the deadline for such a grievance is only 30 days after termination.[71]

My overall impression is that dismissal was a severe penalty for Churchill's unorthodox use of sources, which does not look like plagiarism in any conventional sense (reproducing the words and ideas of others without giving credit). A suspension for a year or two would have been appropriate. In such a scenario, he might have conceded that he had been careless. Of course, he would have continued to sustain his general argument that disease was used as a weapon in white colonization, but this is an argument that should not be dismissed. Nuances got lost in this controversy, under the political pressures to either villainize Churchill or portray him as an innocent victim. Horowitz's encouraged polarized thinking when he dubbed Churchill "incompetent" and "dishonest" and blamed the university for taking so long to fire him, calling this delay a proof of the "corruption of higher education."[72] The ABOR debate and the Churchill controversy conspired to politicize and polarize the discussion of academic freedom in the first decade of our century.

ABOR and the Pennsylvania Hearings: The "Marketplace of Ideas"

The most sustained set of legislative hearings about the ABOR occurred in 2005 and 2006.[73] Through House Resolution 177, Pennsylvania established a select committee "to examine the academic atmosphere" at state universities in the Commonwealth. The resolution reiterates many planks of the ABOR.

Academic freedom and intellectual diversity are values indispensable to the American colleges and universities . . . Students and faculty should be protected from the imposition of ideological orthodoxy . . . students are [to be] graded based on academic merit, without regard for ideological views . . .[74]

Representative Gibson Armstrong, a Republican from Lancaster County and a member of the select committee, stated that it is "time to stop indoctrination taking place under the guise of education on taxpayer-funded campuses."[75]

The transcripts of the Pennsylvania hearings contain some intellectual high points, notably in the testimony of the historian Joan Scott against the ABOR. As for Horowitz's own testimony, it bears out my description of his discourse as compulsively self-referential.

I view this issue in a personal way. I went to Columbia University in the McCarthy Fifties. My parents were Communists and I wrote my school papers from a Marxist point of view. Yet I was never singled out as a Communist the way conservative students are regularly singled out by their professors. In fact, I don't ever remember a professor expressing a political point of view in any class I ever had. I am grateful to my Columbia professors for their professionalism and wish that all students would have the same educational privilege of academic neutrality that I had. I hope you will urge Pennsylvania's institutions of higher learning to give their students a fair shake as well.[76]

Apart from the fact that Horowitz assumes that listeners are interested in his life and will trust his recollections, he conveniently does not mention that his parents lost their jobs because of legislative intervention in academic matters! Horowitz also seemed to be unaware that legislation rarely occurs unless it is supported by extensive factual findings. He provided no statistical basis on which the Pennsylvania legislators could assess the extent to which indoctrination is a problem. He cited only a few interviews, some of which had nothing to do with classroom teaching.

Here is a comment taken from an interview we conducted with a Temple student: "The Chairman of the History Department, who is my adviser, told me during advising that 'If Bush gets re-elected, we will have a fascist country.' He [told me] he will be scared for his survival and will consider possibly moving to Canada." That's scary coming from a history professor.[77]

The select committee held four public hearings. Horowitz spoke only at the last one on January 11, 2006. The initial framing of the case for turning the ABOR into law was articulated by the President of the National Association of Scholars (NAS), Steven Balch on November 9, 2005. He described the NAS as an organization founded in 1987, with about 3,500 members who are professors, administrators, and graduate students "committed to strengthening standards, open marketplace of ideas, and in general higher education improvement."[78] Balch offered no relevant data to justify legislation. He spent much time explaining that Democrats outnumber Republicans in American higher education, a fact that has no necessary bearing on how professors teach, as Joan Scott, who spoke after Balch on the same day, pointed out.

Balch made an intriguing point when he suggested that a similar statistical imbalance as concerns gender diversity would trigger calls for hiring more women and that universities never think of hiring more conservatives in academe. But this was off-topic. Horowitz himself did not claim that universities should hire faculty members on the basis of their political orientation. The ABOR concerns only the tone of the classroom. Balch attempted to prove that certain academic departments within the Pennsylvania public university system were ideologically biased, but his evidence was thin. He pulled ideologically suggestive phrases, such as "social justice," from departmental websites, but had no information about how professors applied such terms in their teaching. As members of the General Assembly pointed out in the questioning period, one cannot make assumptions about how people teach based on what departmental websites say. One Democratic Assembly member commented "To me the promotion of social and economic justice is a good thing and something that's done by conservatives and liberals alike."[79]

Balch's testimony was a miscellany of complaints against leftist bias in higher education. He criticized college summer reading assignments for including the book *Fast Food Nation* by Eric Schlosser. In his opinion, David McCulloch's *1776* would have been a better choice. He faulted universities for making a mantra of "diversity" which "is a big, big time word." He reported that he had done a Google search and found that the website of Pennsylvania State University contained the word "diversity" 31,600 times compared to 17,000 for "scholarship," 4,800 for "truth," and 2,540 for "liberty."[80] Balch called the office of multicultural affairs at one Pennsylvania campus "chillingly totalitarian"[81] because its website said that it "promotes" and "monitors" social justice in the university community. The term "totalitarian" was inappropriate, for administrators in multicultural affairs generally have no control over how professors teach.

Balch meant to prove that classroom indoctrination is taking place in a general academic environment in which leftist ideas about social justice are taken for granted. But his approach was too impressionistic for legislative purposes. Assembly members were justified in pointing out, as they did numerous times, that Balch provided no hard data to demonstrate the scale of the problems to which he referred.[82] Perhaps Balch's best answer to the absence of information was that the legislature itself should require the state campuses to conduct annual surveys of students about the biases of professors.[83] The state of Florida has recently required such a survey to take place. According to the Bill, the survey will discern "the extent to which competing ideas and perspectives are presented" in public universities and whether students and faculty "feel free to express beliefs and viewpoints on campus and in the classroom."[84]

When the internationally renowned feminist historian, Joan Scott, addressed the select committee after the legislators finished grilling Balch, the table was set for a devasting refutation. She did not waste the opportunity. Unlike Balch who spoke without a script and could not find his slides, Scott read from a prepared script and presented the committee members with copies. Her effect was professional and persuasive. Scott is a professor at the Institute for Advanced Study in Princeton, but she was testifying as Chair of the AAUP's Committee A on Academic Freedom. Scott was the clear winner in the Pennsylvania hearings. Its final report concluded that "adoption of a uniform statewide academic freedom policy, which was referenced by several testifiers, was not necessary."[85] Yet, a close examination of her remarks reveals some conceptual sleights of hand that were characteristic of the leftist rejoinder to Horowitz during the entire ABOR controversy.

At the center of Scott's critique of the ABOR is the term marketplace of ideas. Scott repeatedly characterized the academy with this expression, which Balch had also used to describe the NAS. The term is problematic. It's not clear how progressive academics such as Scott can use the market metaphor without implicitly endorsing something they do not actually support: the free market model of society. But if we grant that academics can be selective in choosing spheres of society they construe as a free market, there is still a major problem: the concept of a marketplace of ideas is a very poor fit for universities. A free market is a space in which competitors can easily enter, such as a public square in which anyone can give a speech or a social media site in which anyone can post an opinion. A university classroom is not a market because there is usually only one professor. Members of the general public cannot stream their ideas into this space. In fact, the market metaphor implies that monopolies will be regulated, but an ideologically passionate professor holds a kind of monopoly in the classroom.

Scott's effort to co-opt the market metaphor revealed contradictions in her position. She acknowledged that some academic departments are committed to promoting one theory over all other theories in the field. This is due, she stated, to "market decisions made by departments," which she rationalized as a "decision to specialize and so become distinctive in a particular field." Thus, some English departments, she noted, choose to specialize in "feminist criticism" to gain fame in this area and to attract students with a special interest in it.[86] A problem here is that the only "market" concept that will make this language cohere is the market in which graduate students choose the programs they wish to attend. For undergraduate students, which were of course Horowitz's main concern, this vision of departments branding themselves through specialization and political ideology does not offer much choice.

The impromptu nature of Scott's use of the market metaphor is evident when she attributes the phrase "marketplace of ideas" to John Stuart Mill, who did not use this phrase, and when she asserts that "the marketplace of ideas will sort out the good from the bad"[87]—which Mill patently did not believe. Mill did not suggest that freedom of thought secures the triumph of the best ideas. In fact, he believed that bad ideas tend to gain assent in a democratic society. Freedom of thought is needed so that those few individuals who manage to think independently are not extinguished by the repressive power of public opinion.[88]

The market figures again when Scott denounces Horowitz's appeal to the legislature to reform higher education:

> I said at the beginning of my remarks that the AAUP considers the Academic Bill of Rights . . . to be a misnomer as well as a mistake. In our view, it ironically infringes academic freedom in the very act of purporting to protect it . . . It recalls the kind of government intervention in the academy practiced by totalitarian governments. Historical examples are Japan, China, Nazi Germany, fascist Italy and the Soviet Union. These governments sought to control thought rather than permit a free marketplace of ideas.[89]

Scott mimetically produced the dichotomy used by Balch—open inquiry versus totalitarianism. Both sides were engaging in hyperbole.

From Anti-ABOR to Anti-BDS: Cary Nelson

As President of the AAUP from 2006 to 2012, Nelson defended political activism by professors in Women's Studies, Postcolonial Studies, and other politically radical fields by arguing that their activism accorded with a "consensus" in each discipline. He is now the leading American critic of BDS and argues that militant anti-Zionism has "corrupted" the very disciplines that he used to defend. This is obviously a significant shift, and I explore it in some depth. The change is not in the substance of Nelson's political views about Israel. One can be a leftist and a supporter of Israel. Nelson was presumably supportive of Israel in earlier phases of his career, but he did not write much about Israel. When Israel became one of his central preoccupations, the structure of his discourse on academic freedom changed.

The change lies in the epistemological arguments that Nelson wielded (and continues to wield) in his campaign against BDS. As a supporter of leftist activism in the classroom, it was convenient for him to insulate certain disciplines from criticism by arguing that each discipline determines what shall count as truth. Once combatting BDS became his chief concern, he began to refer to standards of knowing that are not discipline-based but universal.

Nelson's defense of the disciplines, when he was the AAUP President, not only contradicted his later view of the disciplines in his anti-BDS phase. It also contradicted certain views he held prior to becoming a leader of the AAUP, when he was a champion of "anti-disciplinarity." Though not on the scene when Black Studies and Women's Studies were founded, Nelson was a leader in the second generation of "studies" innovation: he was a founder of "Cultural Studies" in North America. In his own words, "There is a field called Cultural Studies that I have some credit for bringing to the United States and it evolved largely in Britain, people like Raymond Williams, Richard Hoggart, Stuart Hall."[90]

Cultural Studies, in the British variant that Nelson promoted, is informed by Marxism. One of its goals is to challenge the notion of high culture or pure culture. By using sociology, media studies, and economics, practitioners of Cultural Studies have aimed to show that aesthetic ideals (such as "great" literature) are inscribed in power relations. Nelson co-organized two large conferences that yielded landmark anthologies: *Marxism and the Interpretation of Culture* (1988) and *Cultural Studies* (1992). The essays in these volumes portray the academy as beholden to right-wing forces spreading capitalism and racism throughout American society. It is necessary to resist these forces by advocating radical social change, including the transformation of the disciplinary organization of the university, which sustains the conservative establishment.

Cultural Studies in the United Kingdom and the United States has been influenced by Antonio Gramsci's idea that revolutionizing the sphere of education is no less important than revolutionizing the sphere of production. The critique of the disciplines is also consistent with Foucault's idea that they underpin systems of classification that de-normalize marginalized groups in society. Since the academy is already politicized—constituted by conservative disciplines which mask themselves as intellectually neutral—it is necessary, for progressive academics to attack the disciplines. In the *Cultural Studies* volume, Nelson and his coeditors wrote that Cultural Studies is "actively and aggressively anti-disciplinary." Cultural Studies seeks not only to understand the world but to change it. And "the classroom" is "one place where cultural studies can make a difference."[91]

In *Manifesto of a Tenured Radical* (1997), Nelson devoted a chapter to "Progressive Pedagogy Without Apologies" The book is informed by Nelson's Marxism; his certitude that "late capitalism" and the corporatization of education is the source of higher education's most urgent problems. College teachers are "looking more and more like migrant factory labor—lacking health benefits, job security, retirement funds, and any influence over either their employment conditions or the goals of the institutions they work for."[92] The classroom should become a site of resistance against capitalism. In making his case for political advocacy in the classroom, Nelson takes an autobiographical approach reminiscent of Horowitz's preoccupation with self. The word "I" occurs ten times in the first paragraph of the chapter of *Manifesto* on teaching. Also, like Horowitz, Nelson portrays academic matters in a good-versus-evil framework. In this book, the evil is denoted by "capitalism" and "the right," terms used indiscriminately for virtually everything that Nelson finds politically and intellectually disagreeable.

The chapter on progressive pedagogy is about an undergraduate course Nelson offered at the University of Illinois on modern American poetry. Amidst many first-person effusions, he does not tell readers what year he taught the course, how large it was, how many times per week it met, what the format was, what the paper assignments were, what the syllabus was, or anything precise about the student demographics. The focus is on himself.

Nelson suggests that a political approach to teaching is not a choice but a necessity.

> With the Left in retreat across much of the postindustrialized world and with the Right—short of economic collapse—increasingly in control of American institutions, a critical and subversive alternative pedagogy seemed essential.[93]

A top-down political approach is evident:

> What I was not particularly interested in doing, I might point out, however, was letting the course be shaped primarily by an effort to honor my students' initial sense of their own needs . . . I had an agenda of discovery and political consciousness-raising for them.[94]

Nelson acknowledges that his political commitment turned off some students. He quotes one evaluation: "If this was to be a left-wing indoctrination course we should have been warned." Nelson does not begrudge the complaint. "For they had no choice about going along with the general program, which was a product of the readings I assigned and the topics I raised."[95] Nelson admits that he transgressed academic convention. "I realize, of course, that many faculty members are immensely uncomfortable with this sort of unashamed advocacy."[96]

Nelson's argument for activism in the classroom hinges on the assumption that there is no middle ground between radical and conservative approaches to poetry. He repeatedly contrasts his own interest in how one can explore racial inequality through poetry with the "canonical" approach that allegedly silences everyone who wishes to discuss the relationship between politics and literature. He also simplifies the attendant visions of academic freedom.

> There appears to be an emerging New Right consensus about the need to restrict academic freedom in universities. The argument goes something like this: these radicals are abusing their free speech privileges; they've given up their right to them. Academic freedom, in other words, is valid as long as you do not exercise it.[97]

According to Nelson, professors who claim they are able to keep politics out of the classroom are part of the conservative establishment. They wear a "mask of disinterested objectivity" only to insinuate their conservative religious and political convictions. Nelson claimed that explicit advocacy is the honest approach. "I prefer to let my students know where I stand."[98] Here again we can see his tendency to exclude the middle ground.

Opposition to leftist political activism in the classroom, he can only imagine, is a form of conservative activism. One wonders what he would make of Jeffrey Wallen (in the Spacks volume), not to mention Edward Said (whose views against politics in the classroom are discussed in the last chapter of this book).

It is hardly surprising that Nelson ends up critiquing his own students. "I was never really successful in getting them to see how cultural investments in race, class, and gender affected the way they evaluated poems." Since only a few students found his anti-capitalist and anti-racist fervor captivating, he characterizes them as "students of rather unreflective prosperity, unaware that their privileges were class specific."[99] He even made a point of polarizing the classroom along political lines.

> [I]t was generally clear where I stood and clear as well that I was politically allied with some students and not others . . . I could live with the resulting tensions more easily than I could live with suppressing my values in the classroom.[100]

The NAS Strikes Back

In 2006, the self-styled tenured radical became the President of the AAUP. Nelson profoundly influenced this organization, which had long upheld the anti-political ortho-doxy. Under his leadership, the AAUP encouraged universities to revise language in their academic freedom policies that came from the 1915 "Declaration," which Nelson bluntly described as outdated. He was especially opposed to that part which exhorted professors to refrain from the one-sided presentation of controversies. Nelson maintained that the "Declaration" was obsolete because America had changed. In 1915, he asserted, American society was predominantly rural; young people came off the farm to the university with little experience of the world. There was no television or radio. Today's students, he argued, do not need to be taught the different sides of a controversy because they grow up in cities and have the internet.[101] "The naive and uninformed undergraduate largely disappeared. Today's students arrive well stocked with their own political opinions and ready to defend them."[102]

Nelson and the AAUP encouraged universities to revise their academic freedom policies. Penn State became a hotly debated case. In December 2010, the faculty senate rewrote "Policy HR64: Academic Freedom." The National Association of Scholars was now led by Peter Wood, a highly accomplished academic. Wood was a former anthropology professor at Boston University as well as former provost of The King's College, a Christian liberal arts college in New York City. The following extract from the revised HR64 is from a version which the NAS put together. The words in bold letters represent additions to the old policy. Deletions from the old policy are in strike-through letters.

> ~~It is not the function of a faculty member in a democracy to indoctrinate his/her students with ready-made conclusions on controversial subjects. The~~ Faculty members **are** ~~is~~ expected to **educate** ~~train~~ students to think for themselves, and to **facilitate** ~~provide them~~ access to ~~those~~ **relevant** materials which they need to **form their own opinions** ~~if they are to think intelligently. Hence, in giving instruction upon controversial matters the f~~Faculty members **are** ~~is~~ expected to **present information fairly**, ~~be of a fair and judicial mind,~~ and to set forth justly, ~~without supersession or innuendo, the~~ divergent opinions ~~of other investigators~~ **that arise out of scholarly methodology and professionalism.**

~~No faculty member may claim as a right the privilege of discussing in the classroom controversial topics outside his/her own field of study. The faculty member is normally bound not to take advantage of his/her position by introducing into the classroom provocative discussions of irrelevant subjects not within the field of his/her study.~~[103]

The title of the NAS article in which HR64 appears with tracked changes is not moderate: "Free to Indoctrinate: The AAUP Applauds Penn State's Retreat from Academic Freedom." But no other news report on HR64 allowed readers to see exactly what was at stake textually. Nelson, in contrast, engaged in the tactic of caricature. He urged Penn State to revise HR66, describing it as

> especially bad . . . McCarthy-era rhetoric . . . Like Horowitz, Penn State failed at the same time to conceptualize the sense in which all teaching and research is funda-mentally and deeply political . . . What Penn State ended up with is nothing less than thought control.[104]

Nelson held the NAS in disdain. He described members of the NAS as "old and irrelevant." The NAS was founded by a small group of Jews" but

> soon began to attract more than its fair share of university WASPS, typically failed academics, buzzing about the decaying remains of their careers. They are professionally and emotionally focused on resentment, and the NAS was founded to tell them it's not their fault.

The NAS "worships at the altar of capitalism."[105]
Wood has persistently denied that the NAS is a politically conservative organization.

> I am used to the NAS being cast as a voice of 'the right,' it isn't. That's a default char-acterization we gain because we frequently criticize positions struck by the academic left. A 'left' by logic seems to require a 'right,' but that's a linguistic illusion applied to the participants in these controversies.[106]

He argued that "an If-you-are-not-for-us-you're-against-us logic" had taken over debate in the American academy. The "political left" has "launched a campaign to narrow the range of legitimate discussion." "If you were not visibly in favor of the new agenda, you stood at risk of being stigmatized as an extremist so far from the intellectual mainstream that your views could be ignored." The NAS favors "not the language of William F. Buckley, but the language of Bacon, Locke, and Montesquieu," and the group draws inspiration "not from Barry Goldwater but from figures such as Jefferson, de Tocqueville, and Weber."

> The disappearance of the intellectual past into a zone that is partly forbidden, partly mocked has occurred . . . across many disciplines. The humanities and the so-cial sciences, in other words, live under not only the reign of political correct-ness writ large, but each has its own microcosm—or micro-prison—of political correctness.[107]

Wood has published scholarly work about the tendency toward extreme polarization in contemporary America. In a *Bee in the Mouth: Anger in America Now* (2006), he argued that

American culture, both popular and intellectual, has recently elevated the public expression of anger into a sign of good character. In a chapter on the rhetoric of political blogs, he wrote:

> Perhaps the dominant form of political blogging in general (Left and Right) is a sassy, hyperarticulate belittling of one's opponents. The blogger's rhetorical stance is one of self-confident control over the facts and sneering disregard for the intelligence and honesty of those he criticizes . . . If in your anger you reduce your opponent to the status of someone unworthy or unable to engage in legitimate exchange, real politics come to an end.[108]

A natural response is to argue that anger is human, and it has been a feature of American culture from the beginning. The point of Wood's book is that "The anger which we see and hear around us differs in character from the anger of previous epochs."[109] Whether Wood demonstrates this convincingly is not the question here. Nor is the question of whether the NAS's opposition to classroom advocacy is the "correct" position. The point is that Wood set out to frame the debate about academic freedom differently than others: less about the self (in contrast to Horowitz and Nelson, his arguments do not take the form of autobiography), and more rigorous in the identification of the issues under dispute.

At its conference on January 9, 2009, the NAS staged a debate between Nelson and Wood on "The Meaning of Academic Freedom." At the center of contention was the role of academic disciplines in maintaining professional standards. Nelson considered himself to be an authority on what "constitutes" knowledge. He repeatedly invoked his own stature as a founder of Cultural Studies and affirmed that it should be considered axiomatic that all truth is "culturally constructed."

> In my view and the view of many others, all human understanding is culturally constructed. We have no unmediated access to any facts, so consequently I teach the cultural construction of gender as true just as I teach the cultural construction of all meaning as a fact of human life. . . [110]

(Though Wood did not make this specific point, one wonders how, if there are no unmediated "facts," one can say that "the cultural construction of all meaning" is itself a "fact" of human life.)

Nelson's strategy was to legitimize the radical disciplines on the basis of their disciplinarity: the shared standards of those in a specialized field. Even though he had called for an "anti-disciplinary" posture before becoming President of the AAUP, he now consecrated disciplinarity. His key move was to link the proposition that all understanding is "culturally constructed" to a vision of the academic disciplines as an array of "cultures," each of which is entitled to uphold its own vision of reality. In the university, he stated, "disciplinary consensus is the only standard around."

> Almost all permanent faculty at four-year colleges and universities have undergone specialized disciplinary training. For better or for worse, an academic discipline provides the primary context and intellectual horizon for the work most faculty members do . . . The reality is the overwhelming majority of faculty are ill equipped to think outside their disciplinary box.[111]

Pressed by Wood, who provided blatant examples of ideological excess in university teaching, Nelson acknowledged that "academic disciplines can pass through periods of relatively unreflective, even dogmatic, conviction and advocacy." But "a period of inflexible and oppositional conviction is sometimes necessary to a field's development." Academic disciplines, he stated, tend to be "self-healing." To support this optimism, he noted that some Women Studies programs had renamed themselves Gender and Women Studies and that some of these were chaired by men.[112]

Nelson conceded to Wood that professors sometimes misused their power in the classroom. But Nelson did not think that any standards for teaching could be defined outside of the disciplines.

> Disciplines are for the foreseeable future the only real models for organizing faculty we have. Thus, Freedom in the Classroom [an AAUP report, discussed below] relies on disciplinary consensus as a guide to what faculty can require their students to master, [and] what students have to comprehend and apply.[113]

Wood did not accept the sovereignty of the disciplines. He argued that some disciplines have more "epistemological warrant"—more rigor, more self-criticism—than others. Nelson replied that epistemological warrant is also "culturally constructed and managed, not an absolute ontological condition."[114] Yet, Wood had not spoken of "absolute" knowledge. He simply held that some disciplines are more reliable and less influenced by political ideology. Nelson would not admit degrees here, and Wood did not hesitate to treat Nelson as he had treated bloggers in his book about anger: he accused Nelson of repeatedly excluding the possibility of a spectrum of positions on any given question.[115] According to Wood, protecting the rights of students is no less important than protecting the autonomy of disciplines.

> Academic freedom needs to protect students from bombastic blowhards and self-righteous bullies in the faculty . . . Academic freedom needs to protect itself against its misappropriation as a mask for anti-intellectual dogmas . . . We want conflicting opinions, lacunae, the things we don't know, the gaps, those areas of continuing uncertainty which account perhaps for most of what we deal with at least in the social sciences and humanities but a fair amount of the natural sciences as well . . . [Academic freedom] doesn't cover advocacy dressed up as scholarship, it doesn't cover ideology of the sort that short-circuits doubts, skepticism, countervailing evidence and fair questions.[116]

This debate also played out in a written form. The AAUP published a "Report on Freedom in the Classroom" (2007) which included, "It is not indoctrination for professors to expect students to comprehend ideas and apply knowledge that are accepted as true within a relevant discipline." The NAS displayed the entire report on its website, with interlinear commentary composed by Wood and Balch. Among the NAS comments:

> Not just women's studies, but many disciplines are today dominated by people who uphold what are easily recognizable as political premises. This is even more true of sub-disciplines, and it should be noted that the AAUP gives no account of what a "discipline" is and where we might reasonably expect to draw the boundaries.

A field such as "post-colonial studies," for example, announces a political premise in its very name. It asserts that the economic and social problems of the third
world are primarily the result of continuing post-colonial domination by the West.
In the AAUP view, post-colonial studies ought to be free to determine on its
own what is "accepted as true," with no regard for any analyses or views developed by experts who may know a great deal about third world history, economy,
and culture but who can be denied a hearing because they are not "post-colonial
theorists."

The contemporary university has many of these self-enclosed enclaves that create
their own islands of "knowledge" and that actively discourage the consideration of
views not derived from the island's own premises . . .

The NAS, along with many other critics, is skeptical of this extreme elevation of
"disciplinary privilege" over shared standards that transcend disciplines. Those shared
standards are a powerful corrective to the tendency of fields to become the comfortable
preserves of "true belief."[117]

The Salaita Affair

Soon after Nelson completed his service as President of the AAUP, he became embroiled
in the storm over the unhiring of Steven Salaita at the University of Illinois, Urbana-
Champaign. The Salaita affair was one of the most publicized academic freedom contro-
versies since the Ward Churchill affair. In October 2013, Salaita was offered a position in
Indian Studies. He was scheduled to begin in August 2014. In July, during a war between
Gaza and Israel, Salaita posted hundreds of anti-Israel tweets, which led to accusations of
antisemitism. When University of Illinois Chancellor Phyllis Wise revoked the job offer,
Salaita sued. The university settled for $875,000.

Nelson was no longer the AAUP president, but he was a member of Committee A on
Academic Freedom. One might have expected him not to comment, as some of his critics
pointed out; but he supported revoking the job offer. He went on to become one of the
leading American critics of academic anti-Zionism. In the process of reorienting from
anti-capitalism to anti-Zionism, he did an about-face on the question of whether academic
disciplines can be trusted to maintain intellectual rigor and professional ethics. He also
walked back on the AAUP's defense of extramural utterances. His views have come to
sound much like those who prosecuted Ward Churchill, and much like those of NAS
President Peter Wood.

Nelson stated that he knew of "no other senior faculty member tweeting such venomous
statements—and certainly not in such an obsessively driven way. There are scores of over-
the-top Salaita tweets."[118] Nelson noted that in response to the kidnapping of three Israeli
teenagers, Salaita wrote, "You may be too refined to say it, but I'm not: I wish all the fuck-
ing West Bank settlers would go missing." Nelson stated:

Salaita condenses boycott-divestment-sanctions wisdom into a continuing series
of sophomoric, bombastic, or anti-Semitic tweets . . . More recently he has said
"if Netanyahu appeared on TV with a necklace made from the teeth of Palestinian
children, would anyone be surprised?" (July 19, 2014) and "By eagerly conflating
Jewishness and Israel, Zionists are partly responsible when people say anti-Semitic shit
in response to Israeli terror" (July 18, 2014).

Nelson argued that the tweets were not merely extramural expressions but reflected on Salaita's qualities as a colleague and teacher.

> His tweets are the sordid underbelly, the more frank and revealing counterpart, to his more extended arguments about Middle Eastern history and the Israeli/Palestinian conflict. They are likely to shape his role on campus when 2015's Israeli Apartheid Week rolls around. I am told he can be quite charismatic in person, so he may deploy his tweeting rhetoric at public events on campus . . . What would he say if the Arab/Israeli conflict were to come up in a class he was teaching on Arab-American fiction? Would he welcome dissent to his views? . . . I see no good reason to offer a permanent faculty position to someone whose discourse crosses the line into anti-Semitism.[119]

Finally, Nelson observed that Salaita had not yet begun his academic appointment. In the period between the job offer and the commencement of the job, the university could revoke the offer.[120]

John K. Wilson, the editor of the blog *Academe*, disagreed. "One thing should be clear: Salaita was fired. I've been turned down for jobs before, and it never included receiving a job offer, accepting that offer, moving halfway across the country, and being scheduled to teach classes."[121] Wilson wrote that Nelson was "completely wrong." "To endorse the firing of a scholar based on the politics of his tweets is not only absolutely intolerable, but it goes against everything Cary has stood for his entire career. It is utterly incomprehensible to me."[122] The President and Vice President of the AAUP released a statement distancing themselves from Nelson.[123]

Stanley Fish's comment on Nelson is also revealing. Fish is an eminent English scholar and postmodernist theorist. He is the rare case, in our time, of a postmodernist thinker who believes that radical skepticism concerning the possibility of truth militates *against* political advocacy in the classroom (his position being very similar to Max Weber's, as described in the previous chapter). The author of *Save the World on Your Own Time* (2012), Fish was in agreement with Horowitz that classroom indoctrination is a widespread problem, created primarily by the academic left; but Fish never supported legislative intervention. At the time of the Salaita affair, Fish was a professor of law at Florida International University. He would soon publish *Versions of Academic Freedom: From Professionalism to Revolution* (2014), a deeply philosophical inquiry discussed in the Introduction of this book. As reported in *Inside Higher Education*, Fish responded to the unhiring of Salaita by stating that

> an appointment should be revoked only if something in the scholar's application, such as a letter from a reviewer, suggests that the professor is professionally incompetent, or uses his political views to "enlist" students, rather than educate them. Tweets alone—however uncomfortable they could make students or colleagues—aren't enough.

Fish said of Nelson, "I'm usually much to the right of him and he's much to the left of me, and in this instance we seem to have traded places a bit."[124]

Since the Salaita controversy, Nelson has published prolifically against BDS. The degradation of academic disciplines is a theme in these writings. In "Conspiracy Pedagogy on Campus: BDS Advocacy and Academic Freedom" (2017), he argued that Women's Studies, Post-Colonial Studies, and other disciplines had ceased to function in an academic manner. These were the same disciplines he defended in the debate with Wood. In fact, he had glibly called postcolonialism "a neutral political category" and flatly rejected the NAS's contention that this field was politicized at all.[125] In contrast, he argued in "Conspiracy Pedagogy" that the radical disciplines are guilty of "the political corruption of the class-room."[126] Political activism has replaced academic inquiry.

> It [BDS] has helped turn some entire academic departments and disciplines against Israel and some faculty members in the humanities and soft social sciences into anti-Israel fanatics.[127]

> What this suggests is that some disciplines—without having the requisite expertise—have reached a virtual consensus about the truth of Israel and the Israeli-Palestinian conflict . . . A political scientist might recognize the need to acknowledge both the Israeli and Palestinian narratives and treat them each as possessing validity. In cultural anthropology, throughout literary studies and ethnic studies, in much of African American studies, Native American studies, and women's studies, and of course, throughout Middle East studies, that is no longer the case.[128]

Nelson's condemnation of the disciplines is now indistinguishable from the position of the NAS: the university is "indoctrinating" students. In "BDS: A Short History," Nelson wrote:

> Antisemitism has found a home in the humanities and social sciences, taking over entire departments and disciplines. The classroom is turning into a space not for exploring the complexities of the Middle East but for *indoctrinating* students to view Israel and Zionism as the embodiment of modern evil.[129] (italics added)

When he believed that political activism in the classroom was in line with his anti-capitalist and anti-racist commitments, Nelson saw no need for limits on classroom advocacy. When the target of advocacy became Israel, which he strongly supports, the politicized classroom became a problem. Having steered the AAUP away from the principles of 1915, Nelson evolved into a defender of intellectual diversity and professional self-restraint. His career as the most prolific commentator on academic freedom over the past thirty years illustrates the trend toward polarization in American academic life. It also illustrates the difficulties we all face in working out a consistent theory of academic freedom.

Notes

1 David Horowitz, *Radical Son: A Generational Odyssey* (New York: The Free Press, 1997), 8.
2 AAUP, "General Declaration of Principles of Academic Freedom and Academic Tenure," in "General Report of the Committee on Academic Freedom and Tenure," *Bulletin of the American Association of University Professors*, vol. 1, no. 1 (December, 1915), 33–34; for the words "impartial" and "disinterested," 22, 25, 29, 30, 33.
3 AAUP, "Freedom in the Classroom" (June, 2007), https://www.aaup.org/report/freedom-classroom.
4 David Horowitz, *Corporations and the Cold War* (New York: Monthly Review Press, 1969), 14–15.
5 Cary Nelson, "The Corporate University," Nelson and Stephen Watt, *Academic Keywords: A Devil's Dictionary for Higher Education* (New York: Routledge, 1999), online at http://www.cary-nelson.org/nelson/corpuniv.html.
6 Cary Nelson, "The Meaning of Academic Freedom," a debate with Peter Wood, January 9, 2009: https://www.youtube.com/watch?v=bQhiuU2Wtns, at minute 24. The debate is captured in four videos. This is the first and will be cited henceforth as Part 1. Nelson's ideas on disciplinarity are discussed in detail in this chapter.

7 Cary Nelson, "Conspiracy Pedagogy on Campus: BDS Advocacy and Academic Freedom," *Academic Engagement Network Pamphlet Series*, No. 2, January 2017, 15. Republished in Andrew Pessin and Dora S. Ben-Atar (eds.), *Anti-Zionism on Campus: The University, Free Speech, and BDS* (Bloomington: Indiana University Press, 2018). Chapter 14.

8 William W. Van Alstyne, "Academic Freedom and the First Amendment in the Supreme Court of the United States: An Unhurried Historical Review," *Law and Contemporary Problems*, vol. 53, no. 3 (Summer, 1990), 137, note 198.

9 More characteristic is Edward Shils, "Do We Still Need Academic Freedom?" *The American Scholar*, vol. 62, no. 2 (Spring, 1993), who upholds the distinction between academics and politics while stating that it is wrong "to conflate academic freedom with freedom of speech" (192).

10 Daniel Gordon, "Is Free Speech an Academic Value? Is Academic Freedom a Constitutional Value?" *Florida International University Law Review*, vol. 14, no. 4 (2021), 717–720 (comparing Van Alstyne and Fish).

11 Van Alstyne, "Academic Freedom," 93 (italics added).

12 Ibid, 106.

13 Ibid, (citing Douglas in *Adler*).

14 *Advocacy in the Classroom: Problems and Possibilities*, ed. Patricia Meyer Spacks (New York: St. Martin's Press, 1996), xiii.

15 Miles Brand, "The Professional Obligations of Classroom Teachers," in ibid, 8.

16 Ibid, 11.

17 Ibid, 14.

18 Ibid, 4.

19 Ibid, 17.

20 Michael A. Olivas, "Fear and Loathing in the Classroom: Faculty and Student Rights in a Comparative Context," in *Advocacy in the Classroom*, Spacks (ed.), 32.

21 Ibid, 29.

22 Ibid, 32.

23 *Cohen v. San Bernardino College*, 883 F Supp 1407 (U.S. District Court of California), at 1418–1420; cited by Olivas, 37–38.

24 Nadine Strossen, "First Amendment and Civil Liberties Traditions of Academic Freedom," in *Advocacy in the Classroom*, ed. Spacks, 72 (citing a 1994 Policy Guide of the American Civil Liberties Union).

25 Ibid, 73.

26 Ibid, 76.

27 Jeffrey Wallen, "Teachers, Not Advocates: Toward an Open Classroom," in *Advocacy in the Classroom*, ed. Spacks, 225–228.

28 Felicia Ackerman, "Be Reasonable and Do It My Way: Advocacy in the College Classroom," in *Advocacy in the Classroom*, ed. Spacks, 290.

29 Helen Moglen, "Unveiling the Myth of Neutrality: Advocacy in the Feminist Classroom," in *Advocacy in the Classroom*, ed. Spacks, 205, 209–211.

30 Michael Bérubé, "Professional Advocates: When is "Advocacy" Part of One's Vocation?" in *Advocacy in the Classroom*, ed. Spacks, 187–188 (italics in original).

31 Ibid, 187, 193–194.

32 Louis Menand, "Culture and Advocacy," in *Advocacy in the Classroom*, ed. Spacks, 117–118.

33 Ibid, 119.

34 Ibid, 121–122.

35 Richard Rorty, "Does Academic Freedom Have Philosophical Presuppositions?" in *The Future of Academic Freedom*, ed. Louis Menand (Chicago: University of Chicago Press, 1996), 33.

36 Thomas Haskell, "Justifying the Rights of Academic Freedom in the Era of 'Power/Knowledge,'" in *The Future of Academic Freedom,* ed. Menand. 73.

37 Ibid, 58.

38 David Rabban, "Can Academic Freedom Survive Postmodernism?" *California Law Review*, vol. 86, no. 6 (December, 1998), 1377–1389.

39 Michael Berubé, "Academic Freedom, Fragile as Ever," in *The Academic Bill of Rights Debate*, ed. Stephen H. Aby (Westport: Praeger, 2007), 42; Rudy Fenwick and John Zipp, "Are Faculty Too Liberal? Are Universities Too Corporate?", in ibid, 92.

40 Aby, "Academic Freedom in Perilous Times," in ibid, 1.

41 David Horowitz, *Indoctrination U: The Left's War against Academic Freedom* (New York: Encounter Books, 2007), 8.

42 David Horowitz, *Reforming Our Universities: The Campaign for an Academic Bill of Rights* (Washington: Regnery Publishing, 2010), 33.

43 Cited by Horowitz, in ibid; Horowitz is meticulous in footnoting the accusations against him; in this case, by William Scheuerman, "Academic Bill of Rights: A Stealth Attack on Truth," March 2005. But the link he provides to the article has expired.

44 Cited by Horowitz in ibid, 80; Larkin's "David Horowitz's War on Rational Discourse," appeared in *IHE* on April 25, 2005.

45 Horowitz, *Reforming*, 7.

46 Ibid, 9–10.

47 David Horowitz, *Radical Son: A Generational Odyssey* (New York: Touchstone, 1997), 102.

48 Ibid, 250.

49 Ibid, 274, 283.

50 Ibid, 315, 321, 360.

51 Ibid, 2.

52 David Horowitz, "Academic Bill of Rights," https://studentsforacademicfreedom.org/basic-texts/academic-bill-of-rights/. Horowitz, *Indoctrination U*, says he wrote it in 2003; see xiv. The version currently online is identical to that which Horowitz presented to legislators in 2003–2006.

53 Gerald Graff, "Advocacy in the Classroom—Or the Curriculum? A Response," in *Advocacy in the Classroom*, ed. Spacks, 426–427.

54 Fenwick and Zipp, "Are Faculty Too Liberal?", 96.

55 David Horowitz, *One-Party Classroom: How Radical Professors Indoctrinate Students and Undermine Our Democracy* (New York: Crown Forum, 2009), 3; citing Bettina Aptheker, *Intimate Politics: How I Grew Up Red, Fought for Free Speech, and became a Feminist Rebel* (Emeryville: Seal Press, 2006), 473.

56 Ibid.

57 Ibid, 5–6.

58 Jacob Gershman, "New Grievance Policy Includes 3 Grounds for Complaints," *New York Sun*, April 12, 2005, http://www.nysun.com/new-york/new-grievance-policy-includes-3-grounds/12052.

59 Quoted in "Report on the Termination of Ward Churchill," by the Colorado Committee to Protect Faculty Rights, a standing committee of the Colorado Conference of the AAUP, November 2, 2011, 27.

60 "General Declaration," 20.

61 The key case is *Pickering v. Board of Education* (1968).

62 AAAUP, "Statement on Extramural Utterances," part of the Report of Committee A, 1964–1965, *AAUP Bulletin*, vol. 51, no. 3 (June, 1965), 239.

63 "Report of the Investigative Committee of the Standing Committee on Research Misconduct at the University of Colorado at Boulder Concerning Allegations of Academic Misconduct against Professor Ward Churchill," May, 9, 2006, 102.

64 Ibid, 4.

65 Ibid.

66 Rubén Hernández-Murillo and John Knowles, "Racial Profiling or Racist Policing? Bounds Tests i Aggregate Data," *International Economic Review*, vol. 45, no. 3 (July, 2004), see esp. 960, note 2.

67 Report on the Termination of Ward Churchill," 14. The late date of this report (2011) stems from the fact the central office of the AAUP, in Washington, DC, chose not investigate Churchill's complaint. The Colorado branch then acted on its own; see ibid, 15.

68 Ibid, 7.

69 Ibid, 10.

70 Churchill v. University of Colorado at Boulder, 2012 CO 54.

71 Ibid, 36. The difference between a trial and the special procedure is that the former allows one to sue for damages; the latter can lead only to reinstatement. And as mentioned, the latter has a strict deadline.

72 Horowitz, *One-Party Classroom*, 37; see also *Reforming Our Universities*, 111–116.

73 Mark Smith, "In Search of a Problem: The Student Academic Freedom Hearings in Pennsylvania," in *The Academic Bill of Rights Debate*, ed. Aby, 134.

74 The General Assembly of Pennsylvania, House Resolution No. 177, July 5, 2005. Printer's no. 2553, 1–3.

75 Cited by Smith, "In Search of a Problem," 134–135 (August 10, 2006, e mail from Armstrong to Smith).

76 While I was able to obtain transcripts of most of the Pennsylvania hearings from state archive, I was not able to get Horowitz's testimony in this form. His testimony on January 11, 2006, was printed in *Front Page Magazine* and then reprinted in the *History News Network*: https://historynewsnetwork.org/article/20387.

77 Ibid.

78 Transcript of Public Hearing of Select Committee on Academic Freedom in Higher Education, The Commonwealth of Pennsylvania House of Representatives, held in Pittsburgh, November 9, 2005, 7.

79 Ibid, 118 (comment by Representative Daniel Surra).

80 Ibid, 74.

81 Ibid, 77.

82 Ibid, 98, 147, 153, 156, 197.

83 Ibid, 154.

84 Ana Ceballos, "New Florida Law Requires Colleges to Survey Students About Their Beliefs: State's Governor Suggests Budget Cuts If Colleges are Found to be 'Indoctrinating' Students," *The Atlanta Journal-Constitution*, June 24, 2021; https://www.clickorlando.com/news/local/2021/06/23/new-florida-law-requires-state-colleges-to-survey-students-on-views-beliefs/.

85 "Final Report of the Select Committee on Academic Freedom in Higher Education," November 4, 2008, 12; https://studentsforacademicfreedom.org/pennsylvania-academic-freedom-hearings/final-report-of-the-select-committee-on-academic-freedom-in-higher-education/.

86 Transcript of Public Hearing, 170–171.

87 Ibid 186.

88 Nishi Shah, "Why Censorship is Self-Undermining: John Stuart Mill's Neglected Argument for Free Speech," *The Aristotelian Society*, suppl. vol. XCV (2021), 71–96; esp. 93.

89 Transcript of Public Hearing, 186–187.

90 Cary Nelson, debate with Peter Wood, "The Meaning of Academic Freedom," 3rd video of the debate, https://www.youtube.com/watch?v=itsfgIgEWBI, at minute 5.

91 Cary Nelson, Paula A. Treichler, and Lawrence Grossberg, "Cultural Studies: An Introduction," in *Cultural Studies*, ed. Nelson, Treichler, Grossberg (New York: Routledge, 1992), 2, 5.

92 Cary Nelson, *Manifesto of a Tenured Radical*, 154.

93 Ibid, 78.

94 Ibid, 79.

95 Ibid, 79–80.

96 Ibid, 80.

97 Ibid, 82.

98 Ibid, 80.

99 Ibid, 82.

100 Ibid, 83–84.

101 Debate with Peter Wood, 3rd video, minute 6.

102 Ibid; see also Cary Nelson, *No University Is an Island* (New York: NYU Press, 2010), 173–174.

103 Ashley Thorne, "Free to Indoctrinate: The AAUP Applauds Penn State's Retreat from Academic Freedom," December 14, 2010. https://www.nas.org/blogs/article/free_to_indoctrinate_the_aaup_applauds_penn_states_retreat_from_academic_fr

104 Nelson, *No University is an Island*, 189–190.

105 Cary Nelson, "National Association of Scholars," in *Academic Keywords: A Devil's Dictionary of Higher Education*, eds. Cary Nelson and Stephen Watt (New York: Routledge,1999), 185–186.

106 Peter Wood, "Is Academic Freedom a License to Indoctrinate?" December 30, 2010. https://www.nas.org/blogs/article/is_academic_freedom_a_license_to_indoctrinate

107 Peter Wood, "Is NAS Conservative?" March 27, 2008. https://www.nas.org/blogs/article/is_nas_conservative

108 Peter Wood, *A Bee in the Mouth: Anger in America* Now (New York: Encounter Books, 2006), 242.

109 Ibid, 2.

110 Nelson debate with Wood, video 1, https://www.youtube.com/watch?v=bQhiuU2Wtns; at minutes 18–19.

111 Ibid, at minute 24.

112 Ibid, at minute 20.

113 Ibid, at minute 23.
114 Ibid, at minute 24.
115 Cary Nelson debate with Peter Wood, video 2, at minute 27.
116 Ibid, at minutes 10–14.
117 Steven Balch and Peter Wood, "A, Response to the AAUP's Report, 'Freedom in the Classroom,' September 21, 2007; https://www.nas.org/blogs/article/a_response_to_the_aaups_report_freedom_in_the_classroom.
118 Collen Flaherty, "In a Hurricane," *Inside Higher Education*, August 14, 2014; https://www.insidehighered.com/news/2014/08/15/cary-nelson-faces-backlash-over-his-views-controversial-scholar (quoting interview with Nelson).
119 Cary Nelson, "An Appointment to Reject," *Inside Higher Education*, August 8, 2014, https://www.insidehighered.com/views/2014/08/08/essay-defends-university-illinois-decision-not-hire-steven-salaita (for all quotations following the previous footnote).
120 Ibid.
121 https://www.insidehighered.com/views/2014/08/08/essay-criticizing-u-illinois-blocking-controversial-faculty-hire.
122 Cited by Flaherty, "In a Hurricane."
123 Rudy Fichtenbaum and Henry Reichman, "AAUP Officers' Statement on Case of Steven Salaita," August 7, 2014; https://academeblog.org/2014/08/07/aaup-officers-statement-on-case-of-steven-salaita/.
124 Flaherty, "In a Hurricane." Of the two quotes, the second is a quote by Fish. The first also appears to be a quote by Fish, for it is preceded by "he said." But since quotation marks are missing, this may be an edited version of a comment by Fish.
125 Nelson, Debate with Wood, video 2, at minute 14.
126 Cary Nelson, "Conspiracy Pedagogy on Campus: BDS Advocacy and Academic Freedom," *Academic Engagement Pamphlet Series*, no. 2 (January, 2017), 4. Republished in Andrew Pessin and Dora S. Ben-Atar, eds., *Anti-Zionism on Campus: The University, Free Speech, and BDS* (Bloomington: Indiana University Press, 2018), Chapter 14, 190–211.
127 Ibid.
128 Ibid, 8. The inconsistent use of capital letters in this quotation derives from the original text.
129 Ibid, but only in the 2018 version where it appears in the abstract, 190.

5 Israel, BDS, and Academic Freedom

Abstract

The Israel/Palestine conflict has proven to be intense and intractable not only in the Middle East but also on the American campus. The BDS (Boycott, Divestment, Sanctions) movement against Israel began in 2004 but became a major force on American campuses only when the American Studies Association endorsed it in 2014. Since then, BDS supporters have promoted a range of boycotts, including the shutting down of study-abroad programs in Israel, which have strained the concept of academic freedom. I examine how responses to BDS have mimetically involved boycotting the boycotters—notably in the anti-BDS laws implemented in 35 states. The result is a "boycott syndrome" extending across academe.

Introduction: Between Free Speech and Academic Freedom

If you boycott Israel, New York state will boycott you. Governor Andrew Cuomo[1]

This chapter explores a question raised by the growth of the Boycott, Divestment, Sanctions (BDS) movement against Israel, a question that has no easy answer. On what grounds can one condemn academic boycotts, such as prohibiting Israelis from attending an academic conference?

One option is to characterize BDS as antisemitic. I suggest, however, that the effort to link BDS to antisemitism relies too heavily on a fragile concept, the concept of "double standards." In addition, the antisemitism argument does not take into account that boycotts are being promoted on both sides of the Israel/Palestine debate. Zionists, for example, have attempted to exclude BDS supporters from speaking on college campuses.[2] Each side believes that it is justified in exiling the other from academe. Is there a case to be made against boycotts in general?

An apparent instrument for criticizing the urge to boycott one's opponents is the principle of free speech. In *The Conflict Over the Conflict: The Israel/Palestine Campus Debate,* Kenneth S. Stern makes a free-speech argument against both supporters of BDS and those supporters of Israel who wish to boycott the boycotters. Stern's penetrating discussion of the campus wars over Israel is a model for the present chapter. For one thing, neither he nor I seek to offer a "solution" to the Palestinian refugee problem. Like Stern, I am concerned not to solve a political conflict in the Middle East but to assess the radicalization of "the conflict over the conflict" in the American university: the tendency to adopt exclusionary policies toward one's adversaries.

DOI: 10.4324/9781003052685-6

However, I do not align with Stern when he upholds free speech as the corrective to the culture of cancelation.

> Students today live on campuses where "trigger warnings," "safe spaces," and a focus on "microaggressions" may be part of the culture. These concepts are not speech codes, but in many ways function to limit expression and intellectual inquiry on campus . . . For education to work, students and faculty must feel comfortable saying what they think, in an atmosphere that allows for testing and recalibration of ideas. It is better to try out ideas and be wrong than to spout what you think others professor be correct.[3]

Is the ideological excess that Stern complains about really an outcome of the *chilling* of free speech? Those who vociferously condemn Israel or defend it are not suffering from a fear of expressing themselves. Supporters of BDS and of Israel do not hold back their inner thoughts. The problem is not the lack of forthright speech; it is that each side is too preoccupied with its own exclusive political agenda.

Stern may well be right that a "testing and recalibration" of ideas is not taking place frequently enough in higher education, but this reluctance to engage with one's adversaries reflects a polarization of discourses—what Stern aptly calls "stridency"[4]—not the chilling of discourses. If the tone of campus life is being damaged by the tendency "to stake a side and fight a battle, rather than to think and learn,"[5] the answer cannot be more free speech. It must be less: a tempering of speech through academic ground rules which promote nuanced, scholarly, civil debate. What Stern really means to defend is a disciplining of free speech.

Again, Stern's book will prove to be exemplary for this chapter, but this one doubtful feature of his argument—his upholding of free speech as the answer—is worth elucidating further. Today there is a widespread tendency to confuse professional academic issues with free-speech issues. Stern devotes a whole chapter to reminding readers that offensive speech in the public sphere is constitutionally protected.

> The Supreme Court has also made it clear that there has to be some sort of emergency, an exigent circumstance, to stop an expression. If I stand at a street corner and say, "I think all blacks should be killed, " as awful as that expression is, it is legally protected.[6]

Really? If repeated over and over, it sounds like fighting words and breach of the peace to me. But more importantly, is a university a street corner? If it were, then by Stern's logic, all the hatred expressed by those who demonize Israel, and by those who attack anti-Zionists in kind, is protected speech. Free speech is not the solution to campus extremism but rather its precondition. The problem boils down to our current tendency to speak of "academic freedom" and "free speech" interchangeably. The advocates of boycotts against Israeli academics are exercising their right to speak. The owners of a journal who decide to purge the editorial board of Israelis are engaging in free speech. Likewise, when Zionist organizations call for the cancelation of courses that portray Israel as responsible for the Palestinian refugee problem, they are exercising their freedom of speech.[7] The effort by Zionists to ban Students for Justice in Palestine (a national organization with chapters on various campuses) takes the form of legal advocacy and is also a form of free speech.[8]

Stern's diagnosis rings true when he argues that too many students and professors are attracted to political ideologies that discourage the recognition of complexity. But nothing in American free-speech jurisprudence suggests that one's right to speak hinges on a duty to tolerate opposing ideas or to engage in complex debate. In *NAACP v. Claiborne Hardware* (1982), the Supreme Court held that politically motivated boycott movements are protected by the First Amendment. Other Supreme Court cases have interpreted freedom of speech under the First Amendment to mean: that students cannot be required to participate in civic ceremonies such as the flag salute[9]; that a newspaper cannot be required to print editorials which counterbalance its preferred point of view[10]; that the organizers of a parade cannot be required to include persons whose opinions they, the organizers, oppose.[11]

There is, in other words, a free-speech right to isolate oneself, a right to refrain from debate, a right to brandish slogans, and a right to belong to organizations whose members speak in unison. When students gather in a university to protest the mistreatment of Blacks by police officers, they are exercising free speech. When students gather to protest the appearance of a speaker whose views they oppose, they are doing the same. *It is not a prerequisite of free speech that one accord speech rights to one's adversaries.*[12]

We are left, then, with the principle of academic freedom as distinct from freedom of speech. If, like Stern, one wishes to admonish BDS supporters and militant Zionists for seeking to purge each other, one has no choice but to distinguish the two concepts. It is not a question of what is the intrinsically "right" definition of academic freedom. It is a question of how academic freedom must be defined, given the kind of work one wants the concept to do. Some may regard Stern's picture of polarization as overstated or will see the stridency on American campuses as nothing new, or nothing to be particularly worried about. Those who are not troubled are free to equate academic freedom with freedom of speech. Yet, those who seek to condemn boycotts as antithetical to the core values of the university need to abandon the commonly used free-speech argument. They must articulate academic freedom as a professional and ethical norm, in the fashion of the American Association of University Professors' founding document, the 1915 "General Declaration of Principles on Academic Freedom and Academic Tenure." This document spoke of the "responsibilities" which accompany academic freedom, such as the duty to include "the divergent opinions of other investigators" when addressing an unresolved controversy. (See Chapter 3 for a full discussion of the "Declaration.")

I suspect that many readers, regardless of their stance on Middle Eastern politics, appreciate the need for limits on the proliferation of exclusionary academic practices. This chapter seeks to be precise about the conceptual and rhetorical foundation of boycott practices in academe. It is by no means certain that these practices are inconsistent with the core values of academic life, and they are certainly consistent with freedom of speech. At the center of contention is the very idea of academic freedom, which has reached a state of intractable ambiguity in the twenty-first century, as I have already tried to show in Chapter 4. Some conceptions of academic freedom serve as a defense for boycott practices, but others serve as a means to reject boycotts. It is ultimately a question of choosing one version of the concept or another and recognizing the kinds of arguments one can make with each and the kind of arguments one cannot make.

Nelson's Case against BDS and the Pathos of Academic Freedom

The ambiguity of academic freedom can be explained in more concrete terms by considering the ideas, once again, of Cary Nelson. As President of the AAUP, he played a key role in opposing David Horowitz's campaign, beginning in 2003, for an Academic

Bill of Rights (ABOR). The ABOR was designed to prohibit professors from engaging in one-sided political advocacy in the classroom. Nelson steered the AAUP to a position quite different from its original position in the 1915 "Declaration." Through much of the twentieth century, the "Declaration" served as the basis for distinguishing academic inquiry and political advocacy. In Nelson's view, which summed up the spirit of political engagement characteristic of the American academic left since the 1960s, academics and politics are intertwined.

Yet, since stepping down from the AAUP, Nelson has emerged as the leading American critic of BDS. He has authored several books on BDS. In his fight against BDS, he has gravitated to the position that academics and politics can and should be separated. *Dreams Deferred: A Concise Guide to the Israeli-Palestinian Conflict and the Movement to Boycott Israel* contains much of Nelson's thinking about BDS. In the Introduction, Nelson makes it eminently clear he does not defend all of Israel's policies and that he supports a two-state resolution of the Palestinian conflict. He argues that the BDS movement is counterproductive to political change and compromise because, "All of the BDS movement's nationally prominent spokespersons make it clear they believe Israel has no legitimacy as a state and no right to exist."[13] He quotes BDS founder Omar Barghouti and several other BDS leaders to support this claim. Nelson also writes, "BDS demonizes, antagonizes, and delegitimates one of the two parties who have to negotiate a solution to the conflict by working together, and BDS uncritically idealizes the other. That will inhibit negotiations, not promote them."[14]

In addition to these pragmatic reasons for opposing BDS, Nelson makes an argument based on professional ethics. In a section of the book composed with Russell Berman, Robert Fine, and David Hirsch, Nelson and his co-authors write:

> Already too many faculty consider themselves to be communicating a fact, not expressing an opinion, when they tell their students Israel is a settler-colonialist state, or, worse still, a genocidal one. The humanities—which have been significantly defunded over a period of decades, and which now resort increasingly to hiring contingent faculty who are not eligible for tenure—will as a whole suffer a loss of public and institutional respect if they make BDS the public face of their disciplines.[15]

Nelson and his co-authors seal the case against BDS with an argument grounded in academic freedom.

> Because it imposes a political constraint on academic activity—prohibiting cooperation with the Israeli academic world based on a set of political judgments and litmus tests—a boycott would interrupt the free flow of ideas within the international scholarly community. That would block the unencumbered pursuit of knowledge, a principle that defines both academic freedom and the academy as a whole. Disciplinary organizations that advocate a boycott of universities have therefore broken faith with the scholarly community and betrayed deeply held academic values."

The authors add, "It is remarkable and disconcerting that scholars who vote for the boycott are so prepared to endanger the foundational principles of scholarly work in the interest of pursuing a political agenda."[16]

The argument is cogent but is also contingent on certain assumptions which Nelson himself was not willing to make in his earlier years. For this reason, Nelson is emblematic of the *pathos* of academic freedom in our time: the difficulty of resolving its meaning in a manner that proves to be consistent across a wide range of cases and controversies. More specifically:

- The argument against BDS rests on a clear-cut distinction between academics and politics which many academics today do not consider to be tenable. Nelson himself played a role in questioning the distinction, as we saw in the previous chapter.
- The argument presupposes that academic freedom is the constitutive and highest value of the academy. When academic freedom collides with other rights and values that are important to professors, they must prioritize academic freedom. We will see that this belief has been questioned.
- Nelson and other critics of BDS fault BDS for violating academic freedom, but they do not observe that the academic freedom of supporters of BDS is often violated: notably, by means of the numerous laws that prohibit state governments from engaging in contracts with anyone who boycotts Israel in any manner.

The above points will be fleshed out later in this chapter. I do not wish to suggest that Nelson is "wrong" when he criticizes BDS. As elsewhere in this book, I am interested in mapping out controversies, not taking sides on them. Nelson's career as a champion of academic freedom is an eminent example of the difficulties that emerge when one person seeks to wield the concept of academic freedom with authority in multiple polemical contexts.

The Boycott Syndrome

BDS is a global effort to oppose the State of Israel's treatment of Palestinians. The original "Call for an Academic and Cultural Boycott of Israel," in July 2004, was framed as an appeal by Palestinian academics and intellectuals to the international academic community. The call asserted that "Israeli academic institutions (mostly state-controlled) and the vast majority of Israeli intellectuals and academics have either contributed directly to maintaining, defending or otherwise justifying . . . oppression." The "oppression" is defined as "the military occupation and colonization" of the West Bank and Gaza since 1967 as well as "a system of racial discrimination and segregation" against Palestinian citizens of Israel "which resembles the defunct apartheid system in South Africa." The "Call" was for a comprehensive boycott of Israeli academic and cultural institutions. Boycotters are supposed to refrain from any form of cooperation with Israeli universities; urge university leaders to disinvest from Israeli businesses; and press academic associations to condemn Israeli policies.[17]

  Later formulations of the "Call" have radicalized the idea of avoiding contact with Israelis and other supporters of Israel. Notably, the guidelines now include an "antinormalization" stricture prohibiting even academic dialogue. The response to Israel's alleged policy of "segregation" is to prohibit the public mixing of pro-Palestine and pro-Israel viewpoints. According to the 2014 "Academic Boycott Guidelines":

> **Normalization Projects.** Academic activities and projects involving Palestinians and/ or other Arabs on one side and Israelis on the other (whether bi- or multi-lateral) that are based on the false premise of symmetry/parity between the oppressors and the oppressed or that claim that both colonizers and colonized are equally responsible for the "conflict" are intellectually dishonest and morally reprehensible forms of normalization

that ought to be boycotted. Far from challenging the unjust status quo, such projects contribute to its endurance. Examples include events, projects, or publications that are designed explicitly to bring together Palestinians/Arabs and Israelis so they can present their respective narratives or perspectives, or to work toward reconciliation without addressing the root causes of injustice and the requirements of justice.[18]

With the addition of the anti-normalization principle, the notion of "boycott" has become elastic. It can apply to the boycotting of economic products or the boycotting of academic institutions and personnel. The academic kind of boycott obviously raises fundamental questions about academic freedom. But we will also see that economic boycotts have academic implications because the anti-BDS laws in many states punish academics who do not buy Israeli products.

Supporters of BDS in the U.S. are at liberty to interpret the boycotting guidelines. Some participants in BDS oppose their own university's study abroad program in Israel, because studying abroad legitimizes the idea that Israel is a normal country.[19] This boycott has an impact on non-Israelis—the American students who wish to study in Israel. There are numerous instances of BDS supporters attempting to cancel the invitation of guest speakers by pro-Israeli campus groups.[20] Jewish students who support Israel have sometimes been cast out of student coalitions for women's rights, prison reform, and other progressive causes. The co-authors of a recent law-review article state, "Jewish students are effectively being told that they can join the progressive community on campus only if they first shed a significant part of their Jewish identity, namely their Zionist beliefs."[21]

When the preferred mode of political engagement is not to engage with others at all, it is difficult to stage debate. An exception that proves the rule was an event entitled "Opposing Views on Israel and Palestine" which took place at the University of Massachusetts Amherst in October 2015. Over 500 people filled one of the largest auditoriums on campus to hear four speakers, grouped into two teams, present their contrasting interpretations of the Palestinian refugee problem. The event was organized primarily by a student club, The University Union (UU), formed a year earlier by some UMass students who were inspired by the model of the Oxford Union, a famous debating society. As the UU's faculty advisor, I welcomed the audience and pointed out that two other clubs, Students for Justice in Palestine (SJP) and Student Alliance for Israel (SAFI), were co-sponsors of the debate. In fact, it was the first time that they had co-sponsored the same event. The motto of the University Union was projected onto a screen before the debate began. It was John Stuart Mill's dictum, "He who knows only his own side of the case knows little of that."

In the *Essay on Liberty* (1859), Mill continued:

> His reasons may be good, and no one may have been able to refute them. But if he is equally unable to refute the reasons on the opposite side, if he does not so much as know what they are, he has no ground for preferring either opinion . . . Nor is it enough that he should hear the opinions of adversaries from his own teachers, presented as they state them, and accompanied by what they offer as refutations. He must be able to hear them from persons who actually believe them . . . he must know them in their most plausible and persuasive form.[22]

The point of my welcome remarks, of course, was that everyone at the debate, including even the debaters, might learn something new about ideas with which they disagreed and thus learn to see their own ideas in a new light.

It was the last time SJP and SAFI worked together. Today, the debate would probably be boycotted by both. The event contravened the anti-normalization guidelines because (1) it included a Palestinian American in dialogue with defenders of Israel; and (2) one of the pro-Israel speakers held out the possibility of compromise based on a recognition of mutual responsibility for the conflict. In the Spring and Summer of 2015, when we planned the event, BDS did not weigh heavily on anyone's mind. The movement was only beginning to gain fame. In June 2014, *Inside Higher Education* reported, "the international BDS movement has only recently become a prominent—and highly contentious—issue at American colleges and universities."[23] Press coverage increased in 2014, after BDS was endorsed by the American Studies Association, but BDS was still little known on the UMass campus in the autumn of 2015.

Since 2015, no one has organized a debate or panel of diverse opinions at UMass on Israel/Palestine. SJP and pro-Israel campus groups such as SAFI and Hillel, far from working together, are now at each other's throats. SJP, which now endorses BDS,[24] and Jewish clubs are on hostile terms; in 2020, it was alleged that SJP tried to disrupt an event featuring an Ethiopian Israeli co-sponsored by SAFI and the Black Student Union.[25] On some campuses, SJP has called for a defunding of all pro-Israel student groups.[26]

Israel as an Alleged Paradigm of Global Injustice

BDS appears to be the primary perpetrator of aggressive boycott practices, but as Stern amply demonstrates in *The Conflict Over the Conflict*, responses from pro-Israel groups often have an exclusionary character. Why is this conflict so intractable? It is because each side envisions the other as incarnating the worst evil of modernity: racism. BDS justifies its boycotts with accusations that Israel is a racist state. Supporters of Israel accuse BDS of promoting antisemitism.

While the intellectual left always had reservations about how Zionism was implemented in Israel in 1948, the critique of Israel was for decades balanced by a recognition of the need for a Jewish state. In 1967, the communist intellectual, Isaac Deutscher, published "On the Israeli-Arab War" in the *New Left Review*. Deutscher, born in Poland, was a child prodigy in the study of Torah; he was ordained as a rabbi at age 13. At 14, he tested God by eating a ham sandwich on Yom Kippur in a Jewish cemetery. Since nothing happened, he became an atheist. At 17, he joined the Communist Party of Poland. He moved to London in 1939 and became a celebrated biographer of Stalin and Trotsky. Deutscher was no lover of Israel, which he regarded as a late expression of the obsolete ideology of the nation-state.[27] Yet, by comparison to the hostility toward Israel today among some leftist academics, Deutscher's old-left framing of the Palestinian refugee problem sounds quaintly nonpartisan.

A man once jumped from the top floor of a burning house in which many members of his family had already perished. He managed to save his life; but as he was falling he hit a person standing down below and broke that person's legs and arms. The jumping man had no choice; yet to the man with the broken limbs he was the cause of his misfortune. If both behaved rationally, they would not become enemies. The man who escaped from the blazing house, having recovered, would have tried to help and console the other sufferer; and the latter might have realized that he was the victim of circumstances over which neither of them had control. But look what happens when these people behave irrationally. The injured man blames the other for his misery and swears to make him pay for it. The other, afraid of the crippled man's revenge, insults him, kicks him, and beats him up whenever they meet. The kicked man again swears revenge and is again punched and punished. The bitter enmity, so fortuitous at first, hardens and comes to overshadow the whole existence of both men and to poison their minds.

You will, I am sure, recognize yourselves (I said to my Israeli audience), the Israeli remnants of European Jewry, in the man who jumped from the blazing house. The other character represents, of course, the Palestine Arabs, more than a million of them, who have lost their lands and their homes.[28]

Deutscher was reluctant to blame Israel entirely for the Palestinian conflict and never did he suggest that the state of Israel should be abolished.

In contrast, some academics on the left today portray Israel as the paradigm of global evil. The charge is that the Palestinian refugee problem is a particularly concentrated form of the worldwide ills of racism and capitalism. According to Columbia University professor of Middle Eastern Studies, Hamid Dabashi, who is also on the advisory board of BDS's American section, "the extended logic of the Palestinian intifada" is "the archetype of all transnational liberations in which the entire spectrum of contemporary liberation geography is evident and invested."[29] Any suspicion that Dabashi's Iranian background may suffice to explain his antipathy for Israel is undermined by the fact some American Jewish academics support BDS and are just as sweeping in their criticism. What is in question here is a pervasive discourse, not a regionally or religiously specific bias.

The writings of Judith Butler, a BDS supporter,[30] have been described as "the intellectual and philosophical foundation of the contemporary anti-Zionist left, both Jewish and non-Jewish."[31] For Butler, it is imperative to "dismantle Israeli state violence and the institutionalization of racism." One must oppose "any state that restricted full citizenship to any religious or ethnic group at the expense of indigenous populations and all other coinhabitants."[32] Her opposition to a Jewish state, and to a religious state of any kind, flows from universal, egalitarian principles. But Butler also claims that Jewish moral tradition weighs against Zionism. An authentic Jew should be anti-Zionist because Zionism's "structural commitment to state violence against minorities"[33] contradicts the ethical teachings of Rabbinic Judaism, which she also calls "diasporic" Judaism (Judaism as it evolved between the destruction of the Second Temple and 1948). The ideas of Butler and of other intellectuals who are highly critical of Israel have helped to convince supporters of BDS that boycotts of Israel are as justifiable as the boycotting of South Africa under apartheid, or the boycotting by Blacks of segregated buses in the South.

The "Double Standard" and Its Discontents

Needless to say, such constructions of Israel are bitterly contested. The charge that critics of Israel are the real racists—because they are allegedly antisemitic—serves to justify efforts to boycott BDS. Butler of course does not regard herself as antisemitic, for she distinguishes between calling for an end to the Israeli state, on the one hand, and calling for the destruction of the Jewish people, on the other. Yet, numerous commentators on the "New Antisemitism" and "Left Antisemitism" argue that anti-Zionism is the primary form which antisemitism now takes. The old antisemitism, based on the construction of the Jews as a race, has been discredited among educated people. The concept of the New Antisemitism posits that much criticism of Israel, though purporting to be based on egalitarian principles, is out of proportion to reality and informed by a passion to demonize something associated uniquely with Jews.[34]

The critical analysis of "Left antisemitism" today by supporters of Israel tends to be discursive rather than psychological. That is, certain linguistic practices associated with leftist anti-Zionism, such as calling Israel an apartheid state, are held to be hateful of Jews on their face, though not necessarily the expression of a given person's intention to harm Jews. The concept of "the double standard" is the linchpin of this critique of anti-Zionist discourse. The argument is that attacks against Israel are antisemitic because these attacks make no mention of gross injustices in other nations and understate the inclusive features of Israeli society (e.g., that Arabs attend Israeli universities and have been in the cabinet, which would not be possible in an apartheid regime). Such attacks portray Israel as uniquely evil and help to create an atmosphere in which antisemitism can flourish.

There is little rigorous analysis of the concept of the double standard as applied to Israel. It is not my goal to discredit or approve of the double-standard argument, but I do wish to suggest that this argument is more fragile than those who rely upon it realize. In terms of the history of this concept, one can find double-standard arguments, without the use of the term, scattered in polemics about Israel. A case in point is Albert Memmi, the Tunisian-born writer who complained about the bias against Israel among European intellectuals in *Decolonization and the Decolonized* (2004). Memmi scolded the new regimes that had liberated themselves from Europe for failing to achieve prosperity and freedom for their own citizens. Memmi argued that leaders of the post-colonial regimes evaded responsibility for their policy failures by pretending that American and European neo-colonialism continued to be oppressive, or by claiming that Israel was to blame. Memmi also assailed Western journalists and academics for overlooking administrative ineptitude and moral failure in the new nations, while never hesitating to single out Israel for criticism.

> The last Palestinian revolt, the second Intifada, which drew significant media attention, cost two thousand lives. That's two thousand too many. But a quick glance at any collection of newspapers will show that, in the past few decades alone, there have been more than a million deaths in Biafra, five hundred thousand in Rwanda, uncounted massacres in Uganda and the Congo, three hundred thousand deaths in Burundi, two hundred thousand victims in Colombia since 1964 along with three million displaced persons, the eradication of Communists in Indonesia, estimated at five hundred thousand, and the terrifying massacres of the Khmer by their own people.[35]

Memmi did not speak of a "double standard." Nor did Harvard President Larry Summers, when he responded to a petition signed by students and professors calling on the university to divest stocks in companies that did business in Israel. Summers stated that while aspects of Israel's foreign policy "should be vigorously challenged," the calls for divestment seek to unfairly "single out Israel."[36] But in 2015, reflecting back upon his response to the petition, Summers deployed the term "double standard."

> There is nothing wrong with criticizing Israel, and I for one believe that aspects of its settlements policy are misguided and potentially dangerous. Yet the U.S State Department was correct when it stated in its 'Anti-Semitism Monitor' that 'while criticism of Israel cannot automatically be regarded as anti-Semitic, rhetoric that demonizes, delegitimizes, or applies double standards to Israel crosses the line of legitimate criticism.'[37]

Summers was referring to the Office of the Special Envoy to Monitor and Combat Anti-Semitism. The particular quotation he references does not appear in any of the Office's archived statements (because few of its statements prior to 2017 are archived), but in a 2010 "Fact Sheet," the Office consecrated the double standard concept for the first time. It included the following among "Contemporary Examples of Antisemitism":

- Applying double standards by requiring of it a behavior not expected or demanded of any other democratic nation.
- Multilateral organizations focusing on Israel only for peace or human rights investigations.[38]

The endorsement of the double-standard definition of antisemitism by governmental agencies has greatly escalated the presence of this concept in political and academic debate. How did "double standard" become so prominent?

Natan Sharansky, the Russian dissident who became an Israeli politician, played a key role in bringing the double standard to the forefront of the discussion of antisemitism. In 2004, he published an article in *Jewish Political Studies Review* entitled "3D Test of Anti-Semitism: Demonization, Double Standards, Delegitimization." In a section called "Recognizing the New Antisemitism," he wrote,

> Whereas classical anti-Semitism is aimed at the Jewish people or the Jewish religion, 'new anti-Semitism' is aimed at the Jewish state . . . Making the task even harder is that this hatred is advanced in the name of values most of us would consider unimpeachable, such as human rights.

He continued:

> I believe that we can apply a simple test—I call it the "3D" test—to help us distinguish legitimate criticism of Israel from anti-Semitism.
>
> The first "D" is the test of demonization. When the Jewish state is being demonized; when Israel's actions are blown out of all sensible proportion; when comparisons are made between Israelis and Nazis and between Palestinian refugee camps and Auschwitz—this is anti-Semitism, not legitimate criticism of Israel.
>
> The second "D" is the test of double standards. When criticism of Israel is applied selectively; when Israel is singled out by the United Nations for human rights abuses while the behavior of known and major abusers, such as China, Iran, Cuba, and Syria, is ignored; when Israel's Magen David Adom, alone among the world's ambulance services, is denied admission to the International Red Cross—this is anti-Semitism.
>
> The third "D" is the test of delegitimization: when Israel's fundamental right to exist is denied—alone among all peoples in the world—this too is anti-Semitism.[39]

Sharansky's ideas were integrated into the "working definition" of antisemitism published in 2005 by the European Union's Monitoring Center on Racism and Xenophobia (EUMC). The previously mentioned State Department "Fact Sheet" of 2010 cites the EUMC as the source for the double-standard principle. Stern played a lead role in crafting the EUMC definition, which was given an additional boost when the International Holocaust Remembrance Alliance (IHRA) incorporated much of the EUMC text into its "working definition" of antisemitism, framed in 2015. Among the examples of antisemitism in the IHRA document is, "Applying double standards by requiring of it [Israel] a behavior not expected or demanded of any other democratic nation."[40]Keith Kahn-Harris, a sociologist at Birkbeck College, states that the IHRA definition "has taken on such to-temic significance" that "its adoption or non-adoption has become an existential question for institutions and individuals."[41]

As it spread from the EUMC to IHRA and to governmental organizations, the double standard argument naturally also made its way into academic discourse. To give but one example, we see the double-standard argument in a 2019 volume of the journal *Israel Studies,* a volume that became controversial because it was pointedly directed against BDS and thus raised questions about the relationship between scholarship and politics. The volume is entitled "Word Crimes: Reclaiming the Language of the Israeli-Palestinian Conflict." In her Introduction, Donna Robinson Divine stated that the contributing authors did not share "a common political agenda."[42] But critics claimed that the volume had an anti-BDS, pro-Israel bias. The two general editors of the journal issued an apology in which they acknowledged that 11 "prominent members" of the journal's editorial board resigned via a letter saying that the journal's volume "deviates sharply from academic standards and acceptable scholarly norms. Its publication clearly crossed the lines between academic schol-arship and political advocacy."[43]

In his contribution to the *Israel Studies* volume on "Enablers of the Demonization of Israel, " Gerald M. Steinberg wrote:

> The singling out of Israel, the disproportionality and the double standards (often referred to as the "new antisemitism") are characteristic of this form of "warfare." While couched and justified as opposition to Israeli government policies, the language and images that are used—apartheid, racism, ethnic cleansing—are clearly referring to and demonizing Israel as the national state of the Jewish people.[44]

In the same volume, Thane Rosenbaum writes:

> Focusing on the alleged evils of Zionism while ignoring the genocide in Syria and the brutality of Israel's surrounding neighbors in stoning women, torching homosexuals, disbanding their judiciaries, and imprisoning journalists is ahistorical and intellectually dishonest . . . What are we to make of this double standard that applies to Israel alone among the family of nations? It is the one nation that, for the entirety of its existence, has had to demand recognition of its nationhood—all on account of having regional neighbors that have continually denied its existence . . . No one seems to question the legitimacy of member states that persecute their citizens—consigning them to desper-ate lives and deplorable living conditions—nations that make not a single contribution to the betterment of humankind and the advancement of global enterprise. How can the Congo, North Korea, and Iran, as just three examples, possibly stand on firmer earthly ground than Israel?[45]

With "double standard" having become a trope in the criticism of BDS and anti-Zionism, it is not surprising that a backlash has occurred. A salient example is the 2020 Jerusalem Declaration on Antisemitism (JDA), which represents an effort to undermine the prestige of the EUMC and IHRA definitions. The JDA is endorsed by an international array of schol-ars, many of them professors of Jewish Studies and historians of Nazi Germany. Signatories included prestigious academics such as Omer Bartov, Daniel Boyarin, Michael Walzer, and Natalie Zemon Davis. As in the IHRA document, the JDA defines antisemitism by means of a list of examples; but the examples are profoundly different. None of the JDA's examples have to do with criticism of Israeli policies. Unlike the IHRA definition, the JDA also includes examples of what is *not* antisemitism, such as "Criticizing or opposing Zionism as a form of nationalism"; "Evidence-based criticism of Israel as a state"; and "Boycott, divestment and sanctions are commonplace, non-violent forms of political protest against states. In the Israeli case they are not, in and of themselves, antisemitic." As for the double standard:

> Political speech does not have to be measured, proportional, tempered, or reasonable to be protected under Article 19 of the Universal Declaration of Human Rights or Article 10 of the European Convention on Human Rights and other human rights instruments. Criticism that some may see as excessive or contentious, or as reflecting a "double standard," is not, in and of itself, antisemitic. In general, the line between antisemitic and non-antisemitic speech is different from the line between unreasonable and reasonable speech.[46]

Clearly, those who drafted the JDA intended to carve out a zone in which academic criticism of Israel will not be equated with antisemitism.

Among the critics of the double-standard test for antisemitism is Peter Ullrich, a German scholar whose complex analysis includes sections on the "Epistemological Status" and "Legal Status" of the idea of double standard. Ullrich finds vagueness, gaps, problems of demarcation, and the use examples without contextualization.

> For instance, other democratic countries that are not occupying powers . . . [cannot] be criticized for a decades-old occupation policy . . . [T]he geopolitical significance of the Arab-Israeli conflict also increase the likelihood of it being a subject of discussion and thus also the likelihood of an unequal distribution of criticism in comparison to other countries . . . One sidedness, endorsing a certain perspective, double standards, and the like are not a sufficient criterion for identifying antisemitism. [47]

But the most compelling criticism of the double standard is that of Stern, for he was a co-author of the EUMC definition of antisemitism which put Sharansky's idea of the double standard into broad circulation. Stern contends that when he helped to forge the EUMC definition, he did not envision that universities would "weaponize" and "abuse" it by turning it into a "de facto hate speech code."[48] Stern opposes the effort by some Zionists to marry the IHRA definition to Title VI of the 1964 Civil Rights Act and the associated concepts of "hostile environment" and "antidiscrimination." That is, he is against Zionist efforts to exclude BDS supporters from the campus dialogue by suing their universities.[49] "I'm a Zionist," writes Stern. "But on a college campus, where the purpose is to explore ideas, anti-Zionists have a right to free expression."[50] As for the double standard, Stern writes:

> Double standards are not unusual in college or in political advocacy, and need not reflect bigotry. Vietnam-era protestors, horrified at the actions of the US government, weren't required to complain about other countries too. Most people advocating freedom for Soviet Jewry in the 1980s weren't also organizing rallies for Tibetan or Chinese dissidents. The 1950s civil rights activists, working to end segregation, usually weren't calling out human rights violations in the Soviet Union (the failure to do so was precisely the complaint of some anti-communists, including some segregationists).[51]

Stern's argument in *The Conflict Over the Conflict* is that each side uses dubious arguments to discredit the other and to call for the elimination of the other's voice from campus life. Supporters of BDS and their Zionist opponents are behaving as if they are combatants in the Middle East, neglecting the fact that they are, first and foremost, co-citizens in a university. The purpose of academic discussion, Stern suggests, is not to "reflect" the political conflict but to "refract" it: to analyze all claims in a civil manner.[52] Dialogue with the other side is essential but cannot take place when BDS supporters boycott Zionists and when supporters of Israel ostracize critics of Israel.

The State Anti-BDS Laws

Supporters of Israel may retort that this battle is a mismatch: that BDS is a huge organization constantly pushing for boycotts on numerous campuses while supporters of Israel are only trying to counteract the demonizing rhetoric of BDS. But it is not self-evident that BDS has more power. In fact, once we factor in the anti-BDS laws that are in place in 35 states, BDS starts to look like it is fighting an uphill battle. The laws and ordinances vary in content, but generally speaking, they prohibit the government from contracting with anyone who supports any kind of boycott against Israel. The laws seem to have little to do with academic life, which is perhaps why so few commentators on academic freedom have discussed them. But many of the complainants against these laws are students and professors.

The anti-BDS laws and ordinances, the first of which date to 2015, resemble regulations from the 1940s and 1950s banning the employment of communists in public institutions, including public universities. As Timothy Cuffman observes in "The State Power to Boycott a Boycott,"

> Many states have written their statutes and executive orders with sensational language so as to demonstrate their staunch support for Israel. New York, for example, claims to 'unequivocally reject the BDS campaign and stand firmly with Israel,' while both Iowa and North Carolina refer to BDS as a tool of 'economic warfare that threaten[s] the sovereignty and security' of Israel.[53]

Courts have not looked kindly upon these laws, but the states have frequently evaded judicial review by backing off when it comes to applying the law to the complaining parties. When specific plaintiffs challenge an anti-BDS law because it has an adverse effect on them, the state will often say that the law was not meant to apply in their case, depriving the plaintiffs of "standing" to sue.[54] Generally speaking, one cannot challenge a law based on principle alone; one must be an aggrieved party, suffering a loss under the law's impact.

In some cases, however, the courts have ruled on the merits, and they have consistently held that the anti-BDS laws violate the First Amendment. The reason for this consensus is a clear precedent: *NAACP v. Claiborne Hardware Co* (1982), a case in which the Supreme Court classified politically motivated boycotts as protected by freedom of association and freedom of speech. The case concerned the boycott of white merchants in Claiborne County, Mississippi. A crucial element in the case was that Blacks boycotted white-owned business to express their dissatisfaction with local *political* conditions. They called for the desegregation of all public schools and public facilities, the hiring of black policemen, improvements of the public amenities in black residential areas, selection of blacks for jury duty, integration of bus stations, and an end to verbal abuse by law enforcement officers.[55] According to Justice Stevens, who wrote for a unanimous Court, "The black citizens named as defendants in this action banded together and collectively expressed their dissatisfaction with a social structure that had denied them rights to equal treatment and respect."[56]

> Speech itself also was used to further the aims of the boycott. Nonparticipants were repeatedly urged to join the common cause, both through public address and through personal solicitation. These elements of the boycott involve speech in its most direct form.[57]

NAACP v. Claiborne figures prominently in recent cases which characterize the anti-BDS laws as unconstitutional.

In *Amawi v. Pflugerville Independent School District* (2019), the U.S. District Court for the Western District of Texas mentioned the *NAACP* precedent about 30 times. Bahia Amawi was a speech pathologist of Palestinian origin who refused to buy Sabra brand hummus. For nine years she had contracted with a school district to provide speech therapy for children, until she refused to sign an addendum in her renewal contract requiring her to certify that she did not boycott Israel. Other plaintiffs in the case were a freelance writer who worked for the Blaffer Art Museum at the University of Houston; he also boycotted Sabra goods. And a sophomore at Texas State University in San Marcos who boycotted PepsiCo, Hewlett Packard, and other companies which he viewed as supporting Israel's occupation of the West Bank; he was denied an opportunity to officiate at a high-school debate competition. A graduate student at Rice University was also not allowed to serve as a judge in debates.

The Court stated that boycotts are a protected First Amendment activity. Expression on matters of public importance is not merely protected by the First Amendment but is on "the highest rung of the hierarchy of First Amendment values."[58] The Court affirmed the classic doctrine that government has no power to restrict expression because of its viewpoint. The Court noted that Governor Gregg Abbot had sent "a strong message" that Texas sided with Israel in the contentious public debate surrounding Israeli-Palestinian relations by saying, "Anti-Israel policies are anti-Texas policies, and we will not tolerate actions against an important ally."[59] In an inversion of the double-standard argument, the Court observed that the Texas law unfairly applied only to those who boycott Israel: "it singles out speech about Israel, not any other country."[60] The Court rejected the argument that anti-Israel boycotters can be penalized for engaging in discrimination against Israelis on the basis of national origin. The Court noted that some plaintiffs boycotted non-Israeli as well as Israeli corporations. Finally, the Court found the Texas law to be unconstitutionally "vague" as to what counts as a boycott under the law. It was impossible to tell if the law applied to people "donating to an organization like Jewish Voice for Peace that organizes BDS campaigns, or picketing outside Best Buy to urge shoppers not to buy HP products."[61] The judge, Robert Pittman, issued an injunction prohibiting the anti-BDS law from being applied to the defendants.

The most recent decision on an anti-BDS law took place in May 2021. It concerned a Georgia law, which became effective in 2017, providing that the

> state shall not enter into a contract with an individual or company if the contract is related to construction or the provision of services, supplies, or information technology unless the contract includes a written certification that such individual or company is

not currently engaged in, and agrees for the duration of the contract not to engage in, a boycott of Israel.[62]

In *Martin v. Wrigley*, the defendant Wrigley, was Chancellor of the University System of Georgia. Abby Martin was a journalist who supported BDS. She was invited to be a paid keynote speaker at Georgia Southern University's 2020 International Critical Media Literacy Conference. She refused to sign a statement saying that she would not engage in a boycott of Israel during the duration of her contract. She was, in fact, working on a film that featured people calling for boycotts of Israel. She was not allowed to speak at the conference. The Federal District Court recognized *NAACP v. Claiborne* as the controlling precedent and affirmed that Martin's speech rights were violated.

> The certification that one is not engaged in a boycott of Israel is no different than requiring a person to espouse certain political beliefs or to engage in certain political associations. The Supreme Court has found similar requirements to be unconstitutional on their face. See, e.g., Baird [v. State Bar of Arizona (1971)], 401 U.S. at 5–6 (holding unconstitutional a state bar question requiring applicants to state whether they had ever been a member of the Communist Party or another organization which advocated the overthrow of the United States Government by force).[63]

The Divided AAUP

In 2006, the AAUP released a clarification of its position on academic boycotts. The document concludes by taking a stand against academic boycotts but displays a great deal of ambivalence throughout the argument. In 2005, the AAUP already issued a clear-cut rejection of boycotts. With a statement that contained only two paragraphs, the AAUP announced, "We reject proposals that curtail the freedom of teachers and researchers to engage in work with academic colleagues, and we reaffirm the paramount importance of the freest possible international movement of scholars and ideas."[64] The 2006 supplement consists of 26 paragraphs. Its title, "On Academic Boycotts," is less categorical on where the AAUP stands than the title of the 2005 text: "The AAUP Opposes Academic Boycotts." The 2006 document describes itself as a "comment" on the previous statement, but in its effort to outline "the complexities of academic boycotts,"[65] the new text seeks to supersede the old with a more sympathetic account of academic boycotts.

Clearly, there was considerable disagreement within the AAUP, and the leadership considered it necessary to reflect publicly the debate. The new document goes to great lengths to demonstrate that reasonable people can disagree about academic boycotts. The authors provide a very long extract from the British Association of University Teachers' 2005 announcement of a boycott of Israeli universities and then observe:

> While a meeting of an AUT Special Council voted to drop its call for the boycott within a month's time of the initial decision, and therefore, no Israeli university was boycotted, we have been urged to give fuller consideration to the broad and unconditional nature of our condemnation [in 2005] of academic boycotts. We are reminded that our own complex history includes support for campus strikes, support for divestiture during anti-apartheid campaigns in South Africa, and a questioning of the requirement of institutional neutrality during the Vietnam War.[66]

The AAUP document continues in this vein. The authors state that the AAUP has traditionally upheld the idea of institutional neutrality but also recognizes that many academics believe that in "perilous situations,"[67] the university should take action.

> Are there extraordinary situations in which extraordinary actions are necessary? . . . Should scholarly exchange have been encouraged with Hitler's collaborators in those universities? Can one plausibly maintain that academic freedom is inviolate when the civil freedoms of the larger society have been abrogated?[68]

The AAUP notes that in 1988, it urged TIAA-CREF (an investment firm for teachers) to divest itself of all companies doing business in South Africa. The authors proceed to distinguish between economic boycotts (boycotting companies and products) and academic boycotts (boycotting universities and professors), but far from condemning the former category as a matter of general principle, the document states that academic boycotts are not an effective "tactic" for achieving a political goal because an academic boycott of Israeli universities can harm Israelis who support Palestine, or Palestinians who work at Israeli universities.[69]

Curiously, the document ends unambiguously by stating that the AAUP opposes academic boycotts because they interfere with "the free exchange of ideas"—roughly the same position as the 2005 statement. The amplified discussion in the 2005 text could be interpreted as the AAUP saying that it has reached its conclusion after fully considering both sides of the question. But I think most readers of this text would agree its discussion of "complexities" casts doubt on its own conclusion and reflects a deep split in the organization about the validity of boycotts. This interpretation is borne out by the aftermath of the 2006 document.

The Chair of the committee that wrote the 2006 document was the historian, Joan Scott.[70] In a 2013 essay, "Changing My Mind about the Boycott," Scott reflected upon the situation in 2006. She accused some leaders in the AAUP of trying to close down the debate about boycotts. Scott noted that in 2006 she was against academic boycotts but also felt "that inflexible adherence to a principle did not make sense without consideration of the political contexts within which one wanted to apply it"[71]—which is exactly the tone of the 2006 statement, minus its final conclusion. Scott announced, in the 2013 essay, that she now supported academic boycotts of Israel, but she indicated that she was already moving in this direction in 2006.

> What did it mean, I wondered [in 2006], to oppose the boycott campaign in the name of Israeli academic freedom when the Israeli state regularly denied academic freedom to critics of the state, the occupation, or, indeed, of Zionism . . . ?[72]

She goes on to describe Israel as "a brutal apartheid system." The boycott of Israel, she argues, "is a strategic way of exposing the unprincipled and undemocratic behavior of Israeli state institutions; its aim can be characterized as 'saving Israel from itself.'"[73]

In a response to Scott's 2013 article, Ernst Benjamin, who held the full-time position of General Secretary in the AAUP and was one of the authors of the 2006 statement, affirmed that he continued to oppose academic boycotts. He argued that the AAUP policies and statements ought to pertain only to academic matters and not to matters of world affairs. Benjamin notes that BDS leaders, such as Omar Barghouti, had argued that the AAUP ought not to privilege academic freedom above other principles, including basic human rights. But the AAUP, stated Benjamin, is not a human rights organization. Proponents of human rights within the AAUP can always pursue their political goals outside the university.[74] They should not deny academic freedom to Israelis, even when Israelis are implicated in the denial of academic freedom to Palestinians. Benjamin notes that Barghouti had questioned whether the AAUP's commitment to the primacy of academic freedom is consistent. Specifically, Barghouti had inquired if the AAUP would support antisemitic speech in the classroom.

Benjamin astonishingly replies, "Yes, the AAUP and I support the right of faculty members to uphold Nazi ideology and other anti-Semitic theories in class if the topic is pertinent to their course."[75] According to Benjamin, Holocaust denial is not protected by academic freedom because it is "counterfactual" (academically refutable), whereas Nazi ideology, shorn of any specific historical and scientific claims, is a pure political opinion, which the professor is free to express. Benjamin is saying that just as professors are free to favor socialism or feminism in the classroom, they are free to support antisemitism and Nazism. This does not sound like a winning argument, but if we limit ourselves to a logical analysis of Benjamin's position, we can simply note that it is an inversion of Max Weber's conception of the academic vocation (see Chapter 3). Weber argued that purely existential commitments which float above academic inquiry simply do not belong in a professor's classroom discourse. Benjamin, in contrast, holds such purely ideological pronouncements to be fully protected by academic freedom, which he seems to construe as interchangeable with freedom of speech in the classroom context.

We are confronted once again with the unexamined assumption that academic freedom and freedom of political speech are the same things. Surely Benjamin did not have to resort to defending the right to preach Nazi ideology in the classroom in order to oppose academic boycotts. Indeed, Benjamin continued with a stronger point.

> [If] we were to agree that each claim of academic freedom should be evaluated on its political merits then the principle of academic freedom itself would be utterly lost. Academic freedom would not be a universal right but a reward to those academics and academic institutions found deserving by self-appointed monitors on the basis of politically defined standards on a case by case basis. Consider the chaos that would ensue if we evaluated each case of a claimed violation of academic freedom on the political merits of the academic institution or aggrieved faculty member. Such a flexible standard could not long be sustained nor should it.[76]

He concludes:

> For those engaged in the struggle for Palestinian rights and their allies the struggle itself is understandably more important than any philosophical argument regarding the merits of academic freedom or academic boycotts. I do not question, nor should the AAUP question, their priorities . . . Many of us may join human rights and political organizations to pursue our concerns . . . But the AAUP is not a general-purpose human rights organization much less a political movement. The AAUP exists to defend academic freedom. We should not compromise this principle in the name of others which though they may be larger and even more important are not the principles specific to our association.[77]

Storm Over Departmental Declarations

In 2021, a new issue pertaining to Israel came to the forefront of academic controversy. It emerged in relation to the Israel–Gaza War in May 2021 and concerned the validity of partisan political statements issued in the name of academic departments and disciplines. Even if one were to grant that it is professionally in accord with academic freedom for a single professor to take a militant political stand in a publication or in a class, political claims made by discipline-based groups raise a separate question. When the representatives of a discipline deploy their *collective* academic authority to endorse a political message, they are suggesting that there is only one uniquely correct way to look at a political situation through the lens of their discipline.

While the debate about departmental and disciplinary declarations reached a new level of intensity in 2021, the issue had been flagged before, notably by Stanley Fish, in relation to the 2016 presidential election. In "Professors, Stop Opining About Trump," Fish responded to an "Open Letter to the American People" composed by a group calling itself "Historians Against Trump." The letter warned against Trump's candidacy and suggested that historians have unique qualifications to assess Trump because "they share an understanding of the past upon which a better future may be built." Fish wrote, "The claim is not simply that disciplinary expertise confers moral and political superiority, but that historians, because of their training, are uniquely objective observers." Fish observed that the historians' letter consisted of standard criticisms of Trump that could be found outside of academe, but these judgments were offered "not as political opinion, which surely they are, but indisputable, impartially arrived at truths . . . Academic expertise is not a qualification for delivering political wisdom."[78]

Fish's argument is reminiscent of Weber's "Science as a Vocation." The focus of both is epistemological: Does political opinion really emanate from the empirical facts which a discipline establishes? If it does not, then is it not dishonest to pass off one's political values as if they were the logical corollaries of an academic discipline? Is it not common for people to agree on certain facts but to draw different lessons from them? Is it reasonable to presume that all the members of a discipline will draw the same political conclusions from the academic knowledge generated by the discipline?

In 2021, such questions became even more pointed than before. The "Historians Against Trump" group did not claim to represent all historians. But in 2021, numerous declarations against Israel were issued in a tone of unanimity by departments, disciplines, faculty unions, and other academic associations.[79] Miriam Elman, Executive Director of The Academic Engagement Network, a group which opposes BDS, raised a procedural question about these statements. She pointed to instances in which faculty members in groups listed as endorsing a statement critical of Israel did not support it or were not even aware of it.

> When there's a letter or petition that speaks for the whole department and its purpose is to represent an official campus unit, it appears like it's speaking for every member of that department . . . Those kinds of formal statements that impose formal positions on all the members are oppressive.[80]

Indeed, discipline-based political declarations raise questions not only about the nature of political allegiance (is it grounded in knowledge or personal choice?) but also about the nature of disciplines (should we expect disciplines to be consensual or centers of legitimate debate and disagreement?).

The Israel-Gaza war began in May 2021, when Palestinians began protests in East Jerusalem over an impending decision of the Supreme Court of Israel concerning the eviction of Palestinian families in Sheikh Jarrah. Many Arabs perceived the legal action as part of a systematic Israeli campaign to force Palestinians out of East Jerusalem—a kind of ethnic cleansing. This prompted Hamas to fire a barrage of rockets at Jerusalem and other major cities in Israel. Israel responded with airstrikes in the Hamas-controlled Gaza Strip. The condemnation of Israel by 130 Gender Studies departments received considerable attention because of its flagrantly partisan language and the apparently tenuous connection between the field of Gender Studies and the situation in Israel.

> We stand in solidarity with the people of Palestine. We unequivocally answer and amplify the call from the Palestinian Feminist Collective for "feminists everywhere to speak up, organize, and join the struggle for Palestinian liberation." . . . We do not subscribe to a "both sides" rhetoric that erases the military, economic, media, and global power that Israel has over Palestine. This is not a "conflict" that is too "controversial and complex" to assess. Israel is using violent force, punitive bureaucracy, and the legal system to expel Palestinians from their rightful homes and to remove Palestinian people from their land. Israeli law systematically discriminates against Palestinian citizens of Israel. Illegal Israeli settlements choke and police Palestinian communities. . .
>
> As gender studies departments in the United States, we are the proud benefactors of decades of feminist anti-racist, and anti-colonial activism that informs the foundation of our interdiscipline. In 2015 the National Women's Studies Association wrote that our work is "committed to an inclusive feminist vision that is in solidarity with Indigenous peoples and sovereignty rights globally, that challenges settler colonial practices, and that contests violations of civil rights and international human rights law, military occupation and militarization, including the criminalization of the U.S. borders, and myriad forms of dispossession." We center global social justice in our intersectional teaching, scholarship, and organizing. From Angela Davis we understand that justice is indivisible; we learn this lesson time and again from Black, Indigenous, Arab, and most crucially, Palestinian feminists, who know that "Palestine is a Feminist Issue." . . . we call for the end of Israel's military occupation of Palestine and for the Palestinian right to return to their homes. As residents, educators, and feminists who are also against the settler colonialism of the U.S., we refuse to normalize or accept the United States' financial, military, diplomatic and political role in Palestinian dispossession. In solidarity, we call for the end of Israel's military occupation of Palestine and for the Palestinian right to return to their homes.[81]

Curiously, professors of Gender Studies, who have spent their careers questioning binary conceptions of gender and sex and promoting complex alternative classifications, cast doubt on the integrity of anyone who sees the conflict in the Middle East as non-binary and complex. The phrase "controversial and complex," is in scare quotes, as if it is the slogan of deceitful and evil people. The phrase is hyperlinked to an editorial in *Aljazeera* which dismisses the notion of complexity as a disguise for anti-Palestinian dogma.[82] The declaration appears to discourage any research or public comment that might contradict the party line decreed in advance.

Such was the argument made by Nelson. In an editorial "Is Academic Freedom A Casualty of the Gaza War?" Nelson addressed the issue of whether political declarations by academic organizations are consistent with academic freedom. He wrote, "Academic freedom protects the right individual faculty have to take aggressive political stands." But he adds:

> This national effort to organize an entire academic discipline—its teaching, research, policies and administration—around anti-Zionism represents a new and dangerous phase in the politicization of the academy. The individual faculty members in these departments have academic freedom; they have the right to express these views without being sanctioned, and faculty and students have every right to study, discuss and debate the views embodied in the statement . . . But for departments to officially adopt one position in such a debate is another matter. A department is an administrative entity, an arm of the university. Academic and professional standards for departments exist, such as that students and faculty members holding opposing views will be free to adopt their own positions and be treated with respect. Departments and their administrators are responsible for a series of professional decisions that are supposed to be politically neutral . . .
>
> Once a department and its chief administrator sign on to a set of political positions, the academic freedom of those who disagree is compromised. Students who hold other views face the bullying power of their professors . . . Will the departments that signed the statement hire or promote someone who disagrees with it? How much extra attention will Jewish candidates receive?[83]

As always with Nelson, the perspective is clear.

Yet, the idea that departmental declarations "speak for the institution" is questionable. Nelson is thinking of the AAUP's 1940 "Statement on Academic Freedom and Tenure":

> As scholars and educational officers, they should remember that the public may judge their profession and their institution by their utterances. Hence they should at all times be accurate, should exercise appropriate restraint, should show respect for the opinions of others, *and should make every effort to indicate that they are not speaking for the institution.*[84]

But the term institution here refers to a university. It is not clear that departments lack the right to represent the viewpoint of their own segment of the university. Moreover, as Nelson would surely know, the AAUP backtracked on this portion of the 1940 statement in a 1970 "comment" on the text.[85] Finally, since the 1940 statement was a caution to professors as individuals, one cannot mobilize this particular text against departments and disciplines without simultaneously calling into question the right of individual professors to be politically active.

This is precisely the point made by John K. Wilson, an independent scholar and a prolific commentator on academic freedom issues, who replied to Nelson in an essay called "In Defense of Departmental Academic Freedom." Wilson argues that one should not presume that Gender Studies departments aim to represent their respective universities. Readers can see that they represent only themselves. He also considers it questionable whether these departments really mean to exclude students and professors who disagree with their declaration. "Absolutely nothing in the statement Nelson denounces suggests in any way that students and faculty in these departments should be banned from disagreeing with the statement. A statement is just a statement. It's not an act of oppression."[86] This is not to say that Wilson is enthusiastic about such declarations; rather, he sees no reason to ban them. Suppressing political speech is a dangerous move in the direction of censorship.

The logic of Wilson's position is evident: he believes that failure to protect the rights of departments and disciplines to speak out politically will lead to further restrictions on the right of professors to speak out as individuals. Of course, Stanley Fish and others, going back to Weber and to the AAUP's 1915 "Declaration," have considered limits on political expression to be of the essence of academic freedom. But Wilson regards professional self-restraint as a matter to be considered in the internal forum of a professor's conscience— not a code to be used by authority figures, inside or outside the university, to punish wayward professors. Wilson tends to equate academic freedom with freedom of speech.[87] From his perspective, the greatest threat to the university is not the political radicalism of professors but the political conservatism of those who seek pretexts to curtail freedom of discussion in the academy.

> The notion that academic freedom requires the silence of anyone with authority is erroneous, impossible, and dangerous. It's an error because academic freedom requires protecting dissenters from punishment, not neutrality and silence from those with power. It's impossible because all sorts of necessary statements and positions by those in authority on campus (supporting diversity or affirmative action or free speech) would violate the rights of any individual students or faculty who might disagree. And it's dangerous because once we accept Nelson's logic that political statements are a form of repression that must be banned, all academic freedom is in big trouble. After all, departments are not the only entities making political statements–individual professors make a lot of political statements. A student is far more likely to feel intimidated by their professor saying something than a departmental statement, since the professor (unlike a department) controls classroom discourse and grading. If departments don't have academic freedom because their political advocacy would silence dissenting voices, then why do professors have academic freedom when their political advocacy could silence dissenting students?[88]

This controversy is a stalemate; I do not think it can be resolved.

To understand this ideological debate is to reach a point where one discerns axioms at work which the participants are reluctant to modify, and which cannot be proven to be false. Nelson's case against political declarations by departments rests on a version of the classic "slippery slope" argument: today departments are denouncing Israel in a tone of imperious academic consensus; next, it's likely they will ostracize all students and professors who do not share their politics. Wilson employs a different version of the slippery slope argument: today, the critics of our universities wish to silence departments which are politically active; next, they will try to silence the unpopular political speech of individual professors. Which possible result is more to be feared: the tyranny of professors, or the tyranny over professors?

Throughout this chapter, I have tried to avoid opining on Middle Eastern politics. Perhaps I have revealed a bias in favor of Israel, a bias that is, admittedly, difficult to eliminate, given my background. Or perhaps I have "over-compensated" for this bias by revealing the constitutional fragility of the anti-BDS laws and the intellectual fragility of the double-standard argument. Yet, even if a bias is apparent, I have tried to make it clear that the challenge of defining academic freedom is separate from forming an opinion about the situation in the Middle East. Suppose one conceded to the most extreme of Israel's critics that Zionism is racism and that Israel is waging a campaign of ethnic cleansing against Palestinians (which I would not in reality concede), whether an American university should boycott all Israeli professors or shut down study abroad programs in Israel would still be open questions: questions hinging on our understanding not of the Israeli/Palestine conflict but of academic freedom.

In the field of law, there is the sub-field of jurisdiction, sometimes called "the law of law" on account of its formal or meta-legal aspect. Which type of court (federal, state, or both) has jurisdiction over a given controversy? The question does not hinge on which of the parties is right in the dispute. Likewise, academic freedom is the "law of law"—the meta-norm in university life. But there is a difference. The axioms governing academic freedom are not grounded in the Constitution and legislation; they are self-implemented by each university. It is to be expected that these principles will be constantly debated. One's conception of academic freedom depends on one's understanding of what it means to call an institution academic. Does it mean that the institution upholds academic exchange and the collective pursuit of knowledge as the supreme good? Or that the members of this institution may be committed to multiple values, some of which weigh more than the collaborative production of knowledge? The lack of agreement about academic boycotts boils down to two things: a difference of viewpoint about what academic freedom means in itself, and about the place of academic freedom in the constellation of values to which academics subscribe.

Notes

1 "Gov. Andrew Cuomo: If You Boycott Israel, New York State Will Boycott You," *Washington Post* (June 10, 2016), https://www.washingtonpost.com/opinions/gov-andrew-cuomo-if-you-boycott-israel-new-york-state-will-boycott-you/2016/06/10/1d6d3acc-2e62-11e6-9b37-42985f6a265c_story.html.
2 See for example "Students File Lawsuit to Stop UMass Israel, Palestine Panel," *Daily Hampshire Gazette,* April 26, 2019, https://www.gazettenet.com/Students-file-suit-to-stop-UMass-Israel-Palestine-panel-25137988. See also discussion later in this chapter of anti-BDS laws.
3 Kenneth S. Stern, *The Conflict Over the Conflict: The Israel/Palestine Campus Debate* (Toronto: New Jewish Press, 2020), 69.
4 Ibid, 53.
5 Ibid, 54.
6 Ibid, 66.
7 One can find numerous appeals to cancel specific course about Israel on the Facebook group: Antizionism on Campus, the University, Free Speech, and BDS: https://www.facebook.com/groups/1740690739327849.
8 See StandWithUS amicus brief in Aw*ad v. Fordham University*, Supreme Court of the State of New York, Appellate Division, First Department, case no. 2020-00843, September 29, 2020; calling for the banning of SJP. Among the arguments is that Students for Justice in Palestine (SJP) "would encourage antisemitic activities" (9). The Appellate Court upheld Fordham's ban on SJP with a very cursory opinion: *Amad v. Fordham University,* December 22, 2020, case no. 2020-00843, index no. 153826/17 (unpublished opinion). The lower court's ruling against Fordham is explained in much greater detail. Awad v. Fordham University, Supreme Court of New York County, Index No. 153826/17, August 6, 2019.
9 *West Virginia State Board of Education v. Barnette*, 319 U.S. 624 (1943).
10 *Miami Herald Publishing Co. v. Tornillo*, 418 U.S. 241 (1974).
11 *Hurley v. Irish-American Gay, Lesbian and Bisexual Group of Boston, Inc.*, 515 U.S. 557 (1995).
12 Frederick Schauer, "The First Amendment as Ideology," *William and Mary Law Review*, vol. 33, no. 3 (Spring 1992), 854.
13 Cary Nelson, "Introduction," in *Dreams Deferred: A Concise Guide to the Israeli-Palestinian Conflict and the Movement to Boycott Israel* (Bloomington: Indiana University Press, 2016), 6. The book is organized like an encyclopedia with numerous brief entries on topics arranged alphabetically. Many entries are written by Nelson; some by Nelson with others; a small number by authors without Nelson.
14 Nelson, "BDS: A Brief History," in *Dreams Deferred*, 63.

15 Russell Berman, Robert Fine, David Hirsch, and Cary Nelson, "Introduction" [to the entry called "Academic Boycotts"] in *Dreams Deferred*, 16.
16 Ibid, 17–18.
17 "Call for an Academic and Cultural Boycott of Israel, July 6, 2004. https://bdsmovement.net/pacbi/pacbi-call.
18 https://usacbi.org/guidelines-for-applying-the-international-academic-boycott-of-israel/ (2014). Here and occasionally hereafter I omit the title of a document when it is evident in the URL. BDS's 2009 boycott guidelines included a similar statement against normalization. The difference is that the 2014 guidelines are for "academic activities and projects" and the 2009 are for "cultural events and projects." For 2009, see https://usacbi.org/guidelines-for-applying-the-international-cultural-boycott-of-israel-2/.
19 Isaac Stanley-Becker, *Washington Post* (September 20, 2018), https://www.washingtonpost.com/news/morning-mix/wp/2018/09/20/a-michigan-professor-supported-a-students-study-abroad-application-until-he-realized- israel-was-her-destination/
20 Israel on Campus Coalition, "2019 Campus Trends Report," https://israelcc.org/wp-content/uploads/2019/11/ICC-2019-Campus-Trends-Report.pdf (on event disruptions from 2011 to 2019); see also Michael B. Atkins and Miriam F. Elman, "BDS as a Threat to Academic Freedom and Campus Free Speech in the United States," *Michigan State International Law Review*, vol. 29, no. 2 (2021), 236–237.
21 Atkins and Elman, "BDS as a Threat to Academic Freedom," 239–240.
22 John Stuart Mill, *On Liberty* (Kitchener, Ontario: Batoche Books, 2001; first pub., 1859), 36.
23 https://www.insidehighered.com/news/2014/06/17/pro-palestinian-student-activism-heats-causing-campus-tensions.
24 UMass SJP website: https://umassamherst.campuslabs.com/engage/organization/sjp.
25 https://www.campusfairness.org/statement-on-the-zoombombing-incident-at-umass-amherst/; https://www.algemeiner.com/2020/06/14/more-antisemitic-activity-at-umass-amherst-is-not-a-surprise/;https://mondoweiss.net/2019/10/umass-sjp-open-letter-to-chancellor-on-statement-attacking-bds/.
26 https://medium.com/jewish-on-campus/rutgers-student-groups-call-for-defunding-of-hillel-and-other-zionist-organizations-83711d97dc77; https://forward.com/fast-forward/400675/sjp-at-stony-brook-university-vows-to-eradicate-zionism-and-oppose-hillel/.
27 Isaac Deutscher, "On the Israeli-Arab War," *New Left Review*, vol. 44 (July/August 1967), 37–38; a revised version appears in Isaac Deutscher, *The Non-Jewish Jew and Other Essays* (London: Verso, 2017; first pub. 1968), Chapter 7.
28 Ibid, 36.
29 Hamid Dabashi, *Can Non-Europeans Think?* (London: Zed Books, 2015), Acknowledgments, vi.
30 "Judith Butler Remarks to Brooklyn College on BDS," February 7, 2013; https://www.thenation.com/article/archive/judith-butlers-remarks-brooklyn-college-bds/
31 Shaul Magid, "Butler Trouble: Zionism, Excommunication, and the Reception of Judith Butler's Work on Israel/Palestine," *Studies in American Jewish Literature*, vol. 33, no. 2 (2014), 237.
32 Judith Butler, *Parting Ways: Jewishness and the Critique of Zionism* (New York: Columbia University Press, 2012), 117, 119.
33 Ibid, 32.
34 For a sample of criticism of "The New Antisemitism," see Bruno Chaouat, *Is Theory Good for the Jews? French Thought and the Challenge of the New Antisemitism* (Liverpool: Liverpool University Press, 2004), 206–223 for criticism of *Butler's Parting Ways*; and *Deciphering the New Antisemitism*, ed. Alvin H. Rosenfeld (Bloomington: Indiana University Press, 2015).
35 Albert Memmi, *Decolonization and the Decolonized* (Minneapolis: University of Minnesota Press, 2006; first pub. 2004), 26.
36 https://www.thecrimson.com/article/2002/9/19/summers-says-anti-semitism-lurks-locally-university/.
37 Larry Summers, "Harvard, Israel, and Academic Freedom," *The Harvard Crimson*, February 3, 2015: http://larrysummers.com/2015/02/03/3850/.
38 "Defining Anti-Semitism: Fact Sheet," U.S. State Department, Special Envoy to Monitor and Combat Anti-Semitism, June 8, 2010: https://2009-2017.state.gov/j/drl/rls/fs/2010/122352.htm.
39 Natan Sharansky, "3D Test of Anti-Semitism: Demonization, Double Standards, Delegitimization," *Jewish Political Studies Review*, vol. 16 (Fall 2004): https://jcpa.org/article/3d-test-of-anti-semitism-demonization-double-standards-delegitimization/.

40 International Holocaust Remembrance Alliance, "What is Antisemitism: Non-Legally Binding Working Definition of Antisemitism," May 26, 2016: https://www.holocaustremembrance.com/resources/working-definitions-charters/working-definition-antisemitism.

41 Keith Kahn-Harris, "Defining Antisemitism—Again, and Again," *Jew Think*, March 25, 2021: https://www.jewthink.org/2021/03/25/defining-antisemitism-again-and-again/.

42 Donna Robinson Divine, "Introduction," in "Special Issue: Word Crimes: Reclaiming the Language of the Israeli-Palestinian Conflict" (cited henceforth as "Word Crimes,"), eds. Donna Robinson Divine, Miriam F. Elman, Adam Romirowski, *Israel Studies*, vol. 24, no. 2 (Summer 2009), 14.

43 Ilan Troen and Natan Aridan, "Statement by Co-Editors on the Recent Special Issue of *Israel Studies*," *Israel Studies*, vol. 24, no. 3 (Fall, 2019), v–vii.

44 Gerald Steinberg, "Uncivil Society: Tracking the Funders and Enablers of the Demonization of Israel," in "Word Crimes," 182–183.

45 Thane Rosenbaum, "Zionism," in "Word Crimes," 122.

46 "The Jerusalem Declaration," 2020, https://jerusalemdeclaration.org/.

47 Peter Ulrich, *Expert Opinion on the 'Working Definition of Antisemitism' of the International Holocaust Remembrance Alliance* (Berlin: Rosa Luxembourg Stiftung, 2019): https://www.rosalux.de/fileadmin/rls_uploads/pdfs/rls_papers/Papers_3-2019_Antisemitism.pdf.

48 Stern, *The Conflict Over the Conflict*, 156, 158.

49 Ibid, 156; for a more positive appraisal of the use of Title VI to sue universities for tolerating anti-Zionism, see Elman and Atkins, "BDS as a Threat to Academic Freedom," 242–256.

50 Stern *The Conflict Over the Conflict,* 172; quoting an article he published in *The Guardian*, December 13, 2019, "I Drafted the Definition of Antisemitism: Rightwing Jews are Weaponizing It," https://www.theguardian.com/commentisfree/2019/dec/13/antisemitism-executive-order-trump-chilling-effect.

51 Stern, *The Conflict Over the Conflict*, 153, footnote.

52 Ibid, 193.

53 Timothy Cuffman, "The State Power to Boycott a Boycott: The Thorny Constitutionality of State Anti-BDS Laws," *Columbia Journal of Transnational Law*, vol. 57, no. 1 (2018), 118; quoting NY Exec. Order No. 157 (June 22, 2016) and Iowa Code, section 12J.1 (2016), H.B. no. 161.

54 An example of such a case, in which the Court had to recognize that the Plaintiffs originally had a strong case but no loger had standing to sue is Ali v. Hogan, U.S. District Court, D. Maryland, Civil No. CCB-19-0078 (October 1, 2019).

55 *NAACP v. Claiborne Hardware Co.*, 458 U.S. 899 (1982).

56 Ibid, 907.

57 Ibid, 909.

58 *Amawi v. Pflugerville Independent School District*, U.S. District Court, Western District of Texas, Austin Division, 373 F.Supp. 3d, at 745, citing NAACP v. Claiborne ("highest rung").

59 Ibid, 731.

60 Ibid, 748.

61 Ibid, 756.

62 Georgia Code Section 50-5-85, May 9, 2017: https://codes.findlaw.com/ga/title-50-state-government/ga-code-sect-50-5-85.htm.

63 Martin v. Wrigley, U.S. District Court, Northern District of Georgia, Atlanta Division, Case 1:20-cv-00596-MHC (May 21, 2021), page 22 of the 29-page unpublished opinion. I have amplified the reference to the *Baird* case because the Court used a short reference, having previously referenced the case in full.

64 "The AAUP Opposes Academic Boycotts," *Academe*, vol. 91, no. 4 (July–August, 2005), 57.

65 "On Academic Boycotts," *Academe*, vol. 92, no. 5 (September–October, 2006), 39.

66 Ibid, 40.

67 Ibid, 41.

68 Ibid.

69 Ibid, 42.

70 The other authors were Ernst Benjamin, Robert M. O'Neil, and Jonathan Knight.

71 Joan Scott, "Changing My Mind about the Boycott," *AAUP Journal of Academic Freedom*, vol. 4 (2013), https://www.aaup.org/JAF4/changing-my-mind-about-boycott#.V8dHL_krJQI; p. 2 of the PDF.

72 Ibid.

73 Ibid, 3.

74 For a similar argument, i.e, that academic freedom should not be sacrificed to allegedly higher values, see Michael Bérubé, "Boycott Bubkes: The Murky Logic of the ASA's Resolution Against Israel," *Aljazeera America*, January 1, 2014. http://america.aljazeera.com/opinions/2014/1/boycott-asa-israelbds.html.

Whenever you make academic freedom contingent on something else, you violate the principle that academic freedom should not be subject to the dictates of church or state, political parties or boards of trustees, corporate funders or irate parents—or even activists in Palestinian civil society.

75 Ernst Benjamin, "Why I Continue to Support the AAUP Policy in Opposition to Academic Boycotts," *The AAUP Journal of Academic Freedom,* vol. 4 (2013): https://www.aaup.org/sites/default/files/Response-Benjamin_0.pdf; p. 1 of the PDF. (For Omar Barghouti's position, see his "Boycott, Academic Freedom, and the Moral Responsibility to Uphold Human Rights," in the same number of *The AAUP Journal of Academic Freedom:* https://www.aaup.org/sites/default/files/Barghouti.pdf.)

76 Benjamin, "Why I Continue," 2.

77 Ibid, 3.

78 Stanley Fish, "Professors, Stop Opining About Trump," *New York Times*, July 15, 2016: https://www.nytimes.com/2016/07/17/opinion/sunday/professors-stop-opining-about-trump.html. The open letter of the historians is no longer on the internet.

79 Elizabeth Redden, "'An Unprecedented Wave' of Palestinian Solidarity Statement," *Inside Higher Education,* June 2, 2021. https://www.insidehighered.com/news/2021/06/02/academic-statements-express-solidarity-palestinians-and-condemn-israeli-actions

80 Elman quoted in ibid.

81 "Gender Studies Departments In Solidarity With Palestinian Feminist Collective," n.d., http://genderstudiespalestinesolidarity.weebly.com/.

82 Mark Muhannad Ayyash, "Break the Fear Barrier and Speak Up for Palestine," *Aljazeera*, May 11, 2021: https://www.aljazeera.com/opinions/2021/5/11/break-the-fear-barrier-and-speak-up-for-palestine.

83 Cary Nelson, "Is Academic Freedom a Casualty of the Gaza War?" *Inside Higher Education*, June 3, 2021: https://www.insidehighered.com/views/2021/06/03/statements-departments-about-gaza-war-have-implications-academic-freedom-opinion.

84 https://www.aaup.org/report/1940-statement-principles-academic-freedom-and-tenure; italics added.

85 Ibid, endnote 6.

86 John K. Wilson, https://academeblog.org/2021/06/07/in-defense-of-departmental-academic-freedom/.

87 This description of Wilson's philosophy is based not only on his critique of Nelson but on his other writings. I am grateful to Wilson for confirming my account of his ideas in an email of October 3, 2021: "Your summaries of my positions are pretty good. I agree with the free speech/AF similarities part."

88 Wilson, op. cit. (per note 78).

6   In Lieu of a Conclusion

An Unpublished Speech on Academic Freedom by Edward W. Said

Abstract

How to end an inquiry that seeks to arrive at no solution to the question "What is academic freedom?" but seeks instead to explain why there are so many different responses to the question? There is no way to end except by continuing the inquiry. In this instance, I have chosen to focus on a leading mind, Edward W. Said, whose ideas about academic freedom defy easy classification.

Introduction

"Unfortunately, the habit of passing judgments leads to a loss of the taste for explanations." (Marc Bloch, The Historian's Craft[1])

Edward W. Said (1935–2003) was one of the most influential academics of the twentieth century. His book *Orientalism* (1978) is an analysis of European representations of Asia, North Africa, and the Middle East. This work, with its critique of Western claims of objectivity and superiority, remains a central text in the field of post-colonial cultural studies. Said was also an activist for Palestinian rights. He played a leading role in framing the treatment of Palestinians under the Israeli occupation as an injustice of the highest order, a wrong that the academic left must integrate into its critique of global inequality. The current popularity of the Boycott, Divestment, Sanctions (BDS) movement in the academy owes much to Said's articulation of the Palestinian cause. Throughout the academy Said's image is that of an activist scholar on the left. Yet, there is one issue on which Said took a position that is generally associated with conservatism. The issue is whether political activism belongs in the classroom.

In December 1992, Said gave a paper to the Modern Language Association (MLA) on this question; it is entitled "Literary Criticism and Politics?"[2] The paper, held in the Columbia University Archives, was unpublished, until I transcribed it and published it in the journal *Philosophy and Literature* in 2020. It is the only text by Said fully devoted to the relationship between humanistic teaching and partisan politics. In multiple interviews, Said mentioned that he never brought his own opinions on political matters into the classroom.[3] Also, in a speech delivered in the year he died, 2003, Said noted that while his political engagement started in 1967, after the Arab Israeli War, "I have never taught anything—I've taught here for almost forty years—about the Middle East."[4] The MLA paper is nevertheless distinctive because Said offers more than a reflection on his own teaching style: he delineates an argument against *anyone* who infuses politics into the teaching of literature.[5]

DOI: 10.4324/9781003052685-7

Said asks if being a political activist can help in literary study. He says, "Yes, but only if one remembers that the spheres are not the same, and that the politics of the classroom are not the politics of the world."[6]

> To use the classroom . . . as a sort of *ersatz* political platform on which to mount an offensive against social ills *out there* is, in my opinion, deeply irresponsible and cowardly. Just as irresponsible is a hyperbolic rhetoric for critical analysis that pretends to be dealing with political issues but which remains a narcissistic exercise in posturing and mock seriousness.[7]

In this essay, I employ the MLA paper to delineate the famous critic's views on the need to separate the political and pedagogical spheres, and I compare his views with other notable intellectuals on this topic.

Fish versus Butler

In the academy today, those who speak out against professors who engage in political agitation in the classroom are likely to find themselves labeled as right-wingers. A public debate has been seething, for about 20 years, over whether pedagogical activism is an expression or violation of the norm of "academic freedom." The controversy became prominent in the public sphere as a result of David Horowitz's campaign, starting in 2002, to convince state legislatures to pass laws against political "indoctrination" in the classroom.[8] As suggested by his book titles, such as *Take No Prisoners: The Battle Plan for Defeating the Left* (2014) and *The Black Book of the American Left* (2016), Horowitz is overtly conservative. As the most well-known critic of the activist approach to teaching, he has contributed to the perception that the debate over advocacy in the classroom is a war between left and right.

The writings of Stanley Fish on academic freedom are an exception that proves the rule. Fish is difficult to classify politically. On some issues, he has aligned with the left. For example, in the 1990s, he deployed his postmodernist sensibility, that is, radical skepticism, to express reservations about free speech; in fact, he outlined reasons for supporting campus hate-speech codes.[9] But in his popular book, *Save the World On Your Own Time* (2007), and his more systematic work, *Versions of Academic Freedom* (2014), Fish converges with Horowitz on one point: they both oppose political advocacy in the classroom and disparage the academic left for promoting this kind of teaching. Fish has opposed legislative efforts to mandate political neutrality and intellectual diversity; this separates him from Horowitz. But their diagnosis is the same: the problem of mixing up politics and academics is created primarily by the left.

Fish, for example, presents Judith Butler as a quintessential example of a thinker who refuses to maintain a distinction between academic inquiry and political agitation. In *Versions of Academic Freedom*, he examines "Critique, Dissent, Disciplinarity," an article of 2009 in which Butler drew upon the thought of Michel Foucault to suggest that one cannot criticize academic authority without criticizing political authority and vice versa.

> Hence, Foucault mobilizes critique against both a mode of rationality and a set of obligations imposed by a specific governmental exercise of authority. The two are clearly linked, but not causally. Modes of rationality do not unilaterally create kinds of governmental obligation, and those governmental obligations do not unilaterally create modes of rationality. And yet to question government authority one has to be

able to think beyond the domain of the thinkable that is established by that authority and on which that authority relies. To be critical of an authority that poses as absolute is not just to take a point of view but to elaborate a position for oneself outside the ontological jurisdiction of that authority and so to elaborate a certain possibility of the subject. And if that domain establishes some version of political rationality, then one becomes, at the moment of being critical, irrational or nonrational, a rogue subject as it were . . . [10]

In other words, since the purpose of academic inquiry is to challenge authority in all contexts, no exception should be made for the authority of the distinction between academic inquiry and political activity.

Fish defends the traditional conception of academic freedom—he even calls it the "conservative" version[11]—as the freedom to engage *only* in activities that are academic, not political, in nature. His response to Butler's perspective is complex because he does not subscribe to a scientific epistemology. Like Butler, he identifies with the theory that reality is constituted by language, which changes over time, rendering all claims about truth conditional upon the standards of one's discursive community. Fish's argument against Butler is pragmatic rather than epistemological. While any proposition can be exposed to theoretical doubts, certain propositions make the existence of certain institutions possible. To make a university's existence possible, some conventional distinctions must be maintained. It would destroy the academy, and all the discursive communities (disciplines) in it, if academic freedom was a license for "going everywhere, ignoring 'do not enter signs,' jumping over all fences."

> [T]o erase any distinction between what questions belong in the academy and what questions do not—would be to make the academy and any usable (because limited) notion of academic freedom disappear . . . Butler, however, wants to go the whole way in the classroom; she wants issues not just to be anatomized, but to be fought out . . . But (as I have been arguing), a diminished—not overly ambitious—concept of academic freedom is precisely what is required if academic freedom is to mean something as opposed to meaning everything. Academic freedom understood as a discipline-based concept, as a professional concept, cannot survive immersion in a sea of critique.[12]

I am not doing justice to the depth of the Fish–Butler exchange. But Fish's point is largely the same as that of Thomas Haskell in his reply to Richard Rorty (see Chapter 4). If we do not separate academics and politics, then nothing prohibits the legislature, in a democratic country, from taking control of the university. If we wish to insulate the university from outside forces which tend to destroy academic freedom, then we must frame academic inquiry as a professional and non-political activity.

My primary point, however, is that Fish is the exception (a non-conservative) who proves the rule (that those who defend the academics/politics distinction are generally conservative). While Fish does not have a conservative political agenda (as Horowitz does), his opposition to activism in the classroom cannot avoid having conservative overtones: because Fish himself uses the word "conservative" to describe his own position; because he singles out for criticism Butler, an iconic figure of the American academic left; and because it is evident that if his concept of academic freedom were taken seriously, social-justice activism inside the university would have to disappear.

Literary Criticism and Politics

We can now appreciate a distinctive feature of Said's MLA paper: he brings us into the debate about teaching from a different angle and makes a political activist's case for neutrality in the classroom. It is because Said was the founder of post-colonial literary criticism, as well as a vehement critic of American policy in the Middle East, that his strictures against politics in the classroom are of special interest. Said's MLA paper, then, allows us to look beyond today's debate about academic freedom, which tends to be framed as left versus right, and to consider the question of activism in the classroom and the meaning of academic freedom from a fresh perspective.

Said insisted on the difference between humanistic education and political commitment. But the former is a prerequisite, not the antithesis, of the latter. To become cultivated and independent, to avoid being an unsuspecting vector of crude class interests and political slogans, the individual must spend a great deal of time immersed in serious reading. Exposure to great writers whose ideas are not reducible to simple formulas is the ideal preparation for independent political judgment and commitment. Said suggested that one can only be as sophisticated, politically and intellectually, as the level of complexity that one attributes to the books that one reads.

As we will see, Said had no reservations about speaking of "great works of literature," even though it was fashionable, by the 1990s, to deny the coherence of the very concept of "literature," not to mention the concept of "great." Great books, for Said, are historical documents reflective of their time, but they also have the capacity to reconfigure our perception of the world, including the world of politics. Said thus wished to preserve, within leftist scholarship, an ideal of canonicity and high culture. Art, for Said, is an edifying realm that refines our sensibility including the place of politics in it. To teach the humanities is to affirm the special role which sophisticated writing and reading can make in the enlargement of our imagination, including, but not limited to, our political imagination.

Said presented "Literary Criticism and Politics?" at the MLA convention on December 30, 1992. The panel in which Said spoke was listed as follows in the MLA conference program:

> Should Literary Criticism Contribute to Politics?
>   1:45–3:00 p.m., Regent Parlor, New York Hilton
>   Program arranged by the American Comparative Literature Association. Presiding: Tobin Siebers, Univ. of Michigan, Ann Arbor
>
>   1   "Poetics or Politics?" Richard Levin, State Univ. of New York, Stony Brook
>   2   "Feminism and the Politics of Identification, " Diana Fuss, Princeton Univ.
>   3   "Literary Criticism and Politics?" Edward W. Said, Columbia Univ.[13]

Said prepared for the panel by writing his paper out by hand. He or an assistant then created a typed version, to which he added handwritten amendments. It was then typed a second time and he added a few more amendments by hand. The third and last version is the one printed in *Philosophy and Literature* and that I quote in this essay. The session took place in the Regent Parlor of the New York Hilton, with a seating capacity of 240. An attendee recalls that the room was "jam-packed."[14]

The paper is ten double-spaced pages. It contains no quotations or footnotes. It is deceptively easy to read. One can easily be riveted by Said's first-person style and end up overlooking the paper's conceptual structure. One is likely to be impressed above all by Said's indignation.

> To use the academy as a place to overturn old orthodoxies in order to instate new ones is, I believe, the end of academic freedom. Academic freedom is accepting the responsibility to explore and read and learn, openly and freely, but is not to be given up just so that a new ascendancy can prescribe and anathematize or hold knowledge down on its terms. I do not believe this point can be emphasized too frequently. There are many things to be said about the inequities and imperfections of our society of course, but these have to be addressed in the public sphere where they exist and where they can be rectified.[15]

Said's tone is reminiscent of Max Weber's denunciation, in "Science as a Vocation," of the professor who acts like a political prophet in the classroom.

> To take a practical political stand is one thing, and to analyze political structures and party positions is another. When speaking in a political meeting . . . one does not hide one's personal standpoint . . . The words one uses in such a meeting are not means of scientific analysis but means of canvassing votes and winning over others. They are not plowshares to loosen the soil of contemplative thought; they are swords against the enemies: such words are weapons. It would be an outrage, however, to use words in this fashion in a lecture.[16]

Weber's consternation stemmed from his insistence on the logical difference between academic facts and analyses, on the one hand, and moral and political values, on the other. Academic discourse is descriptive, not normative. Any deviation from analysis to prescription is an abuse of the professor's authority.

But facts versus values is a distinction that Said never made. Said's anger does not issue from a theory of academic objectivity. The nature of academic discourse as a whole is not in play for him—distinguishing him not only from Weber but from Horowitz and Fish, who argue that academic inquiry across all disciplines can and should be distinct from political activism. Said was speaking specifically as a literary critic to an audience of literary scholars; his topic was how to protect the study of literature from the eroding force of hyper-political interpretation.

More precisely, Said's argument arises from a three-fold classification of the ways in which scholars can envision the relationship between literature and politics. Two of these approaches he considers wrong, and one, of course, is his own view. The first wrong approach is what he calls the "conservative" thesis, that literature is "pure," or not political at all; the second wrong standpoint is the radical tendency to inflate "the politics of pedagogy."[17] It would be a mistake, however, to say that Said considers these two poles to be equally extreme, with his own position being a mean. The key to understanding his argument is to observe a lack of symmetry in the rhetoric he uses to portray the two wrong approaches. He entirely dismisses the view that he associates with conservatism. His relationship to political activism, however, is one of kinship. Activism, he suggests, flows from an authentic source, which is revulsion in the face of the political world's corruption; but activism needs to be tempered and cultivated.

If my assessment is correct, the indignation that Said expresses toward professors who politicize the teaching of literature is also an expression of loving concern, directed at his political allies. The difficulty of balancing his support for political activism in general and his revulsion for politically engaged teaching in particular may be among the reasons that led him not to publish the paper. This is not to say that he had any difficulty articulating his argument. Rather, it is to suggest that he may have been concerned about alienating some of his associates on the academic left. The point is not conclusive, but I will suggest that he was concerned about the rise of "Cultural Studies" yet did not want to fracture the solidarity among progressively minded scholars.

Said focuses his critique of conservatism on Allan Bloom, who represents "the neo-conservative attack on the presumed effort of the academic Left to connect politics and literature."[18] Bloom's concern is "intellectually empty," according to Said, for neither Bloom nor any other conservative scholar "has said in fact what should be taught and how."

> All we get from the neo-cons is a lot of mean-spirited anger at feminism and Black Studies. It is never enough to say that scholars should avoid politics and then advocate something so vague and at the same time so restrictive as what is rather inaccurately called traditional humanism, and a relatively unedifying and basically formulaic one at that.[19]

Said's impatience with "the neo-cons" produces a simplified account of their ideas. Bloom's conception of Great Books is amply explained in the *Closing of the American Mind*, a work that is controversial but not "intellectually empty." The conservative understanding of literature and politics never gets off the ground, according to Said, because conservatives allegedly believe that great literature has nothing to do with politics. But for Bloom, Plato's *Republic*, and Rousseau's *Emile*, two overtly political works, are among the greatest works in the canon.

Said simply moves on to his next target. In contrast to the rhetoric of negation directed toward the person of Bloom, Said conveys more nuanced anxiety about where radical literary criticism is going. He mentions no names, which suggests that he did not wish to discredit any specific scholars. Nevertheless, I venture to suggest that Said could have been concerned about the emerging professionalization of Cultural Studies in the United States. While many American scholars had long been familiar with Raymond Williams, Stuart Hall, and other British Marxists, the creation of a Cultural Studies school in North America, with its own conferences and publications, was a development of the late 1980s and early 1990s. Cary Nelson, a professor of English at the University of Illinois Urbana, was a prominent defender of activist pedagogy and a leader in the Cultural Studies movement. In 2009 he said, "There is a field called Cultural Studies that I have some credit for bringing to the United States."[20] Nelson co-organized two large conferences that yielded landmark anthologies: *Marxism and the Interpretation of Culture* (1988) and *Cultural Studies* (1992, the same year as Said's MLA speech).[21] Essays in these volumes consistently portray the academy as beholden to right-wing forces imposing capitalism and racism throughout American society. It is necessary to "resist" these forces by advocating social change when one is teaching.[22]

For Said, any inquiry into the place of politics in literary criticism must start with the recognition that political ideology does intrude into literature. Hence, "the notion of literature itself" has become "unstable and uncertain in the extreme."[23] Some critics "avoid even the notion of literature for fear that giving it too eminent a privilege or too removed a status prevents free discussion of political forces, questions, interests."[24] Said proposes that we can "mitigate the general volatility to which we all seem to be subject in our endless debate about what literary criticism *ought* to be about." He notes that most societies have a "canon of literature and a pantheon of sages and poets." While these celebrated texts may serve to consolidate authority, societies generally have "a tradition of dissent or heterodoxy which either commemorates rebelliousness or provides a counter-discourse." He adds, "Neither of these two traditions is absent in the United States, nor is one of them likely completely to eliminate the other."[25]

Said means that Western literature does not constitute a unified field of ideology that is subservient to any particular political power. What *is* uniform and corrupt is the current political sphere. Writing during the presidency of George H. W. Bush and during the "War on Terror" in response to 9/11, Said asserts that "the public sphere in this country . . . has been taken over by corporate and governmental powers" which exclude critical thinking, leading to a "degradation of rhetoric" and "shrinking opportunities for intervention."[26]

> The politics of pedagogy have therefore become inflated in importance . . . I believe the acute and disputatious tone of some literary discussion to be a consequence of this attrition in alternative platforms, with the further result that literature and literary study have to bear a greater burden of attention than before, given that there is less of a chance for most of us to participate in the broader discussions of public policy.[27]

Having explained, with sympathy, why leftist literary critics are inclined to transfer their need for political engagement into the classroom, Said then bears down on why such a move is wrong. "I myself do not at all believe that either the classroom or the academy as a whole ought to become a site for the immediate or quasi-mediated settlement of socio-political problems."[28]

The Apolitical Classroom

The first reason for keeping political activism out of the classroom is that the openness of the American university needs to be preserved. Said clearly did not agree with the contributors to Nelson's two anthologies, who maintained that the university had become an arm of capitalism. According to Said:

> The university today still affords us all a very respectable, even luxurious measure of academic freedom, which it would be the rankest folly to abuse or curtail. By that I mean that if scholars use the classroom as a substitute for politics in the real word, then we are at the level not of oppositional politics at all, but of demagoguery and a fundamental betrayal of the teaching ideal.[29]

In a 2003 speech commemorating the 25th anniversary of *Orientalism,* Said remarked:

> For all its noted defects and problems, the American university, and mine, Columbia, in particular, is still I think one of the few remaining places in the United States where reflection and study can take place in almost utopian fashion.[30]

He then goes on to say that he has never injected his political commitments in the classroom.
But there is a logical puzzle here. What is the connection between framing the academy as intellectually open, on the one hand, and trying to insulate it from political activism? Couldn't one just as well argue that precisely because the academy is open to critical ideas, one should seize the opportunity to bring political criticism of our government to the fore? By posting the openness of the academy as if this is *ipso facto* an argument against

politicization, Said is presuming that the justification for political struggle within the academy is based on the opposite claim: that the university tends to shut down free inquiry. This is the Gramscian idea of "hegemony" that practitioners of Cultural Studies employed to justify "resistance" by means of political agitation in the classroom—which adds to the plausibility of my suggestion that Said was concerned about the growing influence of Cultural Studies. In any case, it is evident that while Said believed that political activism is needed to change governmental policies, he did not believe political activism is needed to transform the university.

The second reason for keeping political prescriptions out of classroom discussions comes back to the nature of literature itself. While conceding, or even insisting, that literature is implicated in systems of power and inequality, Said affirms a kind of aestheticism: the capacity of art to create emotional and cognitive effects that nothing but art can create. The tension between the two conceptions of literature—imprinting political ideology versus stimulating the imagination— is a tension that Said refuses to resolve.

Said itemizes the benefits one gets from the close reading of literature, benefits that one cannot get from a précis of the political ideology inscribed in a literary text. First, one can learn how to write in "a jargon-free, clear, direct, and attractive form." The study of literature, Said affirms, is the "best" way to learn how to write. In addition, "great works of literature" avoid "pre-packaged formulas" and "embody a vast range of speculation and questions about human relationships."[31] Said uses certain terms here in a spirit of universality. By studying literature one can learn how to write with good "form" regardless of what one wishes to write about. And through literature, one becomes cultivated in thinking about "human" relationships, not merely about relationships within a capitalist or colonialist system.

Scholarship as Music

Said adds, "literature is unteachable and unreadable without pleasure and affection, although exasperation and anger often enter into the mix."[32] Even when a novel depicts a social ill, such as poverty, in a manner consistent with one of the political parties of the time, "the most interesting questions to pursue" are those which focus on how "the form" of the novel creates impressions that could not be produced in other types of writing, such as the political pamphlet. Said makes the assertion, unusual for today's post-colonial theorists, that the function of literary education is to cultivate "taste and judgment." This includes learning to make distinctions between "good and bad literature." He hastens to say that this distinction does not imply "prohibitions" or "invidious judgments" against popular literature—but his main point is that there are real standards of literary merit.[33]

It is evident that Said considered the most stimulating political effects of art to be those that are not political. The realization that everything is *not* political is essential for becoming a political idealist: one who aspires to make politics something greater than it already is. Said was an accomplished pianist; he taught the course on music appreciation as well as the course on literary classics in the Columbia core curriculum. It is striking that in the following passage, Said presumes that musical performance is the paradigm that literary criticism is based on.

Like musicians, literary critics . . . belong to the class of intellectuals, those people socially entrusted with the production of knowledge . . . with persuading, influencing, and teaching (in the broad sense of the world) people not just to become formally educated but to make decisions, take positions, move, grow, live, die. Literary criticism is not theology or religion, and it is certainly not science. But, in my opinion, it is about not being passive, about being able to think critically using language, and it is about relating language to what isn't language.[34]

The suggestion that musicians are models of how "to make decisions" may seem obscure. But one can understand what Said had in mind through his reflections on European classical music. In dialogue with Daniel Barenboim, Said concurred with the famous pianist and conductor that conductors above all, but also individual musicians, transform the written score into music by making decisions about tempo, volume, the relative prominence of different voicings in the score, and so forth. Said thus associates the ability to "make decisions" not with political action but with the making of art: "Because the score is not the truth. The score is not the piece. The piece is when you actually bring it into sound." (Another noteworthy feature of the dialogues with Barenboim is that Said decries the lack of musical education and taste among young people.)[35]

In a 1987 interview with Imre Saluzinsky, entitled "Literary Theory at the Crossroads of Public Life," Said mentioned his aversion to "the late-1960s notion of the politicization of pedagogical discourse." His interlocutor asked him how he would respond to "Marxist colleagues" who might reply "that it's simply naïve to think that one can separate one's professional life from one's political views." Said responded in a manner that again shows the importance of classical music as a basis for his conception of art and teaching.

> But you're not separating it; you're just leading it in different ways. It's like the voices of a fugue. A fugue can contain three, four, five voices: they're all part of the same composition but they're each distinct. They operate together, and it's a question of how you conceive of the togetherness: if you think it's got to be this *or* that, then you're paralyzed; then you're either Mallarmé or Bakunin, which is an absurd proposition.[36]

This quest for unity is strikingly different from Weber, whose thought is colored by the tragic idea that we cannot harmonize the lives of politicians and scholars; that the various professional spheres of modern life are based on discrete, incompatible value systems: "warring gods." For Said, in contrast, an artistic and scholarly life can contain adventures in political activism. In the MLA talk, he notes that being a political activist outside the university has made him more sensitive to the themes of exile, imperialism, and liberation in literature, but these themes also "enhanced my appreciation of the special, indeed unique role played by the masterpieces of literary art."[37]

No less significant than the term "masterpieces" here is the word "appreciation." In all three drafts of the text, Said wrote "apprehension," which implies cognition but not inspiration. In the last version, he crossed it out and penciled in "appreciation." Given that he uses a variant of the same word in the next sentence, it is likely that he was engaging in intentional repetition. "Far from diminishing or impoverishing the status of the canon, this viewpoint gives the canon, as well as non-canonical, less-known literary work, greater visibility and interest, makes us more appreciative of literature's special status."[38] Said would have known that "appreciation" is one of the preferred terms of traditional humanistic educators. The word is used to this day in course descriptions of classes in the Columbia core curriculum, such as "Masterpieces of Western Literature and Philosophy" (also known as Literature Humanities, one of the courses that Said taught): "Although most of our Lit Hum works (and the cultures they represent) are remote from us, we nonetheless learn something about ourselves in struggling to appreciate and understand them."[39] Said was trying to graft the traditional humanistic goal of appreciation onto post-colonial literary criticism, in order to prevent "criticism" from meaning the negative reduction of literature to imperialist and other pernicious ideologies.

In an interview with David Barsamian, published in *Z Magazine* in its July/August issue of 1993, Said again explained how teaching literature must not devolve into political activism.

> If you have lived through a period of colonial struggle, you can return to the texts and read them in a way which is sensitive to precisely these points which are normally over-looked . . . [But] I don't advocate, and I'm very much against, the teaching of literature as a form of politics. I think there's a distinction between pamphlets and novels. I don't think the classroom should become a place to advocate political ideas. I've never taught political ideas in a classroom.

Barsamian replied that Said's teaching approach is still "political." To which Said responded, "Only in one sense. It is politics against the reading of literature which would denude it." Barsamian was insistent: "But as a teacher you're making certain choices." Said answered, "Of course, we all do." But he explained that while he sometimes shared his own under-standing of texts with students, he never added political prescriptions to his interpretations; he did not even insist on the unique value of his literary interpretations.

> Quite the contrary. I want to provoke new and refreshing investigations of these texts in ways which will have them read more skeptically, more inquiringly, more search-ingly. That's the point.[40]

For Said, the humanistic teacher must leave students free to form political commitments of varying types on their own, outside of class. As he says in the concluding paragraph of the MLA talk, the task of the educator is to create "idealism." The goal is to add the study of literature to politics, as opposed to reducing literature to one's pre-existing understanding of the political field.

> For me, the basic enterprise is how to elucidate, draw, maintain connections [be-tween literature and politics] . . . without losing the delicacy of detail and form, without trying to escape from history, without imposing dogmatic schemes, without sacrificing the deeply held values for which so many individuals have fought, without turning bitter or vindictive, without eroding the fundamentally pleasing enterprise of reading, learning, and using language in the company of one's students and friends.[41]

★

Readers of the speech will likely have varying interpretations. Beyond doubt, though, is that Said participated in a core curriculum based on classic works and that he was dedicated to teaching literature for what it is worth as literature, as distinct from politics. Great works can stimulate political activism, but an instructor must not preordain what kind of activism the masterpieces should mobilize. Said spoke forcefully to the right about its tendency to isolate culture from political and historical reality. He spoke just as forcefully to the left about its tendency to demean the study of culture by infusing political advocacy into the classroom. By taking a position that is difficult to classify politically, Said imbued his speech with the unpredictable vitality that he attributed to art. Although he influenced the political struggles of his day, he also delineated an educational ideal that rose above them.

Notes

1 (New York: Alfred A. Knopf, 1959), 140.
2 Edward W. Said, "Literary Criticism and Politics?" (hereafter abbreviated "LCP") is in the Edward Said Papers, Columbia University, box 75, folder 27. I am grateful to Jeffrey Wallen, professor of Comparative Literature at Hampshire College, for bringing the paper's existence to my attention. In a fine essay, in which he questions the value of political advocacy in the classroom, Wallen includes a quotation from Said's text, based on notes Wallen took when Said delivered the paper at the 1992 MLA conference. To the best of my knowledge no other scholar has discussed Said's MLA paper. See Jeffrey Wallen, "Teachers, Not Advocates: Toward an Open Classroom," in *Advocacy in the Classroom: Problems and Possibilities*, ed. Patricia Meyer Spacks (New York: St. Martin's Press, 1996), 225–231; p. 230 has the extract from Said.
3 Edward W. Said, "Literary Theory at the Crossroads of Public Life," interview with Imre Salusinszky, in *Power, Politics, and Culture: Interviews with Edward Said*, ed. Gauri Viswanathan (Pantheon Books, 2001; interview conducted in 1987), 69–93; the discussion of teaching is at p. 91. "Interview: Edward Said—Culture and Imperialism," with David Barsamin, *Z Magazine*, July/August, 1993, 62–71; the discussion of teaching is at p. 65. A longer version of this interview was reprinted in Edward W. Said, *The Pen and The Sword: Conversations with David Barsamian* (Common Courage Press, 1994), 65–105; the discussion of teaching is the same and is at 77–78. The date of the interview was January 18, 1993. See also Daniel Barenboim and Edward W. Said, *Parallels and Paradoxes: Explorations in Music and Society*, ed. Ara Guzelman (New York: Random House, 2004), 63–64.
4 Edward W. Said, concluding lecture of a conference on the 25th anniversary of *Orientalism*, April 16, 2003: https://www.youtube.com/watch?v=JncXpQQoZAo&feature=youtu.be. At minute 9.
5 In *Pedagogy of the Other: Edward Said, Postcolonial Theory, and Strategies for* Critique (Bern: Peter Lang, 2012), Shehla Burney imputes to Said a pedagogy that is akin to Paulo Freire's "pedagogy of the oppressed." But this is not based on an examination of Said's teaching practices, or his pronouncements on teaching. Burney presupposes that Said's critical writings on colonialism logically entail a politicized approach to teaching.
6 Edward Said, "Literary Criticism and Politics" (henceforth, LCP), *Philosophy and Literature*, vol. 44, no. 2 (October 2020), 399.
7 Ibid, 400.
8 See *The Academic Bill of Rights Debate*, ed. Stephen H. Aby (Westport: Praeger, 2007); and Chapter 4 of the present book.
9 Stanley Fish, *There's No Such Thing as Free Speech, and It's a Good Thing, Too* (New York: Oxford University Press, 1994), 75–76, 78.
10 Judith Butler, "Critique, Dissent, Disciplinarity," *Critical Inquiry*, vol. 35, no. 4 (Summer 2009), 790; cited in. part by Fish, *Versions of Academic Freedom: From Professionalism to Revolution* (Chicago: University of Chicago Press, 2014), 66.
11 Fish, *Versions*, 4.
12 Ibid, 69, 71–72.
13 "Program," *PMLA*, vol. 107, no. 6 (November 1992), 1507; https://www.jstor.org/stable/462653.
14 Jeffrey Wallen, e mail to Daniel Gordon, January 13, 2020.
15 LCP, 400.
16 Max Weber, "Science as a Vocation," in *Max Weber: Essays in Sociology*, C. Wright Mills and Hans Gerth, translators and editors, with a new preface by Bryan S. Turner (London: Routledge, 2009), 145. Weber gave the speech in 1917.
17 LCP, 396.
18 Ibid, 399.
19 Ibid, 399–400. Said criticized Bloom in a similar manner in "Identity, Authority, and Freedom: The Potentate and the Traveler, " in *The Future of Academic Freedom*, ed. Louis Menand (Chicago: University of Chicago Press, 1996), 217. This essay is a critique of nationalism and its impact on academic life. The essay says nothing about the question of whether professors should be political advocates in the classroom.

20 Cary Nelson, debate with Peter Wood, "The Meaning of Academic Freedom," https://www. youtube.com/watch?v=itsfgIgEWBI; at 5:22.

21 *Marxism and the Interpretation of Culture*, ed. Cary Nelson and Lawrence Grossberg (Urbana: University of Illinois Press, 1988); *Cultural Studies*, ed. Nelson et al. (see note 15).

22 See, *Cultural Studies*, ed. Nelson et al., the editors' introduction, p. 5, where they refer to the classroom as a place of resistance. And the contribution of Henry A. Giroux, "Resisting Difference," 199–212.

23 LCP, 395.

24 Ibid, 397.

25 Ibid, 395.

26 Ibid, 396.

27 Ibid.

28 Ibid.

29 Ibid, 400.

30 See note 3 above; at 9:30.

31 LCP, 397.

32 Ibid.

33 Ibid, 397–398.

34 Ibid, 398.

35 Barenboim and Said, *Parallels and Paradoxes*, 24, 32–33, 71, 74–75. "The score is not the truth," is Barenboim, 33. Said not only concurs but takes the point further: "every object is created anew in the reading or performance of it," 34.

36 Said, "Literary Theory at the Crossroads of Public Life" (see note 3), 92. See also the discussion of Bach in Edward W. Said, "The Virtuoso as Intellectual," in Edward. W. Said, *On Late Style: Music and Literature Against the Grain* (Pantheon Books, 2006), 124–132.

37 LCP, 398.

38 Ibid.

39 "About Literature Humanities," https://www.college.columbia.edu/core/lithum/about.

40 "Interview: Edward Said—Culture and Imperialism" (see note 3; the earliest version of the interview), 65.

41 LCP, 401.

Index

Note: *Italic* page numbers refer to figures and page numbers followed by "n" denote endnotes.

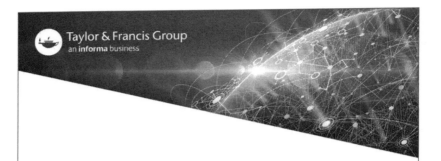